Johnny
Unitas

Johnny Unitas

AMERICA'S QUARTERBACK

Lou Sahadi

TRIUMPH
BOOKS
CHICAGO

Library of Congress Cataloging-in-Publication Data

Sahadi, Lou
    Johnny Unitas, America's quarterback / Lou Sahadi.
       p. cm.
    Includes bibliographical references (p.) and index.
    ISBN 1-57243-610-7
    1. Unitas, Johnny, 1933– 2. Quarterbacks (Football)—United States—Biography.
3. Baltimore Colts (Football team)—History. I. Title.

    GV939.U5S35 2004
    796.332'092—dc22

                                                                2004046095

This book is available in quantity at special discounts for your group or organization. For further information, contact:

Triumph Books
601 South LaSalle Street
Suite 500
Chicago, Illinois 60605
(312) 939-3330
Fax (312) 663-3557

Printed in U.S.A.
ISBN: 1-57243-610-7
Design by Sue Knopf

For Rebecca, Mary, Abby, Hannah, John Bennett,
Sam, Emma, Sarah and Lilly with love,
and the nine best reasons
a Gido could have for writing this book.

Contents

Foreword

Peyton Manning

I FIRST MET JOHNNY UNITAS DURING MY SENIOR YEAR AT THE University of Tennessee when I won the Johnny Unitas Golden Arm Award. The banquet was in Louisville, and it was a great experience. I sat with him at the banquet, and even when people were speaking, he was talking to me, telling me stories about guys like John Mackey and Lenny Moore and Raymond Berry. I just took it all in. Obviously I'd heard a lot about him from my dad, so this was just a special treat and a real treasure. I'm reminded of that evening often because in my house, I've got a collection of pictures of the quarterback and one of my favorites is of Johnny and me: I'm giving him a pair of black high-tops I wore at Tennessee. He thought that was pretty cool. It was a neat, neat moment.

Because the banquet was in Louisville, there were a ton of Tennessee fans there. When it was over, the emcee announced there would be an autograph session, which was news to me because it already had been a lengthy affair. So my dad, Johnny, and Earl Morrall went over to this table and began to sign autographs. Within moments, you couldn't see the end of the line, and I figured we were going to be there a long time, especially with all those Tennessee fans. But about 20 minutes into it, Johnny looked at me and said, "That's enough . . . y'all coming?" Well, if

Johnny Unitas says it's time to go, it's time to go. And that's kind of how he played. We're going to do it my way, and that's the way it is.

Anyway, the Golden Arm Award is prominently displayed in my home and now it's even more special because my brother, Eli, won it this year. I only wish that he could have been able to spend the kind of evening I did with Johnny. It was a special opportunity.

After that, I saw him at a couple of Kentucky Derbies, where we were able to have some brief conversations and, as usual, he was really nice. Then I also got to see him both times the Colts played the Ravens in Baltimore. He'd shake my hand before the game, wish me luck. Then he'd stand on the sidelines. He was one of those guys who, when he's down on the field, everybody knows where he is. Sure, it was a unique situation, the Baltimore Ravens playing the Indianapolis Colts, and obviously he wasn't a big fan of the Indianapolis Colts. But he always took time to be nice to me. He always told me, "Peyton, I like the way you play the game." You know, kind of being a field general, trying to manage everything that was going on out there on the field. That's something quarterbacks should strive for and it's something I strive for. It's the quarterback's responsibility to make order out of all that chaos, and nobody did it better than Johnny Unitas. It didn't matter, either, what the score was or how much time was left. I've heard from his teammates and guys who played against him that, no matter the circumstances, if he was in there, the Colts had a chance. He had the ultimate in belief and trust from his teammates and coaches and the ultimate respect from the opponents, who knew that even if they were up by 14 with three minutes to go, they could look across the field, see Unitas, and feel they're still in trouble.

Of course, I never got to see Johnny play in person, but I've seen films and highlights, and I've heard old coaches talk about the true "timing" passer, which was kind of new at that time. Unitas to Berry. Throwing the timing route. Throwing the out route, throwing the slant route, the true timing passing game. Certainly in today's game, that's what the passing game is all about. Timing. I've heard Raymond Berry talk about the time they spent working in the offseason, just the recall they had on routes, the different adjustments. And that's something I've tried to attain with all my receivers, certainly with Marvin Harrison. Johnny was doing those things 40 years ago.

I'm always hesitant to get into comparisons and put my name in the same category as players of yesteryear. But I take a lot of pride in trying to continue the Unitas legacy as a Colts quarterback, even though we don't play in Baltimore. We still wear the same uniforms and the same helmets. I realize we're not in the same city and the Baltimore Colts fans are disappointed that that team moved, but we're still the Colts.

When Johnny passed away, we were going to play the Dolphins and I wanted to wear black high-tops in his honor, but the league said no. I should have gone ahead and done it. I didn't think it was fair to his family, but his family called me and said they appreciated the gesture. Heck, I think every quarterback in the NFL should have worn black high-tops that weekend.

You hear about players from other eras, and some wonder if they would be as good today. Well, let me tell you, there's no wondering about Johnny Unitas. He was a superstar then. He would be a superstar today. The NFL should name an award after him for all that he's meant. He put the NFL on the map.

—Peyton Manning

Foreword

Art Donovan

I STARTED PLAYING FOR THE BALTIMORE COLTS IN 1950. IN THE first three seasons, I was in only three winning games, but in 1954, things started to change.

The assistant coach from the Cleveland Browns, Weeb Ewbank, came in as head coach for the Colts. We still struggled in that 1954 season, but the next year we had a great draft. We had the first pick and grabbed quarterback George Shaw. That same draft got us Alan Ameche at fullback, Dick Szymanski at center, and George Preas, a lineman.

We knew by the 1956 season that we were forming a great team under the leadership of George Shaw at quarterback. It was during this season that a skinny-ass kid from Pittsburgh came to join the Colts. He'd been their ninth-round draft pick in 1955—number 102 overall—and they had cut him loose. He'd been playing semiprofessional football in Pittsburgh when our general manager, Don Kellett, sent him a postcard inviting him to tryouts.

I was on the training table getting a massage when I first met this skinny kid. He was trying out as a quarterback and had a bad right shoulder. A couple veterans shook their heads and asked how this unknown kid was going to be good enough for the Colts. He made the team, though, right behind our starting quarterback, George Shaw.

In 1956 Shaw got hurt playing against the Chicago Bears in Chicago, and the skinny kid—John Unitas was his name—got the chance to quarterback the team. The first pass he threw was an interception run back for a touchdown by J. C. Caroline of the Bears. His second play wasn't much more impressive—he fumbled a handoff.

Who would believe that from that beginning Johnny would turn out to be the greatest quarterback who ever played football? Who would believe he would earn the nickname "the Golden Arm"? Who would have thought that this skinny-ass kid would become so famous? The beginning of his career didn't start too well, but it ended up as one of the greatest stories in the world of sports.

Johnny was very quiet and unassuming, with a great sense of humor. In the huddle, he was the boss. Every game, he gave us the same speech: "Talk's cheap. Let's go play." He was the coolest player I have ever seen. He would have made a great general or admiral in the service.

From 1957 to 1960, with Johnny Unitas as our quarterback, we were the best football team ever in the NFL. We were the champions in 1958 and 1959, with such players as Gino Marchetti, Don Joyce, "Big Daddy" Lipscomb, and myself forming the defense. We always said that if we could get Johnny the ball, we'd win the game. And we did.

In December 1958, we played in what is now called the greatest game ever played. We met the New York Giants in the NFL championship game. We led at halftime, but the Giants went ahead in the second half. A controversial call ruled that the Giants halfback, Frank Gifford, failed to make a first down. I'd be lying if I said I knew whether he made it, but I don't think he did. Johnny then passed up the middle, setting up Steve Myhra's field goal, tying the game, and sending it into the first sudden-death overtime in NFL history. In overtime, we shut down the Giants and Johnny went to work setting up the plays that ended with Alan "the Horse" Ameche lying on the grass in the end zone with the referee signaling the winning touchdown.

We started the greatest era in the history of the NFL and I mean it—all my teammates will swear by it. We helped put major-league football on the map.

Losing John Unitas in 2002 was a tragedy. He was one of the greatest football players of all time and the greatest thing that ever happened to the NFL. His name is, and ever will be, magical in Baltimore. He's the guy who put the city on the map. It was a pleasure to be on his team. He was a great player and a great guy.

That's why this book is so important and timely—it is a tribute to his greatness and serves as a reminder of all that Unitas did for football. With this biography, we finally have a full-scale portrait of a great man. Lou Sahadi even shares with us previously unpublished material from a personal interview with Johnny, an interview which lets us hear Johnny's own special voice one more time.

It's a voice that will echo through the years as long as football is played.

—Art Donovan

Preface

JOHNNY UNITAS WAS THE QUINTESSENTIAL QUARTERBACK, WHO brought a floundering sport to life and forever changed the pro football landscape. He truly was America's quarterback.

Yet, to my mind, there remains a void: the National Football League has not paid Unitas homage with an award named after him, such as the Johnny Unitas MVP Award. This is perplexing to me. This is my 20th literary work, and I have never experienced a more compelling and inspirational subject as that which unfolds on these pages. This is why I felt compelled to write this profile of one of football's greats.

Acknowledgments

MANY THANKS TO CRAIG KELLEY, CHAD REESE, PETE FIERLE, Joe Horrigan, Kevin Byrne, Ron Wahl, Jeff Gill, Tina Latrella, Melanie LeGrande, Steve Sabol, Kathy Davis, Ryan Robinson, Susan Moran, Bill Houston, Denise Larzo, Joe Mammarelli, Doug Schustek, Lois Nelson, Barry Allen, and especially to Barbara O'Reilly, who prevailed in a battle with an obstinate computer. Finally, to Tom Bast, who let an author run with the ball in the open field without any constraints, and to Blythe Hurley and Kelley Thornton, who kept me in bounds. Thanks also to Linc Wonham, Scott Rowan, and especially Mitch Rogatz.

Finally, a special thanks to those who took the time to do the interviews: Ernie Accorsi, Len Dawson, Frank Gitschier, Bill Glasso, Shirley Green, Lenny Jaffe, Craig Kelley, Tom Matte, Terry Musolf, Buzz Nutter, Jerry Richardson, Chuck Rogers, Dan Rooney, Len Unitas, and Fred Zangaro.

Introduction

THE LEGEND OF JOHNNY UNITAS BEGAN ON A DARK DECEMBER afternoon in Yankee Stadium in 1958 when he led the Baltimore Colts in the NFL championship game against the New York Giants. It was the game that introduced a strange new term—sudden-death overtime—to the American vocabulary. It was a game that captured the country's imagination and set the stage for the pro football boom. It was high drama, and Unitas, as always, was the most compelling figure in the play. He drove the Colts the length of the field to set up a field goal that tied the game at 17–17 with just seven seconds left.

Then, in overtime, he moved his team with remarkable precision. He was like a carnival hustler playing the shell game, mixing up his plays and smirking every time the Giants defense guessed wrong. Finally, on third-and-goal from the 1-yard line, Unitas handed the ball to fullback Alan Ameche for the winning touchdown.

Unitas' performance was even more remarkable considering the physical handicap under which he performed. His ribs were taped and protected by a special brace. Earlier in the season he had suffered three broken ribs and a punctured lung. At first it was feared that Unitas would be lost for the season, but two weeks later, taped and protected, he returned to the lineup to lead the Colts down the road to the championship.

Unitas rode off to the locker room on the shoulders of his teammates. In the crush of the small locker room, a reporter asked Unitas about a daring call he had made during that final drive, a sideline pass to tight end Jim Mutscheller. Wasn't he risking an interception in a situation in which the Colts were in field-goal position?

Unitas answered politely, but with calculated assuredness: "When you know what you are doing, you're not intercepted. The Giants were jammed up at the line and not expecting a pass. If Jim had been covered, I'd have thrown the pass out of bounds. It's just that I would rather win a game like this by a touchdown than by a field goal."

So the image was created. Johnny Unitas became known as "the riverboat gambler." He was so cool, they said, that he could hold an ice cube in his hand and it wouldn't melt. The more pressure there was, the better he liked it. He was the person football fans thought of when they heard the word "quarterback." He led a drive the way an orchestra conductor led a symphony, only Unitas was a bowlegged maestro in black high-top shoes.

Until Unitas' golden performance, professional football had not yet captured the nation's attention; but that one game had been on television. So on a cold, murky December day, professional football made a quantum leap in its incredible spiral to the top of America's sports popularity charts. Unitas' performance left the nation's sports fans sitting breathlessly on the edge of their living room seats. It was not purely coincidental, either, that the NFL enjoyed its greatest boom during the glory years of Johnny Unitas.

"You know, everyone has called it the greatest game ever played," Unitas said. "I calmly approached it as just another football game. Oh, that overtime period and the TV exposure might have given it a little more importance, but I played the game just like any other."

Any wonder why he was also called "Mr. Cool"? From that day on, the quiet, 25-year-old Unitas demonstrated the skill, poise, and artistry that over the next 15 years would earn him a widespread reputation as the greatest quarterback who ever lived.

"Johnny Unitas is the greatest quarterback in the history of the game," said former Chicago Bears star Sid Luckman. "He's better than Sammy Baugh, better than me, better than anybody."

Fame didn't come easily for Unitas. He had to scratch his way out of the obscurity of semipro football that was played on craggy fields that were dimly lit, where he dressed in wooden shacks and wore a soiled and sweaty uniform home afterward to take a shower. Unitas was undeterred, still hoping to sign on with an NFL team. One night in February the opportunity came. The Baltimore Colts found him for the price of an 80¢ telephone call that was prompted by a letter from a fan who extolled the virtues of Unitas to Baltimore coach Wilbur "Weeb" Ewbank. After Ewbank checked with Unitas' college coach, he urged his general manager, Don Kellett, to call the youngster because Ewbank needed a backup quarterback to George Shaw. Unitas was impressive in a tryout, and Baltimore offered him a $6,000 contract.

Whatever others failed to see in Unitas early during his career, they certainly saw later on. "He is uncanny in his abilities, under the most violent pressure, to pick out the soft spot in a defense," the late Vince Lombardi once said. "It may have been Unitas' greatest talent. No quarterback who ever played could pick an opponent apart like Unitas."

It was all so natural to Unitas. "No matter how good a defense is, you can always find a weakness somewhere," said Unitas. "You find it and start hitting it. When they close it up, you have to find the next weakness."

It's a philosophy that is not always shared by some of today's pro coaches. "I think some of them are afraid of throwing the football," said Unitas. "I think they're generally conservative. Maybe they're afraid of losing their jobs; but on a football team, you have to do what your personnel dictates. If you have someone who can throw the ball, you throw it."

And he did so time and time again during a record-breaking career.

Unitas' supreme confidence was infectious. As teammate John Mackey responded when asked what it was like in the huddle with Unitas: "It's like being in the huddle with God." The confidence that Unitas exuded reached into the upper tier of stadiums. The guy in the cheapest seats got the feeling that somehow Unitas would find a way to win and, throughout his long career, he did just that.

His contemporaries on the other side of the field were just as impressed. Merlin Olsen of the Los Angeles Rams described what it was like going against Unitas: "You couldn't shake him. Once in a while the defense got in there, knocked him down, stomped on him, and hurt him. The test of a great quarterback is what he did next. Unitas would get up, call another pass, and drop back into the pocket. Out of the corner of his eye he may see you coming again—and I swear that when he did, he held the ball a split second longer than he really needed to, just to let you know that he wasn't afraid of any man—then he threw it on the button."

Nobody threw it better during the golden years of pro football. That is why all quarterbacks who have arrived on the professional scene are measured against Unitas. He is the standard to whom all are compared: the ultimate. "All things considered," said Bob Waterfield, a great quarterback himself, "I would say Unitas is the greatest quarterback of all time."

As one writer observed when Unitas announced his retirement before the 1974 season, "Superstars are constantly making the scene, but Johnny Unitas may be the last of the real sports heroes. He was the kind of athlete little kids could admire and copy, and whose stories were the kind you could read with your breakfast cereal. We won't see anyone quite like him again."

The Greatest Game
Ever Played

BEFORE JOHNNY UNITAS CAME ALONG, BALTIMORE HAD NOT won a championship in any sport. The city was looked upon as a whistle-stop between Washington and New York on the Pennsylvania Railroad, or the midpoint for motorists making their way north or south on I-95.

When the Orioles baseball team appeared in 1954, the town experienced a sports awakening. But the residents of Baltimore needed something to cheer for, someone to embrace. That person was Unitas.

In 1958 the Baltimore Colts won their first-ever NFL championship by defeating the New York Giants 23–17 in the first sudden-death overtime game ever played in league history. Their leader was a slightly bow-legged quarterback named Johnny Unitas. That championship game has been called the greatest game ever played. That one game captured the hearts of pro football fans around the country, ushering in the era of televised sports and changing Sunday afternoons for millions of Americans.

With that one significant victory over the Giants in 1958, Unitas brought pride and respect to Baltimore. And the city needed both. Unitas won over Baltimore, and they adopted him as their hero.

The Giants

Baltimore faced a Giants team that commanded respect. The Giants joined the league in 1925, two years after the NFL was officially launched. At that time, the 16 teams were formed in such hamlets as Canton, Frankford, Kenosha, Rochester, Dayton, Pottsville, and Columbus. For the shaky league to survive, it needed exposure. And what better place than New York, where such college heroes as Jim Thorpe and Harold "Red" Grange could gallop before record crowds at the Polo Grounds? When a record seventy-three thousand fans showed up to see Grange, the future of the Giants and the league suddenly brightened.

The Giants owner, Tim Mara, was a successful businessman and, of all things, a bookmaker. Back then, bookmaking was legal. Mara made a wise investment when he plunked down $500 cash to join the aspiring league. In only their third season, in 1927, the Giants won their first championship with an 11–1–1 record. However, in the stock market crash two years later, Mara suffered substantial financial losses and looked to his sons to run the team.

Mara's older son, Jack, was 22 years of age, and the younger son was 14-year-old Wellington, who overnight became the youngest owner of a football team. It was the beginning of his storied career as a major player in the Giants organization and in the league as well, which eventually led to his induction into the Pro Football Hall of Fame in 1997.

Somehow the young brothers made it work. By 1933, the Giants played for the championship again, only to lose to the Bears in Chicago, 23–21. However, when they faced the Bears again under the legendary coach and owner George Halas on a frigid nine-degree day in New York, they emerged victorious, 30–13. The game became famous as the "sneakers game" all because of Giants coach Steve Owen's inventiveness. At halftime, when the Giants were down 10–3, he cleverly equipped his players with basketball shoes to provide them with better footing on the icy turf. The results were truly amazing. While the Bears slipped and fell, the Giants scored four touchdowns and turned the game into a rout.

In the next decade, the Giants made it to the championship game three times, only to suffer despair. However, during the fifties, the Giants moved to Yankee Stadium and began to accumulate players that would become household names and be talked about on every sidewalk in New York. Their fans cheered at the mention of Frank Gifford, Kyle Rote, Alex Webster, Pat Summerall, Bob Schnelker, Charles Conerly, Mel Triplett, Sam Huff, Rosey Grier, Andy Robustelli, and Harland Svare. The New York media glorified them. They were indeed the glamour team, and the Baltimore Colts were going up against them.

The Giants had the pedigree, and adoration for them came from Yankee Stadium to Broadway to the sprawling suburbs that comprised the biggest metropolitan area of the country. Baltimore, on the other hand, was not taken too seriously, especially after they lost their final two games of the previous season. But the Colts were different; they were a lunch-bucket team that came to play, as evidenced by their nine victories in their first 10 games.

"We get along so well," said Raymond Berry, Unitas' favorite receiver. "There's a deep and real respect among us."

By late sunset of that game day, everyone in America would have that respect for Baltimore and its Colts. There was no question that the Colts and the Giants were the two best teams in 1958, and whoever emerged victorious would be genuine champions. Nobody in the crowd of 64,185 that made its way into Yankee Stadium that Sunday, or the million or so who watched a championship game on television for the first time, could have known that they would become observers to history.

The Colts

Unitas and his nobodies came into New York as underdogs on an overcast December day. New York was a champion's town. The Yankees, with a new hero in Mickey Mantle, had won the World Series, and the Giants, who had won the NFL championship in 1956, were primed to make it two out of the last three years. Not only had the Giants shut out Cleveland 10–0, but they stuffed Jim Brown, the game's greatest running back, holding him to only eight yards on eight carries. Nobody had ever done that before.

The reason for the Giants' accomplishment was their middle linebacker, Sam Huff, who was the catalyst of a strong Giants defense. He was why they reached the championship game. He had followed Brown's every move, even without the ball, and gunned down the league's greatest running back before he could use his moves and his power to outrun the posse. Huff had joined the Giants as a rookie out of West Virginia, where he played offensive guard, in 1956, the same year Unitas came to Baltimore as a free agent. Huff had already made a name for himself with his stalking play and was the most revered member of the Giants defense.

Unitas was still waiting to make his mark, however. But when that long December afternoon of gut football in New York was finally over in darkness, he had. It was Babe Ruth's hallowed ground, and Joe DiMaggio's, and Mickey Mantle's, and when it was over, it would be Unitas' too.

The Colts had a scheduled 1:15 P.M. workout at Yankee Stadium. For the most part, the players' mood was quiet, almost subdued. After a 4:30 dinner, the players gathered in the team meeting room at 6:30 to discuss the key elements of strategy they would employ the next day. They were very cognizant of the solid Giants defense, Huff in particular, and designed a way to limit his effectiveness. The offensive game plan was to keep good splits along the offensive line, which would benefit the Colts' running game and provide pass protection for Unitas. The split ends and the flanking backs were instructed to keep as wide as possible in order to open up the passing lanes.

For the oppressive Huff, the Colts coaches felt that it would be easier to run away from him if he didn't stay in the middle of the Giants' 4–3 defense. They noted that his tendency was to follow the fullback most of the time, and that a draw play and inside runs would be effective against him. To set the offense in gear, Unitas was urged to go on early counts to discourage defensive moving, especially the blitz, and to help pass protection from any of the Giants' blitzing schemes.

By 10:00 P.M., the players were in their rooms. There were no wives this time. Ewbank was convinced that the Colts had lost to the Giants during the second week of November in New York because the wives were around. None of the players bought into that. They felt they lost because Unitas had been in the hospital having blood drawn from a punctured lung and couldn't play.

Game Day

The team's pregame meal wasn't until 10:00, and the chartered bus for the short ride to the stadium was at 12:30. Some of the Colts got their first look at Huff at the hotel that morning. He lived there during the season and was in the coffee shop having breakfast. None of the Colts players said anything to him. After all, he was a hated enemy, one whose picture would appear on the cover of *Time* magazine a year later and who would be immortalized in 1960 in a CBS documentary, *The Violent World of Sam Huff*, narrated by Walter Cronkite. However, one of the Baltimore writers somehow started a conversation with Huff, who already had on his game face. The writer jokingly suggested to the extraordinary linebacker that he had time to catch the 1:00 train to West Virginia. Huff scornfully looked straight at him. "I can always take the train to West Virginia, but I can't always go out and win the world championship," snarled Huff, who then got up and left.

Running back L. G. "Long Gone" Dupre and sensational end Raymond Berry were the only Colts who didn't appear at the pregame meal. They never liked eating big meals before games—championship or otherwise—and they received permission to eat in the coffee shop. Preferring to spend time in religious meditation, Berry liked the solitude anyway. And before this day would end, he would make believers of anyone who saw him play.

The pregame taping in hotel room 626 had its humorous moments. Naturally, Donovan provided most of it. He had a small hole in his undershorts when he entered the room that trainer Dick Spassoff was using to tape the players' ankles and to provide whatever else they needed medically. It wasn't a large room, and the players entered in groups of 4 until all 33 of them were attended to. Donovan, being the jokester he was, got them laughing. "I feel like I'm going to be so rich today that here's what I'm going to do," he shouted.

At that moment, he looked down, took one of his meaty fingers, placed it in the torn spot in his undershorts, and in one quick motion ripped the pants off his big body. The room howled with laughter.

Dupre added to the fun while having his ankles taped. "Nobody likes your tape jobs, Spassoff, but I do," said Dupre.

Spassoff smiled. "I will give you a two-touchdown tape job."

The taping session was almost over, but Jim Parker, the team's outstanding 270-pound tackle, wished it had ended sooner. He went crashing down to the floor when all four legs of the chair he was sitting on gave way at once. Parker came down with a thud, but fortunately, he wasn't hurt. Laughter again resonated in the room as Spassoff picked up the remaining parts of the broken chair—he wasn't troubled by it at all. "We're going to win, we're going to win!" he shouted.

Buzz Nutter, Unitas' faithful center, wondered out loud about who won last week's game. And that, too, contributed to some laughs. "Who won that game between the Browns and the Giants last week?" he joked. "All that stuff Weeb put us through, and he forgot to tell us who we were going to play."

At exactly 12:30, as scheduled, the Colts' bus made its way to Yankee Stadium. It didn't take long. Before the players could stretch out and get comfortable, they were ready to leave the bus. Some of the Giants fans arrived early and stood watching the intruders from Baltimore. One recognized Donovan: "Hey, Donovan, I hope this team is better than the one you played on at Mt. St. Michael's," he teased. Donovan was laughing too hard to answer, one of the few times he was without words. The good-natured heckler must have been from Donovan's neighborhood.

Once inside the locker room, the Colts found no relief. Ewbank was uncharacteristically irascible in addressing his players after they had finished their pregame warm-ups and quietly waited for the moment of battle.

He was trying to motivate them for the biggest game in the previously moribund history of the franchise—he wasn't about to lose their chance for glory.

Usually a mild-mannered individual, Ewbank was visceral in exhorting his warriors, calling them out individually by name and creating an eerie silence that froze the players. He began by telling them they all had something to prove and the place to do it was New York. But then he jolted them by shouting that they were all a bunch of rejects and started naming names in front of the entire team: "In 14 years, I heard 'em all," said Marchetti. "'Win one for Mother. Win one for Father. Don't disappoint all these people watching on television.' Yeah, he named me and Unitas. He didn't miss anybody.

"Weeb really put it to us. He went down the roster name by name: Ameche, Green Bay didn't want you; Lipscomb, you were released; Berry, people said you'd never be a pro; Donovan, they got rid of you—too fat and slow."

Weeb didn't know it, but Donovan never heard him. He was in the bathroom throwing up when Rechichar, who was in Weeb's doghouse, sauntered in. Rechichar didn't even know if he was going to play or not and couldn't understand why Ewbank was mad at him. Later he got a reprieve when he learned he would kick off.

The Players

The world-championship game had a unique story line associated with it. It was simply the haves against the have-nots. It was blue-collar Baltimore against Madison-Avenue Giants. Unitas was blue collar. He wasn't a suit guy. The glamour that personified the New York team was its defense. If it beat the Browns in the playoff game the week before by humbling Jim Brown to one yard per run in eight carries, then what chance could Ameche and Moore have? It was all up to Unitas, and he accepted the challenge. He had a destiny to fulfill. The daunting Giants defense presented a monumental task. And Unitas would have a balmy winter day to get it done.

There was a great deal more to the Giants defense than Huff. There was Andy Robustelli, a smart, quick defensive stalwart at one end and the rugged Jim Katcavage on the other. The sentinels in the middle of the line were big Rosey Grier at 6'5" and the oppressive Dick Modzelewski. Unitas was told to throw over Modzelewski, who was five inches shorter than Grier. Emlen Tunnell, a savvy safety, and Jim Patton, who had 11 interceptions at the other safety spot, buoyed the defensive backfield.

Indeed, the Giants' hallmark was a magnificent defense. In reality, it was the first defense to have a glamour that their fans really identified with. Defensively, the Giants had limited their opponents to a league-low 183 points during the 1958 season. They won their four final games by yielding a total of 37 points—an average of nine points per contest. The adage that defense wins games was never more evident than during the final month of the Giants' regular season. And they would need every bit of defensive strength if they were to stop Unitas and his band of high-scoring Colts.

Unitas' adversary was quarterback Charlie Conerly, a 37-year-old gunslinger who had a bittersweet relationship with Giants fans. When the Giants won, he was beloved. And, by the same equation, if they lost, he was scorned. Conerly had the respect of his teammates and was also a Mara favorite. He wasn't anywhere near the passer that the younger Unitas was, but he knew how to win on guile and grit. He won some meaningful games with the Giants in the 11 years he was with them. The latest was the 10–0 playoff triumph against the Browns the previous week. Conerly scored the Giants' only touchdown, running 10 yards on his aging legs with a lateral from Gifford. In the 47–7 rout of the Bears in the 1956 championship game, which gave the Giants their first title in 18 years, Conerly threw for two touchdowns.

His craggy looks made him the original Marlboro Man, which explained why he always had a cigarette close by. Although he never was a cowboy, having been raised in Clarksdale, Mississippi, he easily portrayed one in a Western movie. The Giants-Colts game was the biggest game of his career, and it was a showdown between Conerly and Unitas.

Conerly was adept at getting the ball to Gifford on delays coming out of the backfield, an integral part of whatever offense the Giants manufactured. Gifford was the biggest threat to the Colts defense. He led the Giants in rushing, pass receiving, and scoring, and he could also throw the football. Mara cherished him, and Gifford's movie-star looks weren't overlooked by the ladies and Madison Avenue. He was a matinee idol.

Conerly may have been the gunslinger and Gifford may have been the leading man, but Johnny Unitas was certainly the hero that December day. During the sixth game of the season, he had suffered an injury that might have sidelined lesser men.

Unitas was in peak form when the injury occurred. The Colts had opened their season with five straight victories. During a typical game against Green Bay, Unitas had 10 completions in 13 attempts, which resulted in three touchdowns. Then misfortune appeared from out of nowhere. Finding no open receiver, the daring Unitas ran 13 yards to the Packers' 6-yard line, when linebacker John Symank crushed him from behind. Unitas withered in pain to the ground and was taken off the field as his teammates held their breath.

Instead of going to a hospital, Unitas went home. A painful, sleepless night convinced him to see a doctor the next morning. He was diagnosed with three broken ribs and a punctured lung. Blood had entered the lung through a puncture caused by a jutting rib bone and the lung had collapsed.

By 8:00 that night, Unitas was wheeled into the operating room, where a doctor placed a tube in the lung to withdraw the blood. Fortunately, the puncture had healed itself, and as soon as the blood was withdrawn, the lung expanded to its normal size.

The injury had caused some fear that Unitas would be finished for the season. However, he rested for one week and returned to practice the following Monday. He had missed the regular season game against New York and the following game against Chicago. Coach Ewbank always lamented that the reason that the Colts lost the Giants game was because the players' wives had accompanied the team to New York. But the players knew better: they lost by three points because Unitas hadn't played.

After Unitas returned to practice, he was fitted with a nine-pound, sponge-and-rubber-lined aluminum corset to protect his tender ribs. Wearing the coat of armor, Unitas could throw the football without pain. Thus bandaged, Unitas was prepared to play in the greatest game of his life.

The Game

Unitas was hoping that the Colts would win the coin toss when he led two of his teammates to midfield to meet Conerly and two other Giants. The Colts quarterback was primed and anxious to take the first snap from Nutter and lead the Colts uninterruptedly downfield for a touchdown. It would send the vaunted Giants defense a message that they were not impregnable, despite their hyped reputation. But it wasn't to be. The hometown Giants won the coin flip, and they chose to go on offense first, instead of conceding to their defense.

Bert Rechichar, who was worried that he wouldn't be allowed to play because he had missed a team meeting, was the first to touch the ball. His booming kick, soaring with the crowd's roar, was downed by Don Maynard in the end zone.

Conerly didn't join the Giants in the huddle. Don Heinrich did instead. Coach Jim Lee Howell had been opening games with a series or two with Heinrich before turning to Conerly. His theory was that by doing this, he and his coaching staff could observe what the opposing team was doing on defense, especially with its blitzing schemes. That was corroborated by Polaroid film sent down from the press box to the playing field by, of all people, Mara himself. Conerly didn't agree with Howell's strategy of starting the game with Heinrich: "I never knew why they did that," said Conerly. "Don would go in to see what the defense was doing and tell the coaches. They'd change up and I'd go in. Didn't make much sense to me. You always see more when you're in there."

What the Colts defense saw was somewhat surprising. Heinrich normally called some running plays to feel out the defense. However, in his opening series, he surprised the Colts—but didn't fool them—by throwing the ball three times. His first pass to Rote was swatted away by a charging Marchetti. Heinrich's next pass was a flare to Webster that netted seven yards. However, when he tried for a first down to Rote, defensive back Carl "Gaucho" Tasseff denied it.

The Giants defense now had to brace for Unitas. He trotted out to the Colts' 30-yard line and huddled his offense. Would he open with a quick pass to Berry or a long one to Moore, who could run like a gazelle? Close to fifteen thousand Colts fans, who made a weekend out of it in New York by car and train, were looking for the bomb in Unitas' arsenal. Instead, Unitas handed off to Moore on a sweep, and Moore was dumped for a three-yard loss by Carl Karilivacz. Alan Ameche got back some of the lost yardage when he churned inside tackle for seven yards. On the third down, needing six yards for a first, Huff anticipated a pass. He was right. He shot by Nutter on a blitz and slammed into Unitas hard enough to jar the ball loose from his hands. An opportunistic Patton recovered the ball on the Colts' 37-yard line.

It was an unlikely start for Unitas. The menacing Huff had given the Giants a propitious opportunity in the opening minutes of battle. The excellent field position could enable the Giants to score first. Sensing that, the partisan crowd roared approvingly to Heinrich's re-emergence on the field. And if he couldn't deliver a touchdown with a stronger arm than Conerly, there was always the reliable Summerall, who kicked a 49-yarder in the snow to defeat the Browns, 13–10, in the final game of the regular season, enabling the Giants to make the playoffs. But Marchetti, a marvelous defensive end, wouldn't allow it. After Webster lost a yard, Marchetti burst into the Giants' backfield unimpeded, crushed Heinrich, and then recovered the quarterback's fumble.

Unitas was only five yards from midfield when he appeared on the field a second time. He got there in two plays to L. G. Dupre. One was a four-yard flare pass and the other a one-yard run. Unitas was looking for a first down and looking for Berry. The hitch pattern dispatched Berry to the Giants' 40-yard line, but the reliable receiver never got the ball. Defensive back Lindon Crow recognized the pattern and brought back an interception five yards to the 45-yard line.

That couldn't be Unitas: a fumble and an interception in his first two series! Was the reputable Giants defense intimidating him? He came back on the field for the third time in the shadow of his own goal posts on the 15-yard line, a poor location from which to throw. So, the Giants played for the run. And Unitas, being Unitas, the master of the unexpected, called Moore's number for a pass. It wasn't a quick pop. It was a long one, which would enable Moore's speed to get by a defender. Unitas needed enough time for such a cavalier maneuver. What if he got sacked and fumbled again?

Baltimore's linemen executed their blocks, which allowed Unitas to grip the ball firmly and wait for Moore to get open. Parker ensured an opening by taking care of Robustelli. When the moment came, Moore caught the perfectly thrown ball on the Giants' 25-yard line, where he was pulled down by Patton. The catch brought the crowd to its feet and frustration to the Giants defenders.

With one magnificent pass, the Colts were deep in Giants territory and in field goal range. When they could only gain a yard in three attempts, the call for a field goal was issued. Steve Myhra, who wasn't anywhere near as accurate as Summerall was, had only made four of ten attempts during the season. And, true to form, he missed when his kick sailed wide. But the gods smiled on him and gave him another chance. The Giants were penalized for being offside. Five yards closer, Myhra lined up from the 19. He never got the chance to look up when he kicked. Huff rushed straight over the center and blocked Myhra's practically sure three-pointer.

Howell had had enough of Heinrich. He sent Conerly into battle, and the veteran quarterback heard cheers when the fans recognized him. He was a grizzled warrior who had survived three years of mediocre Giants football. In six plays, Conerly marched the Giants to Baltimore's 29-yard line, mostly behind Gifford's powerful 38-yard run. When Webster slipped and fell on Conerly's third-down pass, Summerall surveyed a 36-yard field goal placement and kicked accurately to give the Giants a 3–0 lead.

The Colts hadn't scored yet, and there were only two minutes left in the first quarter when Unitas lined them up from the 21. Three downs only generated eight yards, and the period lapsed with a Baltimore punt.

The Baltimore defense, practically overlooked because of the offense's productivity, forced a turnover on the first play of the second quarter. Conerly completed a pass to Gifford but the glamorous one fumbled, and little-known Ray Krouse recovered the ball on the Giants' 20.

Unitas had to deliver, not only for his own psyche, but for the rest of the team's as well. However, Unitas thrived on such challenges, and he was prepared. He was ready not only with his passing arm, which the Giants respected, but also with his ground forces. On the fourth down, Moore sped around the left end for an eight-yard touchdown. Myhra's conversion gave them a 7–3 lead, and the controlled joy on the sideline was an indication that the Colts scoring machine was primed for more.

After only one first down, New York punted. Rookie halfback Jackie Simpson was in position to gather the kick on the 10-yard line when he fumbled. He dropped the ball without ever being hit, and the Giants recovered it. The joy on the Colts' bench moments earlier was instantly subdued. However, no sooner did the Colts defense assume its alignment than it was relieved after one play. Gifford, trying to run a sweep into the end zone, fumbled, and Don Joyce covered the ball with all of his 255-pound body.

Gifford walked off the field disheartened after his second fumble, a somewhat tarnished idol in front of the hometown fans who adored him. He sat alone on the bench with his thoughts to reflect on what was wrong. "I really felt bad about that one," said Gifford later. "We were going in for a score, but the Colts took it away. If I had to pick a spot where the game began to turn, that was it."

Unitas felt the subtle shift and acted accordingly. He led the Colts on a 15-play, 86-yard gallop into the Giants end zone. This time he made use of his golden arm. He completed four of the six passes he threw, masterfully finessing the Giants for yardage: Berry for 5, Ameche for 10, Berry for 13, and Berry again for the 15-yard touchdown. There was only

1:20 left in the half, and with Baltimore ahead 14-3, New York ran out the clock and trudged somewhat bewildered into their dressing room to regroup in the face of Baltimore's almost 200 yards of offense.

The Giants had to make adjustments. They had only produced 86 yards of offense, which wouldn't get it done in the second half. Assistant coach Vince Lombardi had a solution. He detected that the Colts defense, which had been brilliant during the first 30 minutes, had been keying on Gifford. And it was working. Lombardi suggested using Gifford as a decoy. Although the Giants had been outplayed, they still were within reach, even though they had done almost nothing on offense.

"We were told to key on Gifford," Marchetti said later. "We were told to follow him wherever he went: come up fast, and never lose sight of him when a play began to develop. There were a hundred ways Frank could beat you. We had to be worried about every one of them."

The Giants' faithful crowd was worried now. Unitas was on his game, completing eight of the twelve passes he attempted (one of the four on which he misfired, Berry was ruled out of bounds). Compounding the Giants fans' fear was that the Colts were to receive the second-half kick-off, and Unitas would be there again.

Unitas began the second half the way he left off on the Colts' last touchdown. He threw to his end, Jim Mutscheller, for a first down. However, Giants linebacker Harland Svare read a reverse on the next play and dropped the speedy Moore for a seven-yard loss. The next play turned volatile. Unitas found Berry near the Giant sideline and hit him with a 15-yard throw. Huff ran him hard out of bounds and unleashed his frustrations in a heated exchange with Ewbank. An offsides call cost the Colts a first down, which Dupre had made, and Baltimore had to punt.

The Colts got the ball right back when they stopped the Giants' listless offense on three plays. Unitas had field position on Baltimore's 41-yard line. If the Colts could score another touchdown—one that would provide a 21-3 lead—the spirit of the Giants players would be broken, as well as the hearts of their fans. With that in mind, Unitas, going for the jugular, looked off Berry and opened with a 32-yard strike to Mutscheller on the Giants' 27-yard line. In one seemingly effortless throw, he had the Colts in position to register their third touchdown and probably the game's deciding touchdown. There was no way the docile Giants offense could score three touchdowns.

New York's defense held the Colts to one yard, but on the third down Unitas threw a well-timed sideline pass to Berry for 11 yards to the 15. Unitas came back with a quick pass to Moore, and in just five plays, Baltimore had reached the 3-yard line, to the groans of thousands. This was Ameche territory, and the punishing fullback made it to the 1. When Unitas was stuffed on a quarterback sneak, he turned once again to Ameche, who tried the middle and found nothing. Wanting a touchdown, Unitas engaged in a bit of chicanery with Ameche on fourth down. As the stout Giants defense braced for an inside run, Unitas pitched to Ameche on the outside, but to no avail. Linebacker Cliff Livingston made the play of the game by tackling Ameche for a four-yard loss, which kept the Giants alive.

Huff exhorted the offense to get it going as he ran to the sideline. "There was no way they were going to score," he remarked later. "They weren't going to get a damn thing."

But the Giants offense was isolated on its 5-yard line against a Baltimore defense that had been exemplary so far. On third down, with the Colts needing to stop the Giants from making two yards, they bunched for the run. However, the wily Conerly wasn't done. He dispatched Rote deep, disdaining the short yardage offense. Rote slipped behind the Colts secondary, and like Unitas earlier, Conerly lofted a pass into the receiver's hands. Andy Nelson caught Rote from behind to prevent a touchdown and caused him to fumble. As the crowd screamed and the loose football rolled toward the Colts' goal line, Webster, who was trailing the play, grabbed the ball and was knocked out of bounds by Tasseff on the 1-yard line. In one well-scripted play, the Giants came alive. Then they came within four points of the Colts when Triplett scored two plays later to bring the score to 14–10.

On that one wild play that had practically matched the Giants' entire first-half offensive output, the game's momentum changed again. The crowd felt it and roared deafeningly on almost every play that followed. And the Giants defense responded by stopping the Colts on three downs, with Modzelewski adding to the bedlam by sacking Unitas for a seven-yard loss. That series proved that the game's momentum had indeed switched back to the Giants.

When the third quarter ended, Conerly had taken the Giants to their 39-yard line with an accurate pass to Schnelker. The Marlboro Man was in a groove. With his first two plays in the fourth quarter, he showed his focus. He struck at the Colts' heart with Schnelker again, this time for 46 yards to Baltimore's 15-yard line. Near pandemonium filled the stadium. Giants fans had their own Unitas. Conerly didn't hesitate. He called his buddy Gifford's number and executed a perfect pass for the touchdown that sent the Giants ahead 17–14.

The crowd was nearly delirious. The noise resonated above the three-tiered stadium into the darkness of the Bronx sky. Babe Ruth never created a bigger roar. *Sports Illustrated*'s pro football writer, Hamilton "Tex" Maule, described it as "something you would not believe—a wall of sound."

But Conerly was no Unitas. Starting from his own 20, Unitas got the Colts to the Giants' 39. When two passes failed, Myhra entered to attempt a game-tying 46-yard field goal. His kick fell to the earth harmlessly short, and the Colts remained three points behind with some 10 minutes left in what would come down to a battle of wills: a spunky Colts team versus a proud Giants one, its championship banners waving in the breeze from the bleacher flagpole. All they needed for another banner was to play defense like they had done so wonderfully and run out the clock on offense.

"At that point, we just had to keep the ball, run out the clock, and they'd never get another chance," explained Webster afterward. "We were so hot. Everything was working well. It sure looked like our game."

But the Giants had to keep the ball away from Unitas. They went to work on offense, determined to keep the ball out of his hands. They didn't need any more points. They needed only to keep Unitas on the sidelines, where he couldn't hurt them anymore. Things seemed to be going their way. The Giants had produced two first downs and were trying for a third when fullback Phil King, who replaced a tired Webster, fumbled. Krouse then made his second big play by recovering the ball on the Giants' 42. That meant Unitas would come back in, and he didn't hesitate to make his presence felt.

Unitas was after a touchdown on the first play and called a deep pattern for Moore. They connected on the goal line as the crowd in that section of the end zone leaped to its feet. Was it a touchdown? Moore looked up and saw the referee signal no. He ruled that Moore was out of bounds. Moore insisted that he wasn't, but to no avail.

"I was in bounds. I was, dammit, I really was," Moore claimed for years.

After Unitas got the Colts to the 27, in position to try a game-tying field goal, the Giants defense erupted with fury. First the irrepressible Robustelli dropped Unitas for an 11-yard loss. Then Modzelewski followed with a nine-yard loss, and suddenly, after two heroic Giants plays, the Colts had retreated to the Giants' 47. The Colts' field goal position was gone, and their chances of winning were severely diminished, with only 2:30 left. The Giants needed only a couple of first downs to run out the clock for their 1958 banner.

They got the first when Conerly fooled the Colts with a 10-yard pass to Webster. At that moment in the press box, the writers had voted Conerly as the game's most valuable player. The Giants were only 10 yards away from a title. Webster got a yard, and Gifford, on a sweep, produced five. On third-and-4, Conerly crouched over the center with the biggest play of the game for the Giants. He wanted his sidekick Gifford to deliver the first down from the Giants' 35. Gifford started wide. With Colts defenders in pursuit, he cut back and reached the 40-yard line and appeared to have achieved the down.

A punishing hit by Marchetti and Shinnick helped to knock Gifford to the ground. As a mass of bodies was falling all around, all 288 pounds of Eugene "Big Daddy" Lipscomb crashed onto the pile, landed on

Marchetti's leg, and snapped it like a dry twig just above the right ankle. Marchetti's cry of pain created a referee's whistle for a timeout without anyone knowing if Gifford had made the clinching first down or not. None of the officials gave a signal.

"Frank was hollering," said Marchetti. "I guess he thought I was laying there faking it to get an additional timeout. 'Get your damn butt off the ground, Gino. I was down. The play is over.' I said, 'Frank, I can't get up. I can't.'"

There was momentary chaos on the field as a stretcher carried off Marchetti. He ordered the stretcher bearers to put him down by the goal line because he wanted to watch the end of the game. "As captain, I thought it was important to be there," said Marchetti. When referee Charlie Berry placed down the ball, Gifford was inches short of the precious first down.

"All this hollering is going on, and Gifford's lying on the ground saying, 'I made the first down. I made the sticks,'" said Donovan. "Hell, he didn't even get back to the line of scrimmage."

But Gifford insisted he did even 25 years later. That one paramount play decided the outcome of what has been written about by pro football historians as the greatest game ever played. And, from the standpoint of dramatics alone, it was.

"I made the first down," said Gifford. "I know I made it. But Marchetti broke his leg and he was screaming like a wounded panther. There was a lot of confusion. A lot of time passed by while they carried Marchetti off the field. When they spotted the ball, it was placed short of the first-down marker."

Rote concurred. He was near the play and walked over to the ball held by referee Berry. "The referee was so concerned about Marchetti that he forgot where he picked up the ball," explained Berry. I saw him pick it up by his front foot, but he put it down where his back foot was."

The ball was inches short of a first down, and the Giants players wanted to go for it. Several pleaded with Howell. A conservative, gray-haired guy from Mississippi, Howell decided not to. He had the league's leading punter, Don Chandler, who was proficient in booting high, booming kicks, and because of the hang time they produced, most of his punts weren't run back. Players in battle are emotional at some point in a game, and in a highly charged situation, a coach has to temper feeling with logic. A fourth-down play was a gamble. A punt was not.

"We only needed four inches," said Giants guard Jack Stroud, one of the NFL's outstanding guards with his broad shoulders. "We would have run through a brick wall at that point. Besides, Marchetti was out, and whoever they put in for him couldn't have been as good. And he would have been nervous, tight. It would have gone to him, and dammit, it would have worked."

When Chandler kicked a 43-yard punt that Tasseff had to fair catch on the 14, Howell's decision appeared correct. There was only 1:56 left when Unitas undertook the biggest challenge of his three-year career: he had less than two minutes to conquer 86 yards of earth. It would prove to be the defining moment of Unitas' entire existence.

The Birth of a Legend

A chilly mist began to envelop the field, painting an eerie background for the tired warriors. Everyone on the field knew that Unitas could throw and throw, and he was good at it.

The Giants aligned their defense to abort the big play that would yield the Colts chunks of terrain. When Unitas missed on his first two passes, the Giants players raised their helmets high on the crowded sidelines, which numbered more people than players, coaches, and equipment personnel. But Unitas hurled a bullet to Moore in the center of the Giants phalanx for an 11-yard first down. He would have a fresh set of downs. That was all he needed.

Unitas turned to Raymond Berry, the slow-footed receiver who required contacts for his weak vision, a corset to protect his bad back, and had one leg shorter than the other, which he compensated for by having one shoe with long cleats. It was a wonder that he was a Colt after having been picked in the 20th round of the 1954 draft. Unitas had confidence in him despite his infirmities, and that's all that mattered.

There were two things at which Berry excelled over all the others: he ran precise patterns and had sure hands. Those were two traits that Unitas admired, and the reasons why, over the years, Berry became Unitas' favorite receiver. The other quality that was not lost on the quarterback was that Berry wasn't afraid of patterns that took him to the middle of the field, even though he knew full well that he would be battered by a linebacker or a defensive back. And in Tunnell and Patton, the Giants had two safeties who could punish a receiver.

Before the long day was over, Unitas and Berry would put on a passing clinic. And, of the 12 years they were together, Berry pointed to that afternoon as the most significant. "It certainly was the best game that Unitas and I had together," said the taciturn Berry.

Unitas knew that the Giants were defending the deep ball by protecting the sidelines. That left the middle vulnerable. That meant he could call on Berry. Unitas had realized that the middle was his to exploit when Moore was wide open on the third-down pass that gave the Colts a first down on the 25. Still, Unitas needed to negotiate at least 45 more yards for a game-tying field goal attempt from a kicker who wasn't all that good. Berry was his guy.

Berry caught a pass at midfield with 1:04 left. Then he caught another at the sidelines for 15 more yards. He repeated the play and got an additional 22 yards to the Giants' 16 with the lights on the clock reporting 19 seconds.

Was it possible that, in just over a minute, Unitas had moved the Colts 62 yards to position them for the three points needed to tie the game? He did it all with audibles because time was too precious to be wasted on huddles.

When the shaky Myhra surveyed his kick, the biggest one of his life, there were exactly seven seconds left. His kick would decide the game—one way or the other. If he was accurate, there would be overtime. If he missed, which he did often, time would expire and Conerly and his buddies would celebrate at Toots Shor's. The Colts still needed respectability.

They needed the field goal. Myhra gave them both with a 19-yard field goal, tying the game 17–17.

"I told myself I better not miss it, or it was going to be a long, cold winter on the farm in North Dakota," said Myhra.

By then, darkness had enveloped the stadium, and the weather, which was mild when the game started, had turned cold. Patches of ice appeared on the field, and the players, looking like warriors from the medieval age, huddled under their capes on the sidelines. A five-minute respite was all the players got. There wasn't enough time to take refuge in the dressing room. The players of both teams waited for the coin toss to determine who would get the ball first. The Giants called it correctly and breathed easier. After what Unitas had done, they didn't want to face him again. Getting the kickoff would allow them to turn their backs on him. But he still loomed menacingly on the sidelines. The Giants had to score to keep him there.

Both teams showed signs of weariness from the tense battle. If anything, the Colts had the benefit of an extra week's rest because the Giants had appeared in a playoff game a week earlier in winter weather.

The Giants began the overtime session shakily. Don Maynard fumbled Rechichar's kick on the 10-yard line, but managed to recover the mishap on the 20. With only 10 first downs the entire game, Conerly needed to create some big plays for the Giants to win. But he was tired. He told Gifford on the sidelines that he was beat up and hoped that the game didn't go into overtime because, as he put it, he "[couldn't] go on any more."

Gifford opened with a four-yard run. However, Conerly missed with a pass to Schnelker and came up a yard short with his aging legs when trying to fool the Colts on a keeper play. Chandler had to punt, and that meant that the defense would have to face Unitas again.

Chandler did his best to help with a huge punt, and it was so high that Taseff could only return it one yard to the 20. Unitas had to gain 80 yards, or at least a minimum of 60 to produce the winning points. He choreographed a superlative 13-play progression to establish the beginning of his legendary status as the most feared quarterback in history. In the process, he converted two critical third-down challenges to bring a championship to Baltimore.

Unitas' first pass was an eight-yard completion to Ameche. On the second, he relied on Berry and advanced the Colts to the Giants' side of the field, with a 21-yard sideline toss. Next, he demonstrated his uncanny field perception. Seeing that the Giants second line of defense had split to help on pass coverage, he pointed to Ameche in the huddle to run a trap play. The burly fullback gave him 22 yards to reach New York's 20-yard line and the impending catastrophe that awaited the Giants and their fans.

"Huff was playing for a pass, and the way Modzelewski was crashing, I figured they were right for a trap," was the way Unitas described the call. "I hit it right. Hell, they had been blowing in on me pretty hard on pass plays. They were coming up the middle, so I called a trap and Alan [Ameche] did the rest of it. It wasn't any great call."

Still, Unitas was not thinking about a field goal—not after Dupre failed to gain a yard. He wanted a touchdown, and he indicated as much with a 12-yard pass in the flat to the trusted Berry. Unitas could see the goal posts. They were only eight yards away. But Ewbank was thinking about a field goal and sent in word to Unitas to play it safe and keep the ball on the ground.

"I told him, keep it on the ground, we don't want an interception here," said Ewbank after Unitas called a timeout and conferred with his coach. "We can go for the field goal if the running plays don't work."

Unitas did keep it on the ground—but only for one play, when the weary but audacious Giants defense held Ameche to a one-yard gain. Unitas wanted more, and he got it with a daring six-yard pass to Mutscheller, who was corralled out of bounds on the 1-yard line. The play made the Giants wary of a pass on the third down. Unitas had enough confidence to throw one even from the 1-yard line!

He embarrassingly fooled the Giants on the next play. Instead of having Ameche run behind Parker, Unitas sent him to the other side toward guard Alex Sandusky and tackle George Preas. Brilliantly, Sandusky and

Preas executed the play to perfection and opened a monstrous hole for Ameche. Perhaps out of amazement, Ameche crossed the goal line and fell into the end zone from his own momentum.

The heroic Colts were the champions, 23–17. "They couldn't have stopped us if we needed ten yards," said Unitas triumphantly when he reached the dressing room.

Unitas ran off the field after Ameche crossed the goal line. His work was done. He did what was expected of him, what he expected of himself. He was the consummate pro and didn't want to get enmeshed in the crowd that engulfed his teammates on the field. Looking around, he trotted into the visitor's dugout and to the safety of the dressing room, which in minutes would turn into a bedlam of writers and well-wishers.

The *Sport* magazine red Corvette that had been heading into Conerly's garage was Unitas' now. If the Giants had won, Conerly would have been named the game's MVP because the writers had already voted him as such in the press box 10 minutes before the game had ended. A club official informed Unitas that Ed Sullivan wanted him on his show. His Hollywood-type performance was that good. The *Ed Sullivan Show* was the Sunday-night window on American culture. The Beatles, Elvis Presley, and almost anybody who was somebody, from athletes to movie stars to entertainers, performed on stage or took a bow from the audience when Sullivan pointed them out. But Unitas flatly turned it down. He wanted to be with the team on its return flight to Baltimore. Ameche went instead and picked up $500 for his appearance.

Unitas was swamped by the media. They wanted to know how he did it. How he took the Colts on two long drives in the waning minutes of regulation and the overtime to script such a dramatic finish. In the crush of the small room, a reporter asked Unitas about the gambling play of throwing a pass to Mutscheller and perhaps risking an interception in doing so. Unitas answered politely, but with calculated assuredness: "It wasn't a gamble. They didn't see what I saw. When you know what you're doing, you're not intercepted. The Giants were jammed up at the line and not expecting a pass. If Jim [Mutscheller] had been covered, I'd have thrown the pass out of bounds. It's just that I would rather win a game like this by a touchdown than a field goal.

"It was no sweat. They were playing one on one, looking for a run. All I had to do was flip it up there for Jim and let him catch it. I don't expect a pass like that to fail and it didn't. No matter how good a defense is, you can always find a weakness somewhere. You find it and start hitting it. When they close it up, you have to then find the next weakness."

Unitas just sat calmly answering the questions that kept rolling off the writers' tongues. It seemed that he repeated his answers time after time, but he didn't seem to mind. Not after a game like that. Not after the team's first world championship. It was a golden moment to be cherished. He wasn't in any hurry, and the bus and the plane would never leave without him. Not after what he had done. Unitas continued to explain what made those two dramatic drives work to perfection: "They were just giving us certain things and we were taking them. Berry was working back there on Karilivacz deep on his outside, and then we'd come back inside and work on a linebacker. They were just leaving it there, so we kept going back to it, taking advantage of it. We could just as easily have gone to the other side, but when you got something like that going, you just don't give it up.

"We were also beating the linebacker, Svare. We'd beat him deep, go behind him, and we'd throw it in front of him next. Huff was concerned about that little quick slant-in on the weak side, and he was trying to help Svare and Karilivacz. But he should have never gotten out of the middle. If you can take care of your own responsibilities first and then go back and help there too, fine, but he couldn't do both things at the same time. He never should have gotten so far out of his position. When he did that, he just left open the big play for Ameche."

There was little consolation in the Giants' quarters as Gifford searched for answers. He cried openly. Lombardi bent over and offered comforting words, but they didn't help. Gifford was haunted by the two fumbles that he felt cost the Giants the victory and the championship. And he was still agonizing over his third-down run that was four inches short of a first down.

When the Giants missed by inches, Unitas made them count. A number of quarterbacks could throw long, but the difference was that Unitas could pass long. But the complete quarterback is the one who can also think. Unitas won every inch of that game with his head.

"The man was a genius," said Huff. "I never saw a quarterback that good on those two drives."

He never would. Nor would anyone else, for that matter.

2

The Hill

THE ROWS OF SMALL HOUSES ON BOTH SIDES OF THE HILL IN a remote corner of Mt. Washington are almost hidden and are separated from downtown Pittsburgh by the murky Monongahela River. Back in the thirties, William Street was a winding, unpaved cinder road that barely provided enough space for two vehicles to pass one another in opposite directions. Not that the street was heavily traveled. For the most part, the families that lived on the hill were poor, and automobiles were few in number. Yet the hill, looming like a caretaker looking down on a narrow road, offered security and comfort for its residents, who were underdogs scratching for any way to earn a living.

A Tough Start to Life

It wasn't the best of years when John Constantine Unitas was born on a sunny morning on May 7, 1933, when the hill seemed to welcome spring. It was a turbulent year in America, as Americans were still trying to free themselves from the Great Depression. Money was tight, as America's farmlands were barren. Booze was being imbibed out of flasks, and houses of prostitution were part of the mainstream. Gangsters were in vogue, with the likes of Al Capone, John Dillinger, "Baby Face" Nelson, and "Pretty Boy" Floyd attaining notoriety.

What was most important to the Unitas family, in its remote end of western Pennsylvania, was manufacturing a living from a very modest coal delivery business. Pittsburgh's economy was suffering heavily from the Depression, the visual effects of which were most strikingly noticeable at night, when the steel mills along the river were not lighting up the sky. The steel workers and laborers found comfort in Congress' repeal of Prohibition, and the gin mills were at least doing some business. The Boilermaker, a shot with a beer chaser, became popular.

Leon and Helen Unitas couldn't afford such a swig. John was their third child, and Leon worked hard on his coal truck to make sure that there was enough to eat at 345 William Street. Helen had emigrated from Lithuania to escape the poverty in a country of long, cold winters so that she could experience the American dream, which Leon had already begun. However, Leon's death five years later from pneumonia put an immense strain on the family of five. But the resolve that Helen brought with her to the New World enabled her to be a provider for her four children.

When her husband died on a cool, fall day in 1938, Helen faced her first challenge. The relatives who gathered at the funeral home were convinced that Helen was not capable of running the coal business. They also felt that four children were too much of a burden. The concerned relatives agreed to take some of the children and help raise them. Helen wouldn't hear of it, vowing to keep her family together.

"Nobody is going to take anybody," Helen told them.

She always remembered that day: "John was such a little fellow and too young to be put through all that," she recalled. "But when we returned to the house, he was outside throwing a football with other children. I'll never forget that."

Surviving the Early Years

Helen kept the coal business going with the help of a hired driver. Leonard, her oldest son, who was 10 years old, helped out. When the weather turned warm in the spring and coal orders slowed, Helen took a job cleaning offices in downtown Pittsburgh. She did it four nights per week, from 10:00 at night until 6:00 the next morning. Her pay was miniscule at $3 per night, but she was determined to keep her family together, and no work was too menial.

"My uncle was a bachelor and he lived with us," said Helen. "He was 70 and couldn't work, but at least he could watch the children when I left. We got by all right. Nothing fancy, but I made enough at the cleaning job and the other work I did to make ends meet."

Helen made sure her children made it to school every day. Every morning, John, often accompanied by his younger sister, Shirley, walked to St. Justin's school, which was almost a mile away. The Pittsburgh seasons were harsh, and there were no school buses to offer protection from the snow or the rains of spring. The steep, cinder hill might have contributed to Unitas becoming slightly bowlegged during his formative years.

"John wasn't much of a talker, and there were days when he never said a word," Shirley said. "Mom worked hard, and every day she had a list of chores we all had to do. You always got them done. She had it so hard you would never think of causing her trouble. We were poor and went to school in washed-out clothes, while the other kids had blouses and skirts. No one really associated with us.

"Times were tough. My mother was raising four kids by herself. She had a saying: 'If it's a need, we can talk about it, but if it's a want, don't bring it up.' One time the nuns from school called the house wondering if John and I were malnourished. That's how bad it was. My mother really got mad about that. There was always food on the table. We were just built that way.

"Our neighborhood was rough. You dreamed about making a little more money. Every book John got out of the library was a book about a quarterback. He was always reading something like *The Sid Luckman Story*. All he wanted was football. You could sit in a room with John for six hours and you might get a word here or there. He wasn't a conversationalist. Didn't want any part of girls. He was a late bloomer. The only time I saw him cry was when he was 10 years old. We had a dog called

Weegie, a terrier with a tail like a doughnut, who got hit by a cab and was killed. John just sobbed and sobbed. As we grew older, he became my protector. When I became a cheerleader, he would sit next to me on the school bus."

Unitas didn't grow up without some childhood mishaps. Two of them easily could have destroyed his athletic career, and both involved a gun. One afternoon he was walking near an empty lot where a couple of older boys were playing with a shell, trying to get it to discharge. They succeeded, but John fell to the ground screaming in pain. The cartridge hit him above the knee. A neighbor drove seven-year-old Unitas to the hospital, where a doctor removed as much lead as he could find, but admitted that he didn't get all of the metal.

Ten years later, Unitas suffered another setback, this time of his own doing. There had been a series of robberies in the neighborhood, and his mother, being the protective woman that she was, acquired a revolver to keep in the house. Unitas decided to clean it one morning. He correctly removed the clip and was preparing to treat it with oil and a polishing rag. For some reason, and Unitas never could explain why, he pulled the trigger before clearing the chamber. A single bullet went cleanly through Unitas' right index finger. He was lucky they saved the finger, but he was never able to bend the first joint of the finger for the rest of his life.

An Unlikely Athlete

But Unitas' life was football. He was a junior at St. Justin's, a small Catholic high school. When the doctor told him he couldn't play any football for the remainder of the season, Unitas taped a splint around his finger, played, and threw a 50-yard pass in the very next game. He was a running back, a defensive back, and ultimately wound up at quarterback when the team's starter broke his ankle a week before the season began.

Unitas had dreamed about being a football player ever since he was in the seventh grade. In class one day, a substitute teacher named Mrs. O'Connor asked him what he wanted to be when he grew up. Unitas didn't hesitate. He said, "I want to be a professional football player." He later commented, "I didn't know why I said it."

Unitas at first played baseball in high school. When he appeared on a football field, nobody paid much attention to the skinny youngster with his arms dangling by his side. Little St. Justin's lost more games than they won simply because they were out-manned. "I remember playing Ambridge High," recalled Unitas years later. "That's one of those big schools that sent a lot of players to college. They had four or five teams dressed for the game. Up at our end, there were only 25 of us—and not big either! We just stared up at them. They murdered us."

During his senior year, Unitas was carried off the field with what was suspected to be a severe back injury. It was what his mother always feared, that her son would get hurt playing football. She sat in the stands that day fearing the worst as Leonard rushed to drive him to the hospital. Her first thought was that her son would be paralyzed. On Monday, he was back at practice as if nothing had happened. "He was really driven," said Shirley. "His mother instilled the tough attitude that John displayed," added Joe Chilleo, a neighbor who lived up the street from Unitas. "He was a good athlete, but he didn't walk around with a halo over his head or anything like that. He was just another kid in the neighborhood."

But he was special. Those around him knew it. There was something about a quarterback who could throw a football 60 yards as a senior. "He was a phenomenon," exclaimed his cousin Joe Unitas. "People wanted to come see this skinny, bowlegged kid jump in the air and throw the ball. Of course, he was jumping because he couldn't see over the linemen."

Unitas' center, James Laitta, a little guy who weighed 100 pounds soaking wet, admired Unitas. "I was prone on many plays, but John was thin as a toothpick," he said. "He took quite a beating, but he always got up. He was a commander out there. If people were talking in the huddle, he'd tell them, 'Shut up.'"

Ron Petrelli, another teammate, said Unitas was a natural at any sport. "I thought I was a pretty good boxer, but we put the gloves on and I couldn't hit John," Petrelli said. "He could do anything. He was thin, but he was already throwing a nice ball. And he was tough. One time he got run out of bounds and pushed into a wall and he chipped a tooth. But he kept playing."

Dedication, Destiny, and Promises

Unitas didn't know the meaning of the word quit. It was ingrained in him by his mother, who taught him about courage and perseverance. "She never got discouraged and taught us the same way," said Unitas. His determination to excel paid off during his senior year, when he was named quarterback on Pittsburgh's All-Catholic High School team. It was quite a tribute. He was picked ahead of all the quarterbacks in the bigger schools.

His mother had done an amazing job of getting his brothers and sisters through high school, but that was as far as it got. Unitas had little hope for college. There just wasn't any money for any of the kids to enter college. Despite his accolades, no one would offer a football scholarship to a 6', 138-pound quarterback.

His one hope had been John Chickerneo, an assistant coach at the University of Pittsburgh, who had initially contacted him. But when Chickerneo took a high school head coaching job, Unitas never heard from him or Pittsburgh again. His dream of becoming a professional football player was all but gone. If he couldn't play in college, he wouldn't get anywhere near the 12 professional teams except to sell programs in the stands on game day.

His remaining hopes were his coach, Max Carey, who knew some college scouts, and surprisingly enough, Father Thomas McCarthy, one of the priests at St. Justin's, who had some connections at Notre Dame. Unitas got excited when Reverend McCarthy arranged for a visit to Notre Dame in April.

Unfortunately, Frank Leahy, the legendary Notre Dame coach, was out of town when Unitas arrived by bus in South Bend. Assistant coach Bernie Crimmins saw enough in Unitas to keep him around for almost a week. When Unitas left the Irish campus, he didn't have a commitment nor even a word from Crimmins. That came a week later, when Crimmins phoned Carey and told him that Unitas was too small for Notre Dame football.

The trip that Carey arranged for Unitas to the University of Indiana was just as bad. Unitas worked out for a couple of coaches and wasn't even asked to stay overnight. They simply thanked him for coming and told him to go home. Unitas didn't know what to think. Neither did Carey for that matter. He didn't even get the courtesy of a telephone call about his skinny quarterback. Unitas had visited two schools and didn't receive any encouragement whatsoever. He didn't know what to do, but he had to find a way.

Len Casanova, the head coach at the University of Pittsburgh, invited him back for a workout. Unitas was shocked. He never expected to hear from Pitt again. It was May, and Chickerneo, who had first contacted him, had disappeared. Unitas didn't take the time to sort it out. Instead, he packed his workout clothes for the trip across the river each day for four days. Casanova liked what he saw in Unitas. Besides the fact that Unitas could throw a good ball, Casanova liked Unitas' determination and offered him a four-year scholarship. Unitas couldn't have been happier. He would get the chance to play in his hometown, and his mother, brother, and sisters would be there rooting for him. Maybe the whole Unitas clan of relatives would be there to root for him. Unitas was going to college because he could play football. He liked that, and his mother was proud. At least one of her children would get a college education.

It never happened. The hometown dream evaporated overnight. Unitas failed the entrance exam. He was only a C-average student, but he'd thought that was good enough: Pitt wasn't exactly Harvard. Even though Unitas was a local boy, the administration refused to give him any special treatment. Unitas felt hopeless. It was getting late in the year for college. Spring had turned to summer, and he didn't have anywhere to go.

Unitas' high school football coach, Carey, was still looking for a place for him. Carey contacted John Dromo, an assistant coach at the University of Louisville, about Unitas. Carey knew the kid could play there. Louisville was anything but a football power, but what the hell, the kid had to play somewhere. Frank Gitschier, Louisville's backfield coach, made it happen. He was making a trip to his hometown of Sharon, Pennsylvania, when head coach Frank Camp asked him to stop in Pittsburgh to check out Unitas. Gitschier later became an important part of Unitas' life.

"We didn't have a recruiting budget, couldn't make long-distance phone calls, couldn't do anything," Gitschier said. "What happened was that, simply, coach Camp wasn't happy with the two kids we had. I spent about two hours with John and his mother, telling them what we offered and why John should come to Louisville. I made two promises to Helen: I told her that John would go to mass every Sunday and he would graduate. She smiled and I knew we had a chance. But you know, we didn't get him because of any recruiting coup. We got him because no one else wanted him. Crimmins later told me that he liked John as a prospect, but he knew the fans would run him out of town if he brought in a guy weighing 135 pounds."

James Laitta, the underweight center who couldn't block too well for Unitas at St. Justin's, made up for it by driving him to Louisville in a car that he described as "an old crate." It got them there, and that was all Unitas asked for. He was getting a chance to play college ball and would have walked to Louisville if his skinny legs could have gotten him there. The players' dormitory was no better than Laitta's car, but Unitas never complained about either one.

"It was an old rundown barracks the navy had given to the school," grinned Gitschier, who could never use it as a recruiting tool. "It was terrible. One toilet. A couple of showers. That was it! When I took Unitas to meet Camp, he looked alarmed. Here was this 135-pound kid with hunched shoulders and bowed legs. When John left the room, Camp looked at me and said, 'Boy, you got a project.'"

Camp had earned his reputation as a meticulous high school coach before he came to Louisville. He was hired to build a football program that had fallen on hard times. Being so detailed, he was a stern taskmaster.

Unitas was frustrated one day after practice when Camp chastised him for drinking water. "We had three-hour practices and the players weren't allowed to drink any water, but John thought it was okay because practice was over," explained Gitschier. "Camp yelled out, 'Unitas, that's five laps around the field!' Boy, John was mad. I knew what was about to happen. He was going back to William Street. I ran with him and said, 'John, this is what makes you tough.' He finally calmed down."

Gitschier took a liking to Unitas. He knew where he came from and how much he wanted to play, and he dedicated time to work with him even after practice. He drilled his pupil on all the basics of quarterbacking: how to set his feet behind the center, how to place his hands to take the snap, the correct way to hold the ball when he set up to throw, and the right way to throw the ball without rolling his wrist. "John was really raw when he got there," Gitschier said.

Before classes began that fall, Unitas had to take an entrance exam just as he had at Pitt, with the same result: Unitas failed again. It was the end of the line. Or so Unitas thought. He experienced leniency that he didn't find at Pitt. He appeared before the college board alone. The panel wanted to know why he wanted to attend college and why he should be given the opportunity after not passing the entrance exam. Unitas' future was in his own hands. He had to have the right answers. This wasn't about football. Unitas sat there with the same confidence he had on the football field and assured the board members that he very much wanted a college education and that he could do college work. He wasn't totally convincing, but Unitas was accepted on academic probation with a textbook in one hand and a football in the other. He had to balance the two.

Finding His Way

Unitas' friendship with Fred Zangaro was helpful to him at school. Zangaro, too, was from Pittsburgh and was a few years older than Unitas. Zangaro was married, had gotten out of the army, and was a fullback, not much taller than Laitta, but heavier and more muscular. He lived in a house behind Churchill Downs, and every Sunday Unitas was there for spaghetti and meatballs. "John would come over in that old car of his, the green hornet, we called it," said Zangaro. "He was quiet, didn't drink or smoke, and he loved football. We'd work together after practice all the time. He was a general out there on the field and ran the show. Wow, one time in a game against Dayton, he threw me a pass left-handed that went for 40 yards. I just shook my head in disbelief."

Unitas quickly learned that Louisville was like St. Justin's. The players weren't very good, and there weren't many to begin with. In football terms, Louisville was considered a small school, so small that they played their games on a high school field. They were physically outmanned against practically every team they played. But when Unitas finally got to play, he made the most of the opportunity.

Louisville had dropped three of its first four games that 1951 season when Camp decided to start his skinny, bowlegged quarterback against St. Bonaventure University in Olean, New York. The Bonnies had a pretty good quarterback in Ted Marchibroda, who Unitas met again four years later and who became head coach of the Baltimore Colts in 1975. Marchibroda got St. Bonaventure off to a 19–0 lead before Unitas made his presence felt. Unitas made heads turn when he completed 11 straight passes on a wet field, three of which were touchdowns, to give underdog Louisville a 21–19 advantage. The Louisville players were jubilant on the sidelines until St. Bonaventure converted a last-minute field goal to snatch a 22–21 victory.

That very first game he ever played for Louisville defined Unitas' college career. Camp was so pleased with Unitas' performance that he announced that he would be the starting quarterback the rest of the season. And Unitas showed them how to win. He led them to upset victories over North Carolina State, Houston, Washington and Lee, and Mississippi Southern. When the season ended, Louisville was 5–4, but more important, they had a quarterback for the next three years. Not just a quarterback, but a leader.

Unitas demonstrated his leadership in a game against Houston, when he brought his team back to upset the Cougars 35–28. On a crucial third down play, needing two yards for a first down, running back Bill Pence asked for the ball in the huddle, saying that he could get the two yards. Unitas said, "When I want you to take it, I'll let you know." Unitas instead threw a pass for a touchdown.

Even his cousin Joe, who played with Unitas his freshman year, felt the kid quarterback's wrath. He quickly experienced Unitas' on-field intelligence when he realized that his younger cousin knew he had missed a block not by observing the miscue, but by who eventually tackled him. "If you can't block that guy, there's somebody on the bench who can," growled Unitas.

Unitas' freshman season was his beacon year. However, Louisville's football program was even further depleted as a new administration mandated that 15 scholarships be terminated. Unitas thought briefly about transferring because Crimmins, now at Indiana, wanted him, and Big 10 football was a launching pad for professional football. But Unitas remained loyal to Louisville because Indiana didn't want him at the beginning. Louisville had given Unitas a chance, and he finished his remaining three years there as a way of thanking them. Unitas displayed his exceptional character, a product of his upbringing.

When the 1952 season began, the rallying cry for the beleaguered football team was "Unitas We Stand, Divided We Fall." There was even a sign that read "See Unitas Pass" to attract the fans to the Manuel High School field. However, it wasn't long after it was erected that some mischievous prankster rubbed out the *P.* The Cardinals won their first two games of the season, which was highlighted by a 41–14 win over Florida State. Unitas was brilliant. He completed 17 of 22 passes. "Coach Camp fell in love with him," said Gitschier. "And, what isn't there to love? John was the first of those lunch-bucket quarterbacks to come out of western Pennsylvania. Later on came Joe Montana, Jim Kelly, Joe Namath, and Dan Marino. They were all the same. Guys who didn't have anything.

Guys who knew it was back to the steel mills or coal mines if they didn't get the job done."

The Cardinals won only one more game that season to finish with a 3–5 record. The five losses were not an indictment of Unitas. He had a good season, completing 50 percent of his passes and throwing for 12 touchdowns. Opposing coaches praised him, and he was a hero on campus. He was Louisville's only offensive threat, and as a result, took more hits than the average quarterback.

"I remembered that we played Tennessee, and they came in and beat us real bad, 55–0 or so, and they really jumped on Johnny," said Gitschier. "After the game, their coach, General Bob Neyland, came over and raved about Johnny's guts. He told Johnny, 'Young man, I want to tell you that your play today was as fine a display of courage as I've ever seen. The way you got off those passes with our boys climbing all over you was something to see.' It was the same thing when Sid Gillman came down with that Cincinnati club of his. If you could have seen Johnny stand there and get off those passes you wouldn't have believed it."

Yet, Unitas played in virtual obscurity. Louisville wasn't a member of the NCAA at the time and its football program was small. No more than a couple thousand fans would attend a game. Most of the Louisville residents preferred to drive 80 miles to watch the University of Kentucky on Saturday afternoons. Louisville's home games felt like practice to Unitas. He wondered if anyone in professional football knew anything about him during his final two years. He was a victim of a losing program, and his boyhood, seventh-grade dream of becoming a professional football player was becoming fuzzy.

But he wouldn't give up. He shouldn't have played at all during his senior year. He suffered a hairline fracture of his ankle at practice a week before the season was to open. The doctors informed Camp that he couldn't count on Unitas playing until the final few games. After missing the campaign's opener, Unitas approached Camp. "Coach, I think that if I'm well taped up, I'll be able to play," said Unitas. "I know I won't be able to move around too well, but I'll still be able to pass." Although

Louisville suffered another losing season, a courageous Unitas played on one leg.

After the season, Unitas married his high school sweetheart, Dorothy Hoelle in November of 1954. He had dated her steadily ever since he was a junior and she was a sophomore at St. Justin's. It was a Unitas family wedding. Unitas' uncle, Father Constantine Superfinsky, performed the ceremony in the same church in which the uncle had baptized him.

Things were looking up for Unitas, but he wanted so desperately to fulfill his dream of playing in the National Football League. It wasn't going to be easy, though. He was a thin quarterback out of a small college that played its games on a high school field. His chances of even being selected in the 1955 NFL draft were remote. Unitas knew the odds, but he only wanted a chance to play, to show the pros that he could play in their league even though his background of playing for a tiny Catholic high school and a small college wasn't the least bit attractive to any of the pro scouts. One thing he did have was his bachelor's degree, and he was proud of that. He had kept his promise to the administrators at Louisville that he could do college-level work when he was allowed to enroll as a probationary student. It didn't matter now. No one would know. All he had wanted was a chance to go to college in 1951, and he made the most of it, which pleased his mother. One of her kids had a college degree.

Unitas could only wait. Until the draft took place in March, he went to work. He was married and had other responsibilities, not only to Dorothy, but to his family that had stood by him the last four years. Unitas took a job with a construction firm that was building a hospital in Carnegie, a suburb just outside Pittsburgh. His pay was a lot higher than the $1 minimum wage that President Eisenhower signed into law that year, and it helped take care of two families. Unitas remained close to his mother all the years that she was alive. He always said that he learned discipline and hard work from her. "She never got discouraged and got us to think the same way," said Unitas.

He must have learned perseverance as well. Unitas wasn't picked until the ninth round, which was somewhat disappointing to him. However, the fact that his hometown Steelers selected him buoyed his spirits. He couldn't wait for training camp to begin that summer. He would get to compete on a pro level and show the naysayers what he could do, the Steelers included. Being a ninth-round pick wasn't exactly a vote of confidence. But Unitas didn't gripe and waited until he would walk on the field with the others. The playing field consumed him. It was his life.

Once again, he had to prove himself.

3

Bloomfield to Baltimore

Y OUNG DAN ROONEY, WHO WASN'T QUITE 24 YEARS OLD AND
whose father owned the Steelers, was the catalyst in drafting Unitas.
In 1949 when Rooney was a senior at North Catholic High School and
Unitas a junior at St. Justin's, Unitas and Rooney were ranked first and
second, respectively, on the All-Pittsburgh Catholic football team as quarterbacks. Rooney, who played for a championship team that year, however, never could figure out how he finished second to Unitas. Fresh out
of Duquesne University in 1954, Rooney began his internship in the
family business along with his older brother, Art Jr. Rooney sold advertising for the team's game programs and ran the Steelers' training camp.

Rooney was the one person who was vocal about Unitas, and he succeeded in convincing head coach Walt Kiesling to draft him even though
there were already three quarterbacks on the roster. But Rooney was thinking about marketing: if Unitas made the team, Rooney would have a
coup in the hometown-boy-makes-good angle in selling ads. And it
wouldn't hurt in selling tickets, either. If it weren't for young Rooney,
Unitas might never have been drafted.

Playing for Mr. Pittsburgh

The Rooney name had been synonymous with the city's sporting scene
ever since 1933, when the team, known back then as the Pirates, became

the fifth-oldest franchise in the NFL as a member of the Eastern Division. Art Rooney Sr. was a Pittsburgh legend, who was perhaps the city's most affable and adored personality and who was never without an omnipresent cigar, lit or unlit. He lived in the same house in which he was raised and walked every day to the Steelers offices some 10 blocks away. Everybody in Pittsburgh recognized him, from the saloon keepers to the newsstand operator where he bought a newspaper, to the candy store owner where he purchased his cigars. He was Mr. Pittsburgh.

Actually, the Steelers began their stay in Pittsburgh illegally. Unitas hadn't known that, and it wouldn't have mattered if he had: Pittsburgh was his home. Rooney made a killing by betting on the horses one weekend in New York. On Saturday he won big at Empire City, and then on Monday, he went up to Saratoga and parlayed it all into winnings somewhere between $200,000 and $400,000. Nobody really knows how much he won, but it was a lot of money. When Rooney learned about a professional football league, he called NFL president Joe Carr to ask him about the possibility of starting a team in Pittsburgh.

For $2,500 Rooney bought himself a football franchise. He called them the Pittsburgh Pirates after the city's baseball team. The trouble was that Pittsburgh had a blue law that prohibited the playing of professional sports on Sundays, the day the NFL scheduled its games.

But Rooney's luck was good. An amendment to repeal the law was expected to be passed the week before Pittsburgh's first game, September 20, 1933, against the New York Giants at Forbes Field. The city council became bogged down that week in other legislation, however, and couldn't approve the appeal. The blue law was still effective.

The pro–blue law forces had a rallying point. They organized to protest the scheduled game and arranged a demonstration to take place Sunday at Forbes Field. Rooney acted quickly. He hurried down to city hall to get some answers. First he spoke with Harmar Denny, the director of public safety.

"There are only two people with the authority to stop the game," Denny said. "I'm one of them, but I won't be in town Sunday. I'm going away with the family."

"That's great," Rooney said with a smile. "You need the vacation. Who's the other guy?"

"The other is Franklin McQuade, the superintendent of police," replied Denny.

Rooney thanked him and left. His next stop was McQuade's office. Rooney knew McQuade, too.

"Say, Frank, how would you like to be my personal guest at the game Sunday?" asked Rooney. "You can sit right next to me on the 50-yard line."

"Thanks, it sounds great," replied McQuade.

Rooney managed to pull it off. Some four thousand fans showed up to see the debut of professional football in Pittsburgh. With Denny out of town and McQuade sitting next to Rooney, the antisports protestors couldn't find either of the two city officials they were looking for the day of the game. Nonetheless, pro football in Pittsburgh began on a losing note, as the Giants easily defeated the Pirates, 23–2. "New York won, but our team looked terrible," said Rooney after the game. "The fans didn't get their money's worth today."

In later years Rooney brought a list of colorful characters to Pittsburgh. The first was Johnny "Blood" McNally, a star halfback from the Green Bay Packers. Blood and Packer coach Earl "Curly" Lambeau had had a heated disagreement. Blood had vowed never to play for Lambeau again, which was all right with the Packer coach. Rooney saw Blood as a big box office draw and signed him as a player and coach to replace his departed coach, Joe Bach.

The next year Rooney shook up the sports world by signing Byron "Whizzer" White of Colorado University for the previously unheard-of sum of $15,800. White was easily the most highly paid player in pro football. He played only the 1938 season for Pittsburgh. At the end of it he went to England as a Rhodes Scholar. Blood resigned the following year, and the Steelers continued their losing seasons. They were also losing money. "Only once since we started the team did we make money," admitted Rooney. "Outside of that, we lost. Never any big money, mind you, $15,000 was the worst. But we knew we'd make money if we gave this town a team."

Rooney never stopped trying. It wasn't until 1942 that the Steelers went over .500 for the first time, chiefly on the performance of scrawny rookie running back Bill Dudley. Running from the single-wing attack, Dudley led the NFL in rushing. He carried the ball 162 times for 696 yards, an average of 4.3 yards per run. "If I had to pick my favorite Steeler of all time, it would be Bill Dudley," confessed Rooney. "He didn't know the meaning of the word *quit*."

Dudley was Unitas' type of guy because Unitas was the same way. Unitas could have been another Dudley in Rooney's eyes, but the Steelers never gave him a platform. The Steelers incumbent quarterback was Jim Finks and the backup was Vic Eaton, who could also punt and play defense. The imminent return of Ted Marchibroda from military service, the man against whom Unitas played in that 1951 heartbreaker, made Unitas' chances of staying with the Steelers even slimmer. But Unitas never backed away from a challenge, and he had always dreamed about playing for his hometown Steelers. The problem was that Kiesling didn't give him an opportunity to compete. In the first scrimmage in which he participated, Unitas threw for two touchdowns and broke loose on a run of about 20 yards. It went practically unnoticed.

That was the extent of Unitas' exposure to professional football. He tossed more passes to the Rooney twins, John and Pat, than he did on the football field. And the kids were happy to catch whatever Unitas threw for as long as he wanted after practice. They were certain that Unitas would make the team, and then they could tell every kid in the neighborhood that they helped him make it. Unitas was a hard worker and would stay on the field late with the twins because he didn't get that much work during practice. He even had the kids running patterns.

The twins wrote their traveling father a seven-page letter extolling Unitas' virtues. They wrote about how Unitas wasn't getting a chance and that the coaches were really crazy because Unitas was the best quarterback in camp. Rooney, a prominent horseman, answered with a postcard from

Aqueduct racetrack in New York: "Don't be wise guys. I pay my coaches a lot of money to make decisions." Years later, when he learned about the kids' letter, Unitas remarked, "Those kids had more sense than the coaches."

Sadly, Unitas didn't even get to play in any of the six exhibition games, now known as preseason games. He had thought that he would have an opportunity when the Steelers were preparing to play their first exhibition game against the Rams. Finks got into an argument with Kiesling, and the coach ordered him out of camp. That might have opened up a roster spot for Unitas, but when Rooney learned of Finks' dismissal, he called Kiesling and convinced him that he needed the veteran to run the offense.

Unitas' only exposure as a member of the Steelers that summer came when an enterprising photographer snapped a picture of Unitas showing a Chinese nun how to grip a football.

When Marchibroda joined the team before the fourth exhibition game, Unitas knew his days as a Steeler were nearing an end. After the game it was certain. Unitas still hadn't played. He didn't have to be an A student to figure out what would happen next. No pro team carried four quarterbacks—even a hometown one—and Finks, Eaton, and Marchibroda were starting to sound like an established law firm.

"[Marchibroda] hadn't practiced at all, but Kiesling put him in the game ahead of me," said Unitas. "Just before the season was to start, Kiesling called me in and said he was sorry, but he couldn't use four quarterbacks. I told him, I don't mind if you gave me the opportunity to play and I screwed up. But you never gave me the opportunity. He told me that he would try and put me on the reserve list for $100 a week, but I never heard from him again."

Unitas left with bad feelings about Kiesling. "Back then, Mr. Rooney had very little contact with the team," remembered Unitas. "He was tied up with his gambling and horse racing business. The man who made all the decisions was the coach, Kiesling. And I'm sure he didn't realize I was in camp until the Associated Press ran a picture of me showing a Chinese nun how to throw a football."

A New Plan

Unitas took the $12 bus fare the Steelers gave him, put it in his pocket, headed for Highway 17, and hitchhiked to Pittsburgh. That same morning, his wife, Dorothy, left their baby, Janice Ann, with her parents and went to the Steelers' office to buy two tickets to the regular season's opening game on Sunday. She was unaware that the Steelers had released her husband until she got back home late in the afternoon after some shopping in downtown Pittsburgh. She knew how disappointed he would be when he got home.

"A couple of minutes later, Johnny came walking up the block," she recalled. "He looked like half-past six. He came into the living room and the two of us sat there all night looking at each other. Playing football was his job, at least we thought it was, and now he lost it. I told him, 'I know you're not going to quit. You're going to keep trying. Don't worry, we'll be all right.'"

A week later, Dan Rooney was driving a car in downtown Pittsburgh with his father alongside him and Kiesling in the back seat. He looked over as a car passed him in the right lane. "You know who that is?" he asked his father.

"No, I wasn't looking," came the reply.

"That was Johnny Unitas, Dad."

"Catch him," ordered the senior Rooney.

"I managed to pull up next to Unitas at the next light," Dan Rooney said. "When I did, my father rolled down his window. 'John, I'm really sorry about what happened,' said my dad. 'I hope you get a chance to play and become a big star.' Unitas smiled and said, 'Thank you.' Kiesling didn't say a word."

A day after he got home, Unitas sent a telegram to coach Paul Brown of the Cleveland Browns asking for a tryout. He remembered that a Cleveland scout had seen him play at Louisville and mentioned to Brown that they had planned to draft him on about the 12th round of the draft if he was still on the board. Brown, who was as meticulous as Camp was at Louisville, got in touch with Unitas the very next day. He thanked him for contacting him, but explained that the Browns were set for a quarterback because Otto Graham had decided to play one more season. He also told Unitas to check back with him the next year. With his pro football hopes gone, Unitas took a job as a pile driver with a construction company for $125 per week to support his wife and daughter.

But it wasn't football. And it left a void in his life. Unitas' old friend Fred Zangaro tried to help fill it. He told Unitas that the Bloomfield Rams, a semipro team in the Greater Pittsburgh League, needed a quarterback. Unitas wasn't too receptive, feeling that playing in such a league would hurt his pro chances the following year. Besides, what if he ended up with a serious injury? However, Zangaro insisted. He told Unitas that it wouldn't be good to stay away from football for a year. The Rams had already played two games when Tony Chilleo, a salesman for the Honus Wagner Company, informed Chuck Rogers, the coach and manager of the Rams, that Unitas had been let go by the Steelers.

The Rams played their games on Thursday nights on a field illuminated by four light stations all on the same side of the field at the Arsenal Middle School field. It resembled more of a playground than a football field. It was a barren stretch of earth littered with rocks and broken glass. Before the games, the field was sprinkled with oil to keep the dust down. Rogers was a former sandlot star who helped revive the sport. He ran the team from the basement of Parise's Dairy on Liberty Avenue, and he took the game seriously. The Rams practiced four nights per week, and he fined anyone who didn't show up a dollar. "I had one guy who never made any money because he never made it to the practice," laughed Rogers.

Bloomfield was the biggest draw in the eight-team league, and most of the team preferred to play there because the payout was the biggest. The visiting teams were guaranteed $500 per game, and no other team came close. That is why the Rams played most of their 12 games at home. Admission was $3, and the Rams drew anywhere from 500 to 1,000 fans, who sat on four rows of concrete slabs serviced by two aisles, one on each side. A 6' high canvas running the length of the field was put up on game nights on a 15' high fence to prevent anyone from viewing the game from the street. It wasn't even certain that the field measured 100 yards. But it was a field nonetheless, and a haven for those chasing whatever dreams they had playing sandlot football.

"The league was getting tougher with the addition of two teams from Shaler and McKeesport, and I needed a quarterback and so I called Unitas," said Rogers. "I asked him what his intentions were and he said he didn't have any. I told him I'd pay him $6 a game to play for us because that was all the money I had left from a budget of $350 a game. Besides, I told him that we were the only team that would pay.

"Well, John came by one night with Freddie Zangaro and said that he'd play. There was little equipment left, so John had to pull from a pile of scrap to put a uniform together. He did tell me that he had contacted the Browns and was waiting for the opportune time to try out for them.

"The first game he ever played for us he did so as a defensive back. I had been the quarterback the first three games and knew all the plays because I was the one who drew them up. But John learned them fast and I was glad. There had been a lot of bickering in the huddle and the players would get into arguments on the sidelines that almost turned into fights. It was wild.

"John started at quarterback the next game and immediately took control. He wasn't very big, but I could see that he threw a helluva ball. Well, we won eight straight games and the championship. John was tough. The concrete wall of the stands was only eight feet from the sidelines and he was thrown into the wall dozens of times. But he never complained. He'd get right up and get back in the huddle. I gave him $15 the last two games because he was so good."

The field wasn't much and neither was the pay. But the field was Unitas' refuge. And it wasn't about the money. Unitas would always say that he played because a team wanted him and all he wanted was a chance. Zangaro was right about playing and Unitas enjoyed Thursday nights. "He was the best player the league had," bragged Zangaro. "But when he mentioned that he was aiming for the pros, it didn't sound right. None of the other guys could imagine anyone from the Bloomfield Rams going to the National

Football League. 'Did you hear, I'm going to the Chicago Bears,' they'd say when they wanted to kid him."

Unitas never regretted his experience with the Rams, which he described as "sandlot football" instead of the semipro label the league carried. He was grateful for the opportunity just to play. "I don't think anybody has ever understood that what mattered the most was not the $6, but the fact that there was a football team that wanted me," Unitas said years later.

A New Home in the National Football League

Unitas didn't have to wait until summer to contact the Browns. Rogers had written to Baltimore coach Wilbur "Weeb" Ewbank about a big tackle, Jim Deglau, whom he felt could play for the Colts. The Baltimore team wasn't very good at the time, and it was hungry for players. Ewbank called Rogers and told him to invite Deglau to the Colts' tryout camp held on Saturdays in Baltimore. Rogers then told Ewbank about Unitas. "Send him along, too," Ewbank replied. "And if you have any more promising players, tell them to come too."

At first Unitas was reluctant, which surprised Rogers somewhat. He told Rogers that if he didn't impress the Colts, it might ruin his chances with the other pro teams. Besides Cleveland, the Chicago Bears had expressed some interest, he said. However, Unitas did go and threw passes in what appeared to be nothing more than a public park in Baltimore. He didn't know what to think on the way home with Deglau. And when he didn't hear from Rogers or the Colts in the next month, Unitas forgot about Baltimore and began thinking about Cleveland.

One day in February when Unitas was at work, Don Kellett, the Colts' general manager, called from Baltimore. "I couldn't wait for Johnny to get home," said Dorothy Unitas. "We sat by the phone all night and waited until Kellett called back. It was so important. Football was all Johnny ever wanted. Why, when we were going together, he'd come over to the house for Thanksgiving dinner and sit in front of the television and watch the professional game. I'd stand in front of the set and try to make him pay attention to me. But, he'd make me get out of the way so he could watch football."

Kellett made Unitas a simple offer. He wanted him to report to the Colts in April to work out for Ewbank, and if the coach liked him, he would be invited to the Colts' summer camp. Kellett said that if he made the team at that point, he would give him a $7,000 contract, which was $1,000 more than the Steelers had offered. Unitas agreed.

Ewbank checked on Unitas with his college coach, Frank Camp, whom Ewbank knew. Camp told Ewbank that Unitas had written to him after he was released by the Steelers and said that he wasn't given much of a chance to make the team. Ewbank also checked with his new line coach, Herman Ball, who had been at the Steelers' camp that summer. He confirmed Unitas' story.

Unitas arrived in Baltimore in April and impressed Ewbank enough to get invited to camp. Ewbank admired Unitas' poise and the way he threw a football. He told Kellett that Unitas was good enough to be the backup to George Shaw and to offer the kid a contract. Ewbank went so far as to tell Unitas that he would put him on his summer camp roster. Unitas felt wanted, and he left Baltimore feeling that he would at least have a chance to compete in the exhibition games, something he never did with the Steelers.

"We took pictures of John under center, and when he set up, and right at the last, when he followed through," said Ewbank. "The thing that we noticed right away was the way he followed through. It was exceptional. His arm went through so far that he turned his hand over like a pitcher. It was like throwing a screwball. I often wondered how he kept from injuring his arm. When he followed through, you could see the back of his hand. I worried that he might get what they call a tennis elbow. But, boy, I saw the way he could throw and I never bothered him about it. You knew right away. We knew that as soon as he learned the offense he would be our quarterback."

As training camp approached, Unitas had second thoughts. Dorothy was pregnant with their second child, and he was concerned about leaving her especially because he had no guarantee that he'd make the final roster. He had a secure job as a pile driver and was making good money. Like the others from William Street, Dorothy was strong. She knew how much football meant to John and she encouraged him to attend the Colts' training camp in Westminster.

"John was somewhat dubious because I was expecting a child," explained Dorothy. "He was making pretty good money, at least at the time we thought so, in the construction business. I remember him saying that maybe he should stay around home until the baby was born . . . I told him to go. If he stayed home, he'd always wonder what his chances would have been."

It didn't take long for Unitas to be noticed once training camp opened. "I wasn't nervous about it and the only thing that concerned me was that I might not get a chance," said Unitas. But he got that chance—more than he expected. He got plenty of work on the practice field alternating with Shaw. Fred Schubach, the team's equipment manager, told Kellett, "That new guy Unitas can throw."

Unitas also caught the eye of Don Shula, who was a defensive back. "I was impressed with how well Unitas handled himself and the way he threw the ball," he said. "I commented about it. It was the first time I ever noticed him."

Yet Art Donovan, the Colts' garrulous defensive tackle, wasn't so sure. A veteran, Donovan had an opinion about everybody. He was in the trainer's room, talking with trainer Eddie Block, when he got his first look at Unitas. "I was getting my ankle taped," said Donovan. "There's kind of a skinny kid with a short haircut and buck teeth racked out on the next table with a trainer working on his shoulder. So, I said to Eddie, 'Who is the new guy?' Eddie said, 'He's a quarterback.' 'Holy cheese,' I said, 'Some quarterback! He's not even in a game yet and he's got a bum shoulder.'"

A baby-faced Unitas didn't impress veteran lineman Dick Szymanski either. "The first time I saw Unitas I had asked, 'Where was he?'" recalled Szymanski. "They pointed to a guy in the corner. 'You're kidding me,' I exclaimed. 'That's the locker room boy. That's not Unitas.'" Szymanski and Unitas later became good friends.

Training camp was also the first time Raymond Berry learned about Unitas. He didn't know it at the time, but the two would go on to make Baltimore history with the impeccable precision of a quarterback passing unerringly to a receiver in what was unfailingly described as a textbook pass.

"Weeb brought the rookies and a few other players into camp early," recalled Berry. "The day I arrived, several of us who had just gotten there watched practice from up on the hill. Someone said to me, 'I hear they have a young kid who can throw the ball.' And someone else asked, 'What's his name?'

"The first thing I recall John mentioning to me was that he was married and had a baby daughter. I thought he was kidding because he looked so young.

"Weeb, on several occasions, told me to work with him whenever I could. George Shaw didn't have a very strong arm and would seldom throw after practice. John's arm was tireless, so I began to spend a lot of time with him after practice. I realized that Weeb had spotted something special about John and was anticipating him becoming our regular quarterback."

Unitas got to play more than he had ever dreamed. Shaw came down with a case of pneumonia, and the rookie was suddenly handed the ball to start the first exhibition game against the Giants in Boston, where the New York team had a large fan base. Unfortunately, Unitas' performance that night didn't draw rave reviews in a 28–10 defeat. Unitas admitted later that he was a little nervous. Still, owner Carroll Rosenbloom, who would engender a special relationship with Unitas over the years, never had any doubts about him. The doubt still remained with Art Rooney, however, and he called Rosenbloom one afternoon.

"Rooney called me about something or other," said Rosenbloom. "Then he said, 'Carroll, you got that boy Unitas. I want to tell you something. My sons tell me he was the best-looking quarterback we had in camp, and my coach never let him throw the ball.' After that I watched John in practice. He was so relaxed, so loose, and a very likeable kid. This whole time we were wondering if we needed to trade for another quarterback, or if Unitas could do the job backing up Shaw."

The other players quickly warmed up to the rookie. They saw his potential and what he meant to the club if anything happened to Shaw. Alex Sandusky, a guard, kidded him about driving into camp in a car that "blew smoke out of the back." Unitas found a friendly camp, not like it was with the Steelers: "There were not any cliques in the Colts' camp. With the Steelers, a new guy was lucky if anyone spoke to him. But with the Colts I remember Ameche and Donovan and a few others coming over and introducing themselves."

Still, Unitas wasn't sure if the friendships would last. Shaw had returned to the field and got most of the work for the remainder of the exhibition season. The Colts had scheduled a game in Louisville where Unitas had gone to school. Unitas was asked to do a radio tape to help generate interest and boost ticket sales. He agreed to do so, but then asked with concern, "Do you really believe I'll be with the team when we get to Louisville?"

It was still Shaw's team. When the 1956 season opened, Shaw was the starter. However, after an opening game win against the Chicago Bears, the Colts lost two straight games before meeting the Bears for the second time at Wrigley Field. It would be a game that would change Unitas' life forever and, for that matter, Shaw's. Baltimore was leading by 10 points when Shaw was crushed high and low by several Chicago linemen, who broke his nose and knocked out several of his teeth. But worse, Shaw had to be carried off the field with a leg injury.

A nervous, hesitant Unitas took over and had a shaky start. The first pass he threw was intercepted by cornerback J. C. Caroline and brought back for a touchdown. After the kickoff, Unitas bumped into Ameche and fumbled. The Bears got the ball and scored another touchdown. When the Colts got the ball back, Unitas fumbled again and Chicago scored once more. In three plays, Unitas had personally delivered three touchdowns to the Bears who roared to a 58–27 triumph. It was a despondent Unitas who sat in front of his locker when Rosenbloom approached him.

"John was never one to show his emotions, but he was sitting in front of his locker, still hadn't taken off his uniform, and had his head hanging between his legs so that all you could see was the top of his crewcut," said Rosenbloom. "I walked over and got up under his chin and lifted his head up and said, 'Now look, John, that wasn't your fault. You haven't had an opportunity to play and no one is blaming you. You're not only going to be a good one in this league, you're going to be a great one.'

"Well, I was just trying to build him up, get him out of the dumps. I wasn't even sure right then he'd make the club. But many times over the years John would ask me about that, how I'd been so sure he'd make it. I'd tell him, 'What the hell, John, I'm an old jock. I know talent.'"

Unitas pulled himself together after Rosenbloom's encouraging words. He finished the season leading the Colts to victory in half of the team's remaining eight games. He began by beating Green Bay 28–21 the very next week, completing 8 of 16 passes, 2 of them for touchdowns. A week later, Baltimore upset Cleveland 21–7; they were league champions and a team the Colts had never beaten before. His breakout game against the Los Angeles Rams was two weeks later. He completed 18 of 24 passes for 293 yards and three touchdowns in a 56–21 romp. When the season ended, Unitas had completed 55.6 percent of his passes, a record for a rookie.

Baltimore had a quarterback for the next 16 years.

4

America's Idol

IN THREE SEASONS, JOHNNY UNITAS HAD ACHIEVED THE legendary stardom reserved for great ones. He had risen from free-agent obscurity in 1956 to begin the journey that would lead the Colts to their first championship. He was named the league's rookie of the year in 1956, and in 1957, he received an All-Pro recognition. In 1958, he captured the imagination of pro football fans everywhere when he led his team to the championship and was crowned as the league's most valuable player.

No one else in his first three years on the pro football landscape had ever achieved the reverence that Unitas had achieved. Not only was he idolized by the public, but, to an extent, by his teammates as well.

Lasting Effects

The telegenic Unitas wasn't aware of the magnitude that the overtime win over the Giants created. If he was, he wasn't saying anything about it. Being the competitor that he was, he was only concerned about winning a football game, the challenge of which he carried on his sloping shoulders. It was that way ever since he was a kid at St. Justin's and later at Louisville and the sandlots of the Bloomfield Rams. He was even that way when playing cards with his teammates, which he wasn't very good at, and they would appreciatively take his money. He shrugged off any reference to the records he established that long afternoon. The Colts won 23–17, and they were champions. That was all that mattered to Unitas. His only goal was to win, whether it was on a football field or providing for his family, which now included three little children.

But America knew how significant the game was. Every high school and college quarterback wanted to be like Johnny Unitas. The barber shops put down their combs and scissors and began using electric hair cutters to sculpt crew cuts. High-top shoes were a must for every kid who dreamed about being like him. If there was a cult hero in professional football, it was Unitas. If he had played for the Giants, his photograph would have adorned a poster in Times Square. He was just happy playing and winning for Baltimore.

To some degree, Raymond Berry recognized the game's importance. Long after the contest's conclusion, Berry walked out of the stadium and noticed Commissioner Bert Bell, who had marshaled his tenuous legions for 14 years. Bell had watched the sudden-death drama like a fan, sitting at midfield behind the press box with his son, Bert, and his daughter, Janie. Before he became commissioner in 1946, he had been a coach and an owner. Bell was happy for Colts' owner Carroll Rosenbloom and felt justified knowing he had persuaded the dashing Rosenbloom to buy the franchise for Baltimore after a two-year absence. It paid off for Rosenbloom and the league.

Bell was doubly satisfied that a five-year-old team, such as Baltimore, rose so quickly to win a championship, ahead of the more established cities. Only months before, in October, Bell had appeared in Congress to defend the league's college-player draft, which was deemed illegal by opponents. He convinced the lawmakers that the draft was a democratic process that enabled lesser teams to compete with the stronger ones. He specially cited Baltimore as an example of a team becoming a championship contender in a short period of time.

Personally, he was also happy that he had fought with many of the owners to establish a sudden-death period strictly for championship games, in the event of a tie such as the one he had just witnessed. The result was what he and sixty-five thousand people in Yankee Stadium and perhaps 10 million more on television observed: the best football game ever played. Pro football and television formed a union that December day. It was high theater, a monumental struggle of excitement, and its catalyst was Unitas—a new hero who was adored by all who observed him.

When Berry saw Bell standing alone on the sidewalk, he quietly approached him. Berry was a big reason why the Colts were champions, as his 12 receptions and 178 yards were both new title-game records. But his thoughts were with the short, solitary figure whom he wanted to address. In his own quiet way, Berry wanted to pay him a tribute.

"Here was a guy who had midwifed the NFL and shepherded it through all the tough times," said Berry. "I walked up to shake his hand, and he had tears in his eyes. He knew what the game meant. The rest of us, we had no perspective on the big picture. But the commissioner, he knew his baby grew up that day."

Hours before, Bell had mentioned to a writer that he thought he would never live to see sudden death. He did, but sadly, he died a year later. Fittingly, he died while attending the Eagles–Steelers game at Franklin Field in his hometown of Philadelphia on October 11, 1959. He suffered a heart attack during the final two minutes of the game, the same amount of time Unitas, only the year before, had needed to force the first overtime—Bell's overtime—at Yankee Stadium.

The Unitas-to-Berry artistry left an indelible mark on the nation's pro football memory. Unitas, like Berry, had established new records with his magnificent performance in completing 26 of 40 passes for 349 yards— both new championship-game marks. And yet, Unitas appeared unaffected by them and by all the stories and radio talk heralding the overtime thriller as the greatest game ever played. For the still-growing NFL and its fans, it was. But not exactly to Unitas.

A frank and honest individual, he admitted that he got a bigger bang beating the San Francisco 49ers that season in Baltimore, 35–27, on a bitterly cold afternoon. "I got a bigger thrill in helping to win that game that got us into the playoffs," said Unitas in an exclusive interview in

1989. "We trailed at halftime, 27–7, but we got hot in the second half, offensively and defensively, and won. If we hadn't, we would never have had the chance at the championship."

Back to Training Camp

Unitas had given Baltimore the title, and nothing could be bigger than the NFL championship. But what about the follow-up season in 1959? The city of Baltimore was intoxicated by a year-long celebration, but could Unitas and the Colts do it again? The players were certainly thinking that way when they gathered for training camp at Westminster College that summer.

Because the Colts were champions, they were accorded an extra exhibition game, one against the College All-Stars in Chicago, a charity game sponsored by the *Chicago Tribune*. It wasn't a game the veterans looked forward to, but for anxious rookies trying to make the team, it was an opportunity. Trying to crack a championship team made it that much harder for any rookie.

Jerry Richardson, a tall, shy, good-looking receiver, was one of the newcomers. Like Unitas, he came from a small college. He had played college football in South Carolina at Wofford College, and Richardson always seemed to be explaining just where Wofford was. He was the third receiver taken by the Colts in the 1958 college draft that Bell had preserved that day in Congress the year before. And Richardson could have been ready to explain to the congressional members where Wofford was after he first put on a Colts practice jersey.

There were approximately one dozen other receivers running around trying to make a lasting impression, one that would enable them to fill the sole spot on the roster. Richardson's chances, arriving from tiny Wofford College in Spartanburg, South Carolina, were not exactly promising. Richardson was taken in the 13th round and was the 153rd player overall. However, defying the long odds, Richardson showed enough promise for the Colts to keep him on the team's reserve list for $100 per week, which allowed him to practice with the regulars during the 1958 season.

Richardson was having a very good camp a year later, which earned him a trip to Chicago for the All-Star game. And he got more than he ever would have imagined—his roommate for the All-Star game was Unitas! That alone would have been enough to write home about even if he never played in a regular season game with the Colts. Richardson never figured why they roomed him with Unitas. And he was smart enough not to ask, either. No one, especially a rookie, would ask Unitas why. And when writers asked too much, Unitas gave them icy stares.

Being the NFL's new idol meant that Unitas, a private person, was subjected to an entire new world of incessant interviews. He averaged four radio, television, or banquet appearances per week because of his newly acquired fame, and more often than not, he had to explain the six-yard pass he made to Mutscheller. The 13-play, 80-yard drive in overtime had been discussed, detailed, and diagrammed as no other drive in pro football history had ever been. It certainly was a Hall-of-Fame moment, but unfortunately, there was no such building in Canton, Ohio, back then. Unitas and the media preserved it instead.

In Chicago, *Sport* magazine was waiting for him. After all, he drove away their Corvette as the MVP of the 1958 championship game. They didn't know it, but Unitas, with a wife and three kids, didn't have any use for a Corvette and traded it for a bigger car. There were three or four representatives of the magazine in Unitas' room assigned to do an in-depth feature on the star. After an hour or so of bantering, the *Sport* representatives invited Unitas to dinner. They did so without any mention of Richardson. The slight wasn't lost on Unitas. And he didn't hesitate in responding, "No thanks, I have other plans." After the magazine entourage left, Unitas looked over at Richardson and said, "Let's get something to eat."

Unitas saw the underdog in Richardson, who had married his high school sweetheart, Rosalind Sallenger. When training camp opened for the 1959 season, Richardson had no way to get to practice, so Unitas helped him out. He picked him up in front of his rented house every morning to drive him to camp. They got along fine: Unitas didn't talk, and neither did the rookie, which suited them both. Further, Rosalind picked up her husband at the end of the day, so Unitas considered it to be a good arrangement.

The compassionate Unitas helped Richardson earn the only remaining receiver spot on the roster, as well. During an exhibition game against the Cardinals in St. Louis, Berry wasn't going to play much at all, and the Colts' game plan was to alternate Harold "Big Thunder" Lewis, the prohibitive favorite to make the team that year, with Richardson. At halftime, Unitas approached Richardson.

"How are you doing?" Unitas asked.

"I didn't do too good," Richardson said.

Unitas didn't say another word, but in the second half, Richardson saw more balls than he ever could have imagined. He caught seven passes, which left an impression on the coaches. Richardson was a Colt.

"Catching seven passes in an exhibition game was a lot for a rookie," said Richardson. "John helped me again the following year too. Against the Eagles, near the end of the exhibition season when the final cuts were made, I caught six or seven passes and kept my place on the team."

Unitas' help may have been because he still wanted to pick up Richardson and take him to practice in 1960—Unitas did not like change. But 1961 was Richardson's final year—not only as a Baltimore Colt, but also as a professional football player. He became involved in a contract dispute with the team's management and quit.

"My first year I received a $750 bonus and a $7,500 contract," said Richardson. "The second year, my contract was $8,750, and I had been the Colt Rookie of the Year in 1959. In my third season in 1961, they offered me a contract for $9,750—a $1,000 swing. I felt I should get $10,000, which was only a $250 differential. After five weeks in camp, I packed it in."

Richardson quit on principle. Yet that miniscule $250 gap changed his life forever and enabled him to reach a bigger goal than playing pro ball for perhaps 10 more years. He took the $4,674 bonus money he earned from the 1959 championship game, went back to North Carolina, and got into the food business. But his biggest dream of all was to own a pro football team. In 1994, he secured an NFL franchise when the Carolina Panthers became the league's 29th team.

Unitas was, in every sense of the word, a perfectionist. He demanded perfection of himself and asked it of others. That's why he worked endlessly with Berry on timing and patterns. They would remain after practice for an hour or so after everyone had left, seeking and developing perfection. He distilled the infinite hours of practice in those two long drives against the Giants, which made it appear that he and Berry were an extension of the practice field in Baltimore. Those two drives were the hallmark of their dedication to excellence.

"I knew the precise instant I broke free from my coverage that the ball would be there," said Berry. "We had drilled long and hard ever since John joined the club in 1956. By this time, we could reach each other pretty good. He sure didn't miss me in that title game. His accuracy was amazing.

"There was no time for huddles. We were trying to beat the clock. The plays were called from the scrimmage line and we stuck with the basic stuff. We merely reacted the way we've been trained to react all year. I recall that one of the big gainers developed from a slant that I ran inside a Giant linebacker who was playing on my nose. We'd practice it many times."

A Dream Team

It appeared that the 1959 season offered a bountiful promise of a second straight NFL championship. The offensive team of Unitas, Berry, Moore, and Ameche remained intact. But just as compelling was the defense, which didn't garner the recognition the Giants' unit got. Although the offense generated the accolades, the defense was coming together as one of the best in the league and was certainly efficient enough to be mentioned in the same breath as the Giants. Up front, Marchetti, Donovan, Lipscomb, and Joyce were on the top of their game. They were seasoned, rugged sentinels. Behind them were the linebackers, Pellington, Shinnick, and Szymanski. The secondary was savvy with Tasseff, Nelson, Davis, and a brash newcomer, Johnny Sample. They would be heard from.

In New York, everything happened big. It had sports heroes such as Joe DiMaggio and Mickey Mantle and the glorified Giants. Sure the Colts won the championship, but they were only from Baltimore. The Giants and New York were everything. As the 1959 season approached, the town that had been ridiculed looked to Johnny Unitas for more. In New York, DiMaggio was eternally called "the Yankee Clipper" and Mantle was "the Mick." Unitas now became "Johnny U," and appropriately, the shape of the horseshoe on both sides of his helmet accented it. Baltimore had a love affair with Unitas, but love can sometimes be fleeting unless it is extended by winning. Unitas knew that. He was ordained to lead and he took it upon himself to do just that.

With Unitas, the Colts' rich offense remained lush with Berry as the go-to receiver and Moore as the breakaway weapon not only on the ground, but also with a pass in his hands. The Unitas–Berry tandem was now the league's most potent combination. The offense was a force from anywhere on the field. Ameche was still around to do the heavy legwork between the tackles, and Mutscheller was as good and dependable as any end in the game. Unitas used him well, and often unexpectedly, to catch opponents off guard.

Baltimore's offensive line, with its granite-like protectors led by tackle Jim Parker, provided protection for Unitas. "I'll say we block for Johnny," said Parker, who had to learn the intricacies of pass blocking, at times with Unitas' help. Parker had played in Ohio State's run-emphasized offense and now was pushed, along with the other linemen, to provide Unitas with three seconds from the snap of the ball so that he could set up and throw his deadly passes. "He's a wonderful leader and he inspires a guy to do his best. Then, too, if we're going to make any extra money out of this game, he's the guy that's gonna get it for us and we try to take good care of him."

Unitas got everyone $4,718 as a bonus for their championship victory over the Giants. To a great many of the players, it was as much as half of their season's pay. If Unitas was money in the bank, the players wanted more. And why not? Nobody had believed in Baltimore, and overnight, Unitas converted the nonbelievers by beating a revered team in the NFL's biggest city. Suddenly, with that single, cathartic victory, the Baltimore Colts, with their euphoric fans, became beloved underdogs.

5

Another Championship

T HE MOST HERALDED CHAMPIONSHIP GAME OF 1958 NEEDED
an encore, and what better one than the Colts and Giants glaring
at each other for a second straight year? The killing fields in 1959 weren't
in stately Yankee Stadium, but instead in Baltimore's raucous Memorial
Stadium, which had twenty-five thousand fewer seats. The frenetic Colts
fans were beside themselves; more than fifty thousand of them rocked
the old stadium known as "the world's largest outdoor insane asylum."
There they experienced a championship football game for the first time
in the city's history only four years after Unitas' arrival as the biggest
football god of all. It was metropolis New York against diminutive Baltimore, and the big city invaders were consumed with revenge—none more
so than Sam Huff. Huff had spent the season recalling the previous
championship game: "It just seemed like Unitas-to-Berry, Unitas-to-Berry,
Unitas-to-Berry over and over again—like a nightmare."

Earning Their Chances

No one disagreed that the Colts and the Giants were the two best teams
in the NFL in 1959. The Giants finished with a 10–2 record with a defense
that allowed only 14 points per game. However, up until midseason, the
Colts had been a question mark. All they had produced was a 4–3 record,

and it looked like they weren't going anywhere with the heavy part of their schedule ahead of them. Then, with Unitas showing them how, the Colts caught fire. Baltimore swept its final five games with a performance of prodigious offensive zeal by scoring 187 points to beat both the Los Angeles Rams and the San Francisco 49ers twice, averaging 39 points per game against their two Western Conference rivals after beginning the streak with a 28–24 victory in Green Bay.

The incomparable Unitas had had his best season ever. He not only threw for 2,899 yards, but he established a record with 32 touchdowns and suffered only 14 interceptions. His resilient right arm threw the football 367 times, and his favorite ally, Raymond Berry, caught 66 of them, with 14 resulting in touchdowns. The impeccable Unitas-to-Berry combination, over which Huff agonized, reached its zenith in generating 959 yards as Unitas made the All-Pro team for the third straight campaign: one more than his receiver.

Unitas and Berry were a destructive force all because they worked together for hours at a time after practice to refine their craft. Berry was slow, with bad vision, and needed perfection to compensate for his shortcomings. Unitas understood and unabashedly helped him to become a dependable receiver in clutch situations. It was all part of Unitas' blue-collar work ethic. He had had to scratch for anything he ever got since he was a skinny high school quarterback that none of the colleges wanted. In a sense, the same was true for Berry, and they bonded like no two underdogs ever had before.

The championship rematch was eagerly awaited by the New York media. They trumpeted the game as a duel between Unitas and Conerly: the league's newest star versus an aging one. Conerly was 38 years old, but 1959 had been his best season in years, and the Giants felt they could score behind the reinvigorated veteran. The old gunfighter wouldn't be standing on the sidelines this time, while his deputy Don Heinrich started the game. He would be there from the beginning, matching his arm against Unitas', the way it should be. Surprisingly, Conerly won the league's passing title—not so much because of his 14 touchdowns, but because of his accuracy, which surrendered only four interceptions. His 1,706 yards paled in comparison to Unitas' total, as did his 194 passing attempts.

One championship wasn't good enough for Unitas and never would be. As an underdog, he had an insatiable appetite to win and keep winning. He had demonstrated that much during the 1958 overtime game against New York to beat the odds with two long, flawless drives that forever would be enshrined in pro football lore. That seminal game, that artful performance, was the quintessential Unitas. He had moved his team with precision. That historic game would always be the defining moment of Unitas' career, and now he was challenged to do it again.

Business as Usual

On the morning of the second biggest game of his life, Unitas awoke at 7:00 as usual. As far as Unitas was concerned, it was just another Sunday. He had a game to play all right, like he did on 12 other Sundays during the regular season, and it didn't matter that this one was for the NFL championship. It was a game, and just like any other game, Unitas always played to win. He got dressed, walked into the living room of his Towson, Maryland, home and looked down at his kids, Janie, four, and John, three. They were playing with an electric train, bounty from Christmas two days earlier. And in the few minutes that he stood there, whenever the train derailed, Unitas bent down to align the train wheels on the circular aluminum tracks. Having done that for the last time, he slipped on his topcoat and headed for church, telling his family that he would return in a little while for breakfast.

Unitas was a regular churchgoer. He tried to attend Catholic mass almost every morning and he made certain that he didn't miss Sundays. When he arrived at the Immaculate Conception Church for the 8:00 mass, one of the parish priests approached him in the parking lot to inquire how his wife Dorothy was doing following the birth of their fourth child just nine days before.

"The doctor doesn't think she should go to the game today because the baby is only nine days old," answered Unitas. "But really, she's feeling fine and there's nothing to worry about."

Moments later, a little boy looked up at Unitas and asked, "Johnny, are you going to win today?"

"That's what we're going to try to do," said Unitas.

When Johnny returned home, Dorothy had breakfast ready. Over eggs and sausage, the conversation revolved around the weather. Late December's precipitation wasn't snow, but rain instead. Dorothy had her thoughts about that: "Since it was raining before 7:00, it will be clear by 11:00."

Unitas quickly scanned the sports section of the *Baltimore American*. He saw his picture on the front page and showed it to his son John. "Do you see your old man? What's that?" asked Unitas.

"It's Daddy," exclaimed the youngster. His older sister, Janie, didn't agree. "It's not," she insisted. "It's Bert Rechichar."

It ended there. Dorothy and her mother, Mary Hoelle, were ready for church and took the two older children with them. Unitas was left to care for 18-month-old Bobby, who waddled around with his security blanket tucked in his hands, and nine-day-old Christopher, who required a diaper change. When Dorothy returned an hour or so later, little John ran up to his father and put his hand in his pocket. "There's nothing there," joked Unitas. "Santa Claus cleaned it out."

It was just a normal game day in the Unitas household. Unitas put on his topcoat a second time, bid each of his family members good-bye, and prepared for the 20-minute ride to the stadium. He said that he would be back at dinnertime. Dorothy told him that she would cook a ham. There was no mention of any victory celebration if the Colts won or anything of that nature. Unitas was off to work, and when his day was done, he'd be home for dinner like any other working husband.

By 11:30, Unitas emerged from his car in the Memorial Stadium parking lot, an hour and a half before the kickoff. He stopped for about five minutes, long enough to sign autographs for a number of youngsters. Unitas always held a soft spot in his heart for kids. He didn't disappoint any of them, and when he finished, he made his way into the stadium through the players' entrance. Once inside the locker room, it was just another routine Sunday, low-key and workmanlike. Unitas knew all too well his opponents from last year, but he didn't know anything about Rechichar, who had been operated on for cartilage damage to his knee.

The Rematch

Weeb Ewbank didn't need the attention-grabbing oratory that he invoked so successfully before the previous year's game. He was a mild-mannered person better known as a player's coach, and the 10-minute tirade in Yankee Stadium just wasn't him. However, it worked and it extracted a Herculean one-hour, six-minute, and 45-second effort from his players. In the end, the tenacity the Colts players exhibited over the tired Giants team was the difference. Before the rematch, Weeb reminded his players that they were the world champions and told them to go out and play like they were. And he added that they had the chance to win again—this time in front of the loyal Baltimore fans.

As fate ordained it, the weather was mild. And, as Unitas' wife Dorothy predicted, the morning rain ended by game time and gave way to a mild afternoon. That worked to the Colts' advantage. A dry, fast turf would benefit Unitas' receivers and be a plus for Lenny Moore's swift legs. He could turn on a dime and run behind the Giants secondary if Unitas needed him deep.

"I remember Alan Ameche unable to get the proper footing in the third period when we were close to the goal line," said Moore. "The play could have worked. If we scored then, it's all over, a blowout. You know, for most of that game I was a decoy. I had hurt my back and couldn't get my arms up in the air. I don't honestly believe we knew how good a team we were."

To a man, the Colts wanted to win the second game unequivocally. The Giants wanted retribution from last year's defeat. Psychologically, the Colts had a bigger edge than the Giants did: a second-straight championship would forever eradicate the naysayers and put an indelible stamp on the

Colts as genuine champions. They had come far in their short existence, but they needed just one more win to be recognized around the league as a force and not the ragamuffins they were made out to be. With Unitas, they were confident that they could earn that respect after 60 minutes of battle. They didn't want to wait for another time, another year. They wanted it then.

It was a late December day in Baltimore, only two days past Christmas, and the temperature for the 1:00 kickoff was close to 60 degrees. The preceding season's success, combined with the crowd's high spirit and exuberance, suggested that the noise level at Memorial Stadium would be the loudest ever for a sporting event in Baltimore.

Giants coach Jim Lee Howell wanted no part of Memorial Stadium until the game. The Giants had arrived by train from New York on Saturday, but Howell did not conduct any workout in anticipation of the noisiest crowd they had ever faced. Instead, the wary Howell briefed Conerly on the use of hand signals to combat the expected volume.

The noise wasn't any impediment to Donovan, who was loud and garrulous to begin with. What concerned Donovan was any appearance of his father on the Colts' bench. Donovan's father, the celebrated referee, and Donovan's best friend, John Brady, sat on the Baltimore bench last year. "I had some problems before the game, then during it," said Donovan. "Brady was a police captain and responsible for security that day. He had a bottle and got drunk, and he also kept passing the bottle to my father. I said, 'Cut it out, Jack. I got enough problems on the field without having to worry about my father getting drunk.'"

There was no such problem in 1959. For the second championship game, Donovan and the rest of the defense were angered that they were overlooked by the media. The defensive accolades all went to the Giants' unit. The Colts players felt they were every bit as good as their big city counterparts and had even gotten stronger with Dick Szymanski replacing Leo Sanford at linebacker and Johnny Sample taking over for Ray Brown at safety. The Colts' secondary had a total of 40 interceptions, which far outnumbered any other in the league. They were confident that Unitas would put points on the scoreboard as he had done all season long. What the defense wanted to accomplish for their day in the sun was to prevent the Giants from scoring a touchdown.

It was a more confident Giants team because of Conerly's resurgence. It was evident in their dressing room, which sharply contrasted the Colts'. The players were visibly relaxed as big defensive tackle Rosey Grier napped on the floor while his teammates put on their war gear without any signs of tension or trepidation. The defense was still the soul of the team and the reason why the Giants finished 10–2, one game better than the Colts, and why Grier was so at peace with himself.

Baltimore's locker room was a bit more tense. The players were on edge and really couldn't wait for the game to start so they could fulfill their mission of a second straight championship. The players were dressed 30 minutes early, and they sat in front of their cubicles in strained silence. A photographer, wanting to take some photographs, was rebuffed at the door by Berry: "They are pretty keyed up and you might make them mad," he advised the man.

For the second straight year, the Giants won the coin toss, and as they had in the previous encounter, they wanted the ball first. Only this time it was different: Conerly led them out onto the field. He established his presence on the very first play with a 22-yard completion to Kyle Rote. When Gifford swept the right side for another additional 22 yards, the Giants reached the Baltimore 36 in two plays. It certainly wasn't an encouraging beginning for a defense that had something to prove.

Eugene "Big Daddy" Lipscomb then took charge. On a third-and-6 play, he crashed through the Giants' front wall to embarrass the doughty Conerly with a 17-yard loss. That one play provided inspiration for Unitas and the offense. The field general moved his legions to the 40-yard line and wanted a quick strike. On a second-down play, Unitas turned to Moore. Unitas was at his guileful best. He faked one way and feinted another, waiting for Moore. The running back started down the right sideline then sharply cut to his left between two defenders and reached up for Unitas' perfectly timed pass to make a 59-yard touchdown. After less than five minutes of play, the Colts had a 7–0 lead, and all of Baltimore was cheering.

The game had begun with a quick tempo, and the Colts looked capable of a rout. However, after both teams failed to generate a first down to sustain an offense, the Giants found themselves with decent field position on their 40-yard line. They finally showed some offense. With Mel Triplett encouraging them on a 28-yard run on a draw play, the Giants reached the Colts' 3-yard line and were poised for a tying touchdown. If Marchetti and his gang wanted respect, they had to earn it then. Charged with emotion, they corralled Gifford for a 6-yard loss and then overwhelmed Conerly for seven more. The Colts defense drew cheers as the Giants had to settle for Summerall's 23-yard field goal as the quarter ended minutes later.

Baltimore's offense was docile in the second quarter. They only produced five first downs as Unitas was unceremoniously sacked five times. They managed only one scoring attempt, but Myhra's field goal from the 42-yard line in the opening minutes of the period sailed wide to the left. The last time the Colts got the ball was an aberration. Unitas was a fallen idol as his protection imploded. He was smothered three times for a total of 22 yards as Andy Robustelli, the Giants' premier end, led the assault by getting the best of Jim Parker, which wasn't easy to do. When Summerall booted another field goal, this one for 37 yards, 11 seconds were left in the half, the crowd noise had abated, and the Colts walked off the field with a thin one-point advantage, 7–6.

Yet there was no need for panic. Although their running game was pathetic, with only 27 yards, Unitas was still in control and displayed his usual accuracy. When he had time, he completed 12 of 17 passes for 129 yards and was responsible for seven of the Colts' eight first downs with his arm. Hindering Unitas was the New York secondary. They were doing a yeoman job on the Colt receivers, who experienced a difficult time eluding the Giants' tight man-to-man defense. The fact that Berry caught only three balls said a lot.

Although the Colts received the second-half kickoff, the offensive inertia continued. Baltimore had four possessions in the third quarter, yet they could only manage a single first down, and that came when time expired. What had happened to the high-octane offense that Unitas had directed throughout the season? Meanwhile, the grizzled Conerly had taken the Giants on a 72-yard drive that culminated with a 23-yard field goal that pushed the Giants ahead for the first time, 9–7.

There was some apprehension as the Colts offense returned to the field to begin the final period. They hadn't scored a point since their opening march in the first quarter. And in the period that had just ended, they had only moved the chains once. A solitary first down! Concern? Yes. Defeat? No.

Unitas, with all his unwavering panache, decided to take matters into his own hands and, ultimately, his own legs. As far as he was concerned, crunch time was at that very moment of the struggle. He began the Colts' comeback with a key third-down pass to—who else?—Berry to gain 17 yards and a big first down near midfield to awaken the crowd. On the second down, he wanted speed and got it with a 36-yard burner to Moore on the Giants' 14-yard line. On the third down, he completed the enormous 85-yard touchdown drive himself. As the Giants defense, which had been brazen all afternoon, braced for Ameche's bullish charge from the 4-yard line, Unitas outsmarted them. He faked the handoff, turned to his right, and held the ball triumphantly as his bowed legs carried him into the end zone to reclaim the precious lead, 14–9.

The master of chicanery wasn't finished. It was only the beginning of a bizarre and whirlwind fourth quarter, which the beer vendors in the stands appreciated. The Colts defense rose to the challenge and stuffed the Giants twice without a first down, the second magnified by an interception by Andy Nelson, who carried the ball 17 yards to the Giants' 14. The Colts fanatics were on their feet, their emotion carrying their team for another touchdown. Ameche got only two yards and Unitas looked to the sidelines for the next play.

Was Ewbank thinking of a field goal to give the Colts an eight-point lead? That would present the visitors with the task of scoring twice. Or was he contemplating going all out for a touchdown to put the game beyond the reach of the New Yorkers? Jerry Richardson, the rookie receiver Unitas chauffeured during training camp, was waiting to return the favor by bringing in the play that Ewbank wanted.

"I stood next to Weeb and looked at him for the play," said Richardson. "He kept mumbling to himself. I finally asked him what the play was and he remarked, 'Just tell Unitas to score.'" I ran into the huddle and Unitas looked up at me and asked, 'Whatta ya got?' I replied, 'He just said just score.' 'Aw shit,' was all Johnny said."

Given the opportunity to score a seemingly safe field goal or a touchdown, Unitas would always go for the six points. "I get paid to score touchdowns," he would always say. Unitas called for a pass. Years later, Richardson took delight in remembering his biggest moment as a Colt: "Berry was split on the left and would make his cut into the middle underneath the linebacker," said Richardson. "I lined up close to the tackle and would swing wide to the outside. It really was Berry's play all the way. He's done it a hundred times. But Unitas looked off Berry. I looked around and saw the ball coming to me. I squeezed it tight and went into the end zone standing up. I never expected the ball and neither did the Giants. But that's John."

The rookie's touchdown was the clincher. The Colts moved closer to the championship with a 21–9 lead. There were less than eight minutes remaining to glory, so it was highly unlikely that the Giants could manage two touchdowns. And the way the Colts defense was playing, it would be a monumental task. Johnny Sample made sure of that. He picked off a desperate Conerly pass and rambled 42 yards for a 28–9 bulge. Then the speedy Sample came up with another interception to position Myhra's 25-yard field goal for a 31–9 Colts rout. Baltimore had awakened from its slumber with a 24-point fourth-period explosion. A meaningless Conerly-to-Bob Schnelker 32-yard touchdown pass only made the score somewhat more respectable, 31–16. The Colts proved that they were for real because they had a defense every bit as good as the Giants'.

Due Credit

"The defense did it," was the resounding yell in the overcrowded Colts dressing room. They had indeed, and Unitas knew it out there on the field during the waning moments of the game. He hadn't wanted a field goal; he wanted a touchdown. And it wasn't to run up the score either. He wanted to extend homage to the defense, that was all, but the play he called for misfired from a lack of communication. The field goal was supposed to have been a fake instead, so that Marchetti could score a touchdown. Ray Brown, the holder for Myhra's kick, was supposed to throw the pass to Marchetti. But he didn't hear the signal for the changed play.

Ameche was one who realized what the defense did. "After that talk about the Giant defense, I'm certainly glad our defense came through the way it did," he said. "Our defense set us up. It held the Giants to three field goals. We gave them that last touchdown. Now who has the best defense?"

Ewbank, who had almost been fired three years prior, had coached the Colts to a second straight championship. No other coach had done more. And although Unitas had only 207 yards and two touchdowns, Ewbank praised his quarterback for his generalship in a gutsy performance. Unitas had picked himself up off the ground more than at any other time in his career, even more than he did during the regular-season Rams game in 1958 when he was sacked seven times. Unitas unfailingly got up, a warrior of the gridiron.

"I stressed to John he couldn't throw before he was ready," said Ewbank. "So, the losses he incurred, you can blame on me. I believe his cautiousness led to the victory. We had no interceptions and I believe that was the key to the game. I told him not to throw until he had someone clear. The Giants were forcing him and he just had to eat the ball. I think that eventually paid off for us."

Unitas was less reticent than usual with the media. But he concurred with Ewbank's assessment: "The Giants did a great job on our receivers," he said. "That's why I lost yardage several times. I had the time to throw, but no one could get clear."

Vice President Richard Nixon was in attendance for the 1959 championship game as a special guest of Colts owner Carroll Rosenbloom. A mass of people filled the entrance to the Colts' locker room, and Nixon had to wait some 10 minutes before security could clear a path for him to enter. The room was notably quiet for a championship celebration, and Nixon described the contest with the eagerness of a sports fan: "Carroll Rosenbloom said that since I went into the Redskins' dressing room when they beat the Colts, I was obligated to visit the Colts. And it's a pleasure."

As he exited the room, one of the well-wishers outside yelled, "Nixon and Unitas for president." It brought a grin to Nixon's face. "Not a bad team," he quipped. "But if we do it, I'll let Johnny call the signals."

Lenny Moore gave further insight on why Unitas was Unitas and why there was no one better. He described one particular play, in the opening minutes of the game, when Unitas created a play that produced a 59-yard touchdown. "I wasn't the primary receiver on that one," said Moore. "I wasn't supposed to run any particular pattern, just get clear in case the short men were covered."

It was clear that the Colts were somewhat of a Horatio Alger story. They transcended obscurity five years prior to achieve an unbelievable second consecutive NFL championship and gave every underdog in America a reason to strive. Unitas came unknown and unwanted from a poor, remote neighborhood in Pittsburgh. He took the championship in stride, knowing that he had made it happen. But an hour after the game, it was all in the past for Unitas, who was never one to dwell on yesterdays. All he thought about was going home to a ham dinner. That was celebration enough. He was just a meat and potatoes guy: there was no champagne when he was growing up.

Measuring Unitas' Worth

What more could Unitas do? In four years he had won two championships for a bunch of misfits who had been laughed at and scorned around the league for being a bunch of jokers who came out of the doomed All-America Conference with the diminutive 5'6" running back Buddy Young as their star. Indeed, the Colts were orphans looking for a place in the sun. They had been so downtrodden that the NFL had given Baltimore special consideration in the allocation draft, allowing them 15 players compared to the 10 the other teams got in 1950.

Despite the boost, the Colts only won one game out of 12 that year. After an opening day crowd of 26,267 hungry fans, attendance dwindled every week for the rest of the season. The following year, owner Abraham Watner had enough. He returned the Baltimore franchise to the league. And with it, he received $50,000 for the players' contracts and was happy to get some money back. The entire roster was made available for drafting on January 18, the same time as the college players, which meant that the bewildered pros on that list had to start all over again—only they didn't know where.

It certainly didn't appear that Baltimore was a pro football town. However, a resolute Carroll Rosenbloom was convinced he could make professional football work in Baltimore. After two empty years, pro football returned to Baltimore in 1953 when Rosenbloom was awarded the holdings of the defunct Dallas team. Rosenbloom didn't wait long to stack his club. In one of the biggest trades in NFL history, a fifteen-player transaction, he acquired ten players from Cleveland for five of his own. Any way you looked at it, two Cleveland players were worth one Baltimore player.

Baltimore remained a loser's town. In Keith Molesworth's only year as coach in 1953, the Colts went 3–9, which was exactly what Weeb Ewbank did when he took over for Molesworth the following year. Then Ewbank gave them a glimmer of hope in 1955, when the Colts finished 5–6–1 after losing their final two games on the road in Los Angeles and San Francisco—to just miss their first winning season. The stigma of losing still remained.

That's what Unitas encountered when he arrived for his first season in 1956. But he wasn't one to look back: he could only concern himself in what was given to him, and the past didn't concern him, especially if it was bad. The stigma was not his doing. But he didn't know if he could do anything about it, especially because Baltimore had a star in quarterback George Shaw.

Fate had brought Unitas to the Colts. He wasn't on anybody's mind after the 1955 season. If reserve quarterback Gary Kerkorian hadn't decided to return to college to earn a law degree, Unitas would never have made it to the NFL and perhaps would have worked on a construction job for the rest of his life in Pittsburgh. And fate also interceded to make Unitas the starting quarterback for the rest of his time in Baltimore: 17 years.

Unitas had four children and wanted more money to play. He got together with Don Kellett on a new contract and asked for $25,000, which was a large sum of money in the league at the time. Kellett told him he couldn't talk about that amount unless he went to Rosenbloom first.

Kellett returned with the owner and the three of them sat down. "John, what seems to be the trouble between you and Kellett?" asked Rosenbloom.

"I don't have a problem," answered Unitas.

"Don?" asked Rosenbloom.

"God, Carroll, the kid wants $25,000," said Kellett. "We don't pay anybody who's been in the league 10 years that amount of money."

"Wait a minute," said Unitas. "Are you paying on the amount of time you spend in the league or the ability to get the job done?"

Rosenbloom began to laugh. "Don, I believe he's got you there."

Rosenbloom knew the intrinsic value of his quarterback. Unitas was more than a star. He was Baltimore. He was an original.

6

Christmas in Cleveland

J OHNNY UNITAS AWOKE A LITTLE AFTER 7:00 ON A COLD, LATE-
December Saturday morning in Cleveland. He dressed, put on a rum-
pled raincoat for whatever warmth it offered, and walked a couple of blocks
to the 8:00 mass at St. John's Cathedral with Gino Marchetti and head
coach Don Shula. The blustery wind off Lake Erie made it feel even colder,
and Unitas hunched his shoulders and stuck his valuable hands in his pock-
ets. Cleveland winters, at times, could be the coldest anywhere, and if a
howling wind off the lake remained the next day for the 1964 NFL
championship game between the Colts and the Browns, it could create
havoc for Unitas' passes. Shula, having played college ball at John Carroll
University and for a couple of years with the Browns, knew all about the
Decembers in Cleveland.

Marchetti never expected to be there, especially not on Christmas
night when the Colts arrived a day earlier than planned because of the
weather. He was almost 38 years old, and he had actually retired following the 1963 season. He had a Hall-of-Fame career as one of the most
feared defensive ends in the league and had made the All-Pro team nine
times. Shula, who wasn't much in the way of superlatives, claimed Marchetti
was "the best defensive lineman to ever play the game of football." When
he was voted the Most Valuable Player of the 1963 Pro Bowl, Marchetti

decided that it would be the opportune time to retire after 11 years of menacing every quarterback and running back who got in his way. He definitely didn't need the money to hang on for another year. Marchetti had
a 25 percent stake in a Baltimore hamburger drive-in that was doing an
$8-million business, which was more than Marchetti ever envisioned the
day Rosenbloom staked him $100,000 for his end.

Shula knew he had a championship team in place for the 1964 sea-
son—only if Marchetti played. "Just having Gino in there helps," said Shula.
He spent the entire summer during training camp trying to convince
Marchetti to play just one more year. Finally, in desperation, he convinced
Rosenbloom to apply pressure on Marchetti, who was no stranger to pressure on the playing field. When Marchetti flew to New York to meet with
Rosenbloom, who was prepared to call in a favor, he took his 13-year-old
son, Ernie, with him, perhaps contending that the owner, seeing the kid,
would relent in his demand that he play football one more time.

"What do you think about your father playing football again?" asked a
smiling Rosenbloom.

"Oh, Mother and I want him to play," answered the youngster
innocently.

Marchetti was blocked. Rosenbloom offered him a blank contract and
told him to fill in the amount with which he was comfortable. Marchetti,
thinking about all the hamburgers his joint was selling, deferred. He, in
turn, told Rosenbloom to put down whatever he wanted, and at the same
time, honestly mentioned that he didn't think the team had any kind of
a chance for a championship. Marchetti had missed several weeks of the
season to get his body in shape for trench warfare. When he played, he
performed as adroitly as he had before, and when the season was over, he
was named to the All-Pro team for the 10th time and was a big reason
why the Colts were in Cleveland in December.

Baltimore would need the fulminating presence of Marchetti and the
excellence of Unitas, who had a great season throwing for 2,864 yards with
19 touchdowns and only six interceptions, to extinguish the Browns on
their home field. The oddsmakers, who thought highly of the Colts for

winning 10 straight games in a 12–2 campaign, established Baltimore as a seven-point favorite. It was Shula's second year as head coach, and indeed, he was the youngest one in the league. And it didn't get past the odds-makers that Unitas was named MVP of the NFL for the season.

It was expected to be a high-scoring game. The Colts had finished second in scoring with 428 points during the season, and the Browns were right behind them with 415, making them two of the highest-scoring teams in the history of the 45-year-old league. Only the 1950 Los Angeles Rams with 466 points, and the 1963 Giants with 448, had scored more. Led by Unitas, Baltimore had scored the most touchdowns, 54, and led by Marchetti, the Colts had a league-high 57 sacks.

Preparations and Problems

Unitas was content to spend Saturday afternoon after practice relaxing in his room watching television. He came out only to have dinner at about 7:00 and then returned to the TV set in his room. He analyzed some plays and went to sleep at about 11:00. While he was asleep, Bernie Parrish, Cleveland's defensive back who called the team's formations, was in another hotel studying film. Less than 24 hours later, he would figure prominently in Cleveland's much-maligned defense, which had surrendered the most points in the league.

"I [was] looking at films of the Colts and saw that the defensive backfield men they were up against kept dropping off on plays," said Parrish, who was a wily veteran. "I felt the Colts expected us to back off too and give them the short yardage. I thought we could do better by playing their receivers closer. I know that I had been playing closer the last six or seven games and I found it better." Parrish shared his observations the next day in the dressing room of old Municipal Stadium with the other defensive backs and formulated a new defensive game plan only hours before taking the field.

On Sunday morning, Unitas again dutifully left the hotel for 8:00 mass, this time with Marchetti and his son. Walking back afterward with Alex Sandusky, Unitas spotted Marchetti and Shula jaywalking, and in a playful mood, yelled to some nearby policemen, "Hey, officers, arrest those guys for crossing against the light!" The cops easily recognized Unitas, and one of them, apparently a Colts fan, replied, "Get a few points today, John."

"Gonna need more than a few points today," said Unitas who appeared relaxed despite the cold in his wrinkled raincoat. Little did he ever imagine that he wouldn't get any points at all.

Shula was confident. He had taken a moribund team and turned them into championship contenders. He remarked to Unitas at the time, "How well I do depends on you." Shula was asked to take over a Colts team in 1963 that had had only one winning season, 8–6, since winning their second world championship in 1959, and in the interim three years, had a mediocre 21–19 record.

During that time frame, Unitas' game had noticeably suffered. He had thrown more interceptions, 71, than touchdowns, 64, and had not been in agreement with Weeb Ewbank's conservative offensive philosophy. Ewbank even began to question how Unitas ran a game, which hurt the quarterback who had given him back-to-back championships. The decline of the team started with the loss of Ameche, who retired in 1960 from injuries despite only playing six years. He had been a vital member of the backfield, a punishing blocker who protected Unitas, and a powerful, straight-ahead fullback who kept the defenses reasonably honest. He was never sufficiently replaced, and the Colts' running game wasn't dangerous anymore.

"You lose a guy like that," said Unitas, "you can't replace him. 'The Horse' was a tremendous blocker as a fullback. And he was also a great runner. They couldn't key on me alone. They'd have to watch for Ameche slipping up the middle on a draw or taking a screen pass."

There were other contributing factors to the team's decline. The reliable Berry had a knee operation before the opening of the 1961 season, missed a couple of games, and never did catch a touchdown pass all that year. Mutscheller, another of Unitas' favorite receivers, limped throughout the campaign. Art Spinney, a key member of the offensive line, left a hole when he retired. With Ameche gone, the Colts moved Moore, the most dangerous flanker in the league, to running back, which negated his explosiveness as a feared receiver.

Moore caught the final pass of Unitas' incredible touchdown streak in 1960. Beginning in 1956, Unitas had thrown a touchdown pass in 47 straight games before his streak ended on December 11, 1960, in the last game of the season against the Rams in Los Angeles in a 10–3 loss. The five-year run had spanned the time when games were increased to 14 per season and pro football underwent a transition from a running offense to a passing one. Unitas' streak has been equated to the 1941 hitting streak of Joe DiMaggio, which reached 56 games. And rightfully so. No other quarterback has come close to breaking Unitas' record—not Joe Montana, not Joe Namath, not Dan Marino, not John Elway, and not Peyton Manning.

During the streak, Unitas put up gaudy numbers. He completed 713 passes in 1,336 attempts, accounting for 10,827 yards, 103 touchdowns, and 62 interceptions that resulted in a completion average of 53.4 percent. The average yardage per game was 230.3, which translated into an average of 8.1 yards per pass. He was a force that brought fear to opposing defenses.

The offensive line, which had been considered the best in the league, had begun to age, which didn't bode well for Unitas. He staunchly believed that if his blockers didn't give him more than two and a half seconds to throw, he'd have to pull down his arm and eat the ball. But, he emphasized, if they did provide him with three full seconds, he'd have an excellent chance to complete a pass. "There's never been a doubt in my mind that I couldn't do the job again if given adequate time," said Unitas. His throwing hand middle finger, which was dislocated in 1961, had become permanently swollen. Some observers felt that the injury affected his passing. "Nah, I throw the same," Unitas said. "It's no problem at all."

Unitas had begun to have problems with Ewbank in 1962. Weeb was convinced that Unitas' gambling style was now wrong after two disappointing seasons. Yet much of Unitas' success was the result of his daring and improvisation, and he needed the freedom to continue. Unitas wasn't about to change. He would still do the things he always did during a game, calling plays he felt were appropriate. Although they never took their disagreements into public, there was an air of tension between the two and Unitas didn't let it extend beyond that. Still, it bothered him.

"As a quarterback, I have to take orders and do what the hell he wants," said Unitas. "Before the season started, in training camp, I'd been under a lot of criticism from newspapers, maybe it was from Weeb. I don't know. He came out and said I never followed game plans to the letter. I guess you get a little touchy because the man says you don't do what the hell he tells you.

"In '58 and '59, I'd throw from the end zone if I knew I could hit the man and get him open. I had a situation against Green Bay when we beat them in Baltimore. Fourth down and a yard to go. We were on their 35-yard line, score tied. Weeb sent in a quarterback sneak. I couldn't get through with a bulldozer. We lined up and faked the fullback into the line on an off-tackle play and I told Lenny Moore to slant in and take off, then bust the sideline out for about 15 yards. I held for half a count, then spun around and hit him on the 12-yard line. We got the first down and went for the score on the next play.

"The thing that hurt me was that he kept out of there. I know I could do what I had to do. One of the games in Baltimore, the first 10 times I threw the ball, I completely missed. But I ended up 18 of 32. If the man doesn't have enough confidence in you to let you go, he only hurts himself and hurts you at the same time.

"Against San Francisco in Baltimore, we had the ball 20 plays in the first half. They just killed us. Our defense couldn't hold them. So he took me out and put Lamar McHan in at the beginning of the third quarter. I didn't play any of it. I never stayed out of a game that long. The little time I was in the fourth quarter, we scored two quick touchdowns and we were on the way to another when the game ended."

After 12 games of the season, the Colts were 5–7 and headed for another losing season when an angry Carroll Rosenbloom took charge. He had all he could stand from Ewbank's conservatism. In a drastic move, he confided with Unitas. "Look, you're the boss," he said. "Call the plays any way you want to. You're in complete charge on the field once the game starts." Unitas rallied the Colts with two season-ending victories to finish 7–7. Ewbank was finished two days later.

The Game

Two years after that, with Unitas in control the way Rosenbloom ordered, the Colts were in the 1964 championship game. The day before, they went through a short workout to test the Cleveland Stadium field to determine if there would be any problems with the footing. Unitas was one of the last to leave the bus and walk onto the field. He found his teammates staring silently around the cavernous stadium. "Hey," he yelled, "haven't any of you seen a football field before?" Marchetti, who was standing next to Unitas, laughed. It broke the tension. Suddenly, other players started laughing. "A football field is 120 yards long," continued Unitas, "and it's about 50 yards wide, and it's got goalposts." Unitas was relaxed.

The wind that was prevalent on Saturday remained throughout the night and into the next day when the Colts arrived at the stadium for the second time. On game day, it was colder and the wind off nearby Lake Erie howled even louder. Unitas' counterpart at quarterback was Frank Ryan, a prematurely graying quarterback with a brilliant mathematical mind. If anyone could analyze the velocity of the wind and its effect on a leather ball, it would appear that Ryan could. On a day like that, the ground game became a prominent factor, and the Colts would have to watch out for Cleveland's Jim Brown, the league's best running back. The weather conditions definitely favored Cleveland.

The Browns won the coin toss, and coach Blanton Collier, factoring in the wind, elected to have the strong element at their backs. His decision meant that the Browns would have the wind again during the third quarter instead of the final period, which most teams prefer. "Most of the time you want the wind with you at the end of the game so you can rally if you have to," explained Collier. "But I decided that maybe we better take the wind while it was still blowing." It would turn out to be the right strategy.

And it turned out to be an abysmal first half—almost to the point of spectator boredom. Neither team could move the ball to create any excitement as the ominous wind made its presence felt. The only serious moment for a score of any kind occurred early in the second period when Baltimore lined up a field goal. However, Bob Boyd, the holder, fumbled the snap from center, which botched the attempt. The snap was good, but apparently the cold numbed Boyd's hands.

Unitas, too, was experiencing difficulties—not only from the cold, but from the Cleveland defense as well. He not only threw an interception, but he was also guilty of two fumbles. The prodigious Baltimore offense was as docile as a falling leaf, and the first half of what was expected to be a high-scoring game ended scoreless.

The Loss

After failing to do anything with the second-half kickoff, the inept offense forced the Colts to punt from their 23-yard line. However, Tom Gilburg, a big offensive tackle, didn't have much leg, and got off a weak 25-yard kick that was downed on Baltimore's 48-yard line. Marchetti and the rest of the defense then limited Cleveland to a field goal try, and Lou Groza, the oldest player in the league, booted a 43-yard one with a 20-mile-an-hour wind at his back. Baltimore's offensive futility continued on the next series of downs and Cleveland got the ball back on its 32-yard line.

A running play netted nothing. Ryan then used deceit to fool the Colts. He set up in a double wing with Ernie Green spread out to the left as a flanker, leaving Brown behind Ryan. On a quick pitch, Brown swept around the left side, with three blockers in front. He wasn't caught until he reached Baltimore's 18. The 46-yard run shocked the Colts. Ryan was thinking of calling another sweep. Instead, he threw a pass to flanker Gary Collins. On a hook-and-go, Collins ran free in the end zone and

Ryan's perfect pass gave the Browns a 10–0 lead. The Colts' Boyd acknowledged the blown coverage later. "We couldn't hear our calls," he said.

At that point, the Colts appeared rattled. Ryan and Collins took advantage of the team's loss of focus and combined for another touchdown pass, once again on a missed defensive assignment. Jerry Logan admitted that he misread the Browns' formation on the 42-yard play that left the Colts questioning themselves. The 17–0 lead escalated to 20–0 in the fourth quarter when Groza kicked a 10-yard field goal and then to 27–0 when Ryan connected with Collins a third time for 51 yards. The rout was evident. The game ended in a 27–0 Cleveland masterpiece.

The Colts had arrived in Cleveland as one of the best offensive teams and had not scored a single point on the worst defensive team in the league. The plane ride back to Baltimore was a long one.

Bernie Parrish's late night at the movies was unquestionably a major factor in the Brown's plays. "Bernie called a beautiful game," praised Cleveland safety Ross Fitchner.

Unitas was pressured the entire game and threw two interceptions. He appeared somewhat befuddled by the Brown's defense, which produced an implausible shutout. But he offered no excuses, which was his way.

"We knew that the Colt pass patterns were built on precision and timing, and that if you [take] away the first receiver and force Johnny Unitas to go a second or third, you are forcing them out of a pattern," said Cleveland defensive coach Nick Skorich. "We took away Unitas' first target and he had to hesitate and look again for another. We got a strong rush inside and he couldn't get away. We crowded him especially when he was throwing into the wind and knew he couldn't throw long."

Unitas never had a pocket to throw from all afternoon. When he stepped up away from the rush, the pocket was too shallow. He was forced to throw the ball quickly, or if he wasn't able to move, was easily tackled. "That was not the way I wanted it to go," said Unitas. "I wanted to go out and gun them down, but their defense didn't allow it. They shut off the bombs. They just beat the heck out of us. They played a good ballgame. We didn't."

It was so bad that the Colts could only produce 11 first downs and an anemic 171 yards of total offense. Although he was 12 of 20, Unitas' passes accounted for only 89 yards as the Browns took away his long ball and yielded on the short ones.

Shula was visibly upset and kept the dressing room door closed for almost 15 minutes before letting in the media. He placed the blame for the defeat on the offense. He offered no excuses for any of the players, including Unitas. "We had zero points on the scoreboard and I wasn't satisfied with anyone," he fumed. "We couldn't get anything done." A writer asked if it was Unitas' fault. That was sacred ground, but Shula didn't hold back. "He killed our own drives by giving up the ball twice on fumbles and twice on pass interceptions. We never gave our defense a break. Heck, when you can't move it and keep putting pressure on the defense, you can't expect to win."

Except of course, Unitas always expected to win. When the Colts' charter made a two-bounce landing in Baltimore, one of the players shouted, "Touchdown!" Another one added, "First one we made today." It wasn't supposed to be that way. Not for Shula, not for the players, especially not for Unitas.

7

An Injured Arm

IT WAS NOT THE BEST OF SPRINGS FOR JOHNNY UNITAS IN 1968 in the weeks before he got ready for his 13th training camp. He had expressed a desire to play for another five years when the question was posed to him by those around the team. But age and the bruising hits he had absorbed over time hinted that the seemingly indestructible Unitas, who had missed only four or five games in his career, was only human after all. Not even the nectar of the gods could heal him now. Unitas' arm was weak and hued black and blue, unlike anything he ever experienced before. But the great ones, like Joe DiMaggio with his torn Achilles tendon, never complain. They have too much pride, which sets them apart from the others. Unitas endured his injury without a murmur, but there was reason to suspect that he might have been through at the age of 35. The game had become faster and more injurious with bigger, stronger athletes.

Before the summer grind was even over, 1968 evolved into the worst season of Unitas' legendary career. Inexplicably, he discovered he couldn't throw. The unerring arm that brought him and, in turn, the Colts to glory, betrayed him. He was like a bird with a broken wing as his passes flopped forlornly to the ground. He was puzzled by the inability because he had had a good 1967 season; he threw for 3,428 yards, made the Pro Bowl for the second straight year, and led the Colts to an 11–1–2 campaign which resulted in a first-place tie in the Coastal Division, although not an advance to the playoffs.

Breaking Down

When he reported to training camp after that marvelous season in which he threw 436 times—the most of his career—his arm, increasingly, began to swell. At first, Unitas appeared unconcerned and stoically accepted the condition. Treatment and the summer heat would be the balm that would correct the ailment, and it would be like 1967 all over again. All a tennis elbow needed was a rubdown and rest, just like he had done for the past two years, only this time it was much more painful and severe and took longer to heal. It became a concern with every passing day. "I can't raise it or straighten it out, and it hurts when I try to do something with it, like lifting," he told trainer Eddie Block.

By early August, Unitas' arm strength hadn't improved. A vigilant Don Shula needed assurance about whether Unitas' arm would be able to open the season. Shula's offensive theory always began with the quarterback. He needed Unitas now, but became wary after seeing Unitas' daily struggles. So he reached out to New York and Earl Morrall, who had basically been a career backup for San Francisco, Detroit, Pittsburgh, and the Giants during his 12 years in the league. Morrall confided to Shula that he was considering retirement, but Shula was persuasive. He convinced Morrall to join the Colts.

"If you come to Baltimore, you'll join a team with a great chance to win a championship," said Shula. "And, you may get more action than you think."

The Diagnosis

In lay terms, Unitas' ailment was simply described as a tennis elbow. But it was much more serious than that because he had structural damage inside the elbow. The condition was caused by the nature of Unitas' follow-through after he zinged a pass. Every time he threw, he not only felt pain, but aggravated the elbow even further. Although his delivery was a normal, straight, overhand pass, the way he turned his hand inward for the follow-through created the problem, much like a baseball player throwing a screwball. After a throw, Unitas' right thumb turned counterclockwise, putting a reverse strain on the elbow with his right hand ending up facing the left. Ewbank noticed it the first time he threw a pass at a Colts practice in his rookie season in 1956.

In Unitas' condition, he couldn't be anybody's quarterback. The team's orthopedic doctor ruled out surgery, which wasn't what Unitas wanted anyway. There wasn't any remedy except rest. The team doctors were of the opinion that not only had Unitas torn a muscle, but he had also aggravated the chronic tendonitis. What's more, the tendons in his million-dollar arm were now starting to rebel from years of strain. Unitas' high threshold for pain over the past several years had been Spartan. A warrior, he had been able to live with the pain and never accepted cortisone shots for relief. Eventually, the swelling and pain had always lessened. But that was then. Now he needed the cortisone.

"I've known my man John since 1956 and that's the first time I've ever heard him admit he had pain," said Lenny Moore.

A Legend's Courage

During his 12 years with the Colts, Unitas had thrown 4,097 passes that counted, and at least 4,000 more in practice to Raymond Berry, Moore, John Mackey, Jimmy Orr, Willie Richardson, and Ray Perkins. The arm that had served him so well now deceived him. His passes were like a feather wafted by the wind, flowing harmlessly to nowhere. It was sad to watch him throw, asking his arm to give him more. In essence, he really couldn't. He couldn't go deep anymore, and even the short ball that he threw at times was barely worthy of Pop Warner League football. As Shula had indicated, Morrall got to play sooner and much more than he expected.

It was also a lonely summer for Unitas. His pal Berry retired and so did Moore, whom Unitas referred to as "Spats" because of his heavily taped cleats. Both were vital components in Unitas' success over the years.

The great quarterback's arm was a liability. Shula was hoping to get one more year out of Unitas, and he even began to have doubts. He needed to see his quarterback in a preseason game, but he had to wait until training camp was almost over.

Unitas' debut was in the final preseason game on September 7 in Dallas. The magic of Unitas' name was still alive in the area. A crowd of 69,420 turned out in the Cotton Bowl to see Unitas when they learned that he would start. And he didn't disappoint at first. Early in the opening period, Unitas and Mackey hooked up for an 84-yard touchdown when the mobile tight end pulled down a short pass and ran away from the secondary. Backing up from center Bill Curry's snap, he got off a pass that wobbled and fell to the earth like a dying duck. That was enough for Unitas. He walked to the sidelines holding his elbow and fearing the worst.

"Are you hurt?" asked Shula.

"Yeah, but not bad. I can still play," answered Unitas. There was no quit in him even in a preseason outing.

Unitas managed to split the game with Morrall. Late in the fourth quarter of a 10–10 tie, Unitas was on the field. A shanked Dallas punt left the Colts on the Cowboys' 40-yard line. Who better than Unitas to deliver the winning points? Mixing runs and two complete passes, he got the offense to the 14, and it looked like old times again with more of Unitas' patented two-minute magic. However, a holding penalty handicapped Unitas and left him with third down and needing 25 yards for a first down. It would be the final test of his crippled arm. The pass he attempted failed miserably. It was weak and uncatchable. The pain in his arm was more excruciating than ever before and he walked over to Shula with his head down. "I can play, but I can't play well," he said.

The pain lingered longer than at any time in the past. It was worse. There was no possible way he would be ready to play in the season's opener the following week. Even Unitas was beginning to harbor doubts about his ability to continue. When writer Larry Harris of the *Baltimore Sun* asked Unitas about his arm, he said, "I'm through. They got all they could out of me. With this arm, I couldn't knock a sick cat off a flower pot."

The Sins of the Crowd

Morrall opened the season, and he did so with éclat. He performed like he never had before in directing the Colts to five successive victories. And he did so impressively, averaging 33 points in those wins. However, in the sixth game, against Cleveland, he faltered. He could only throw for 63 yards, which enabled the Browns to take a 14–7 halftime lead. Shula walked over to Unitas in the dressing room and succinctly asked, "Can you make it?" As usual, Unitas didn't hesitate in answering: "Yeah."

But he really couldn't. His arm was still weak after five weeks of rest— too weak to throw a football with real ferocity. Unitas was a sad, solitary figure on the field, far from the paladin of a year ago. If his performance on that October day could be characterized by one word, *disaster* would be it. His very first pass was intercepted and set up Cleveland's third touchdown. Unitas continued to try. He threw 10 more times, and his feeble attempts translated into two more interceptions. It was the worst performance of his life. He connected on only one pass of the 11 he gamely tried in the 30–20 Baltimore loss. "Unitas was the guy that won it for us," exclaimed one of the Browns players in a dressing-room interview.

That had to hurt the proud Unitas. But not as much as what the Colts fans did: a great many of the sellout crowd in Memorial Stadium booed Unitas as he solemnly walked off the field during the fourth quarter when Morrall returned to replace him. The fans' behavior was execrable. How could they ignobly turn away from their hero, one who had brought the whole city together with heart-pounding victories and two championships? Unitas was in agony with his wounded arm and didn't ask for pity. He wanted to do more, produce more vivid memories, but couldn't.

Unitas was unfazed by the crowd's venom. "I don't give a damn whether they cheer or boo," he said. "I'm not surprised either way and it makes no difference to me."

But John Steadman of the *Baltimore American,* who was perhaps Unitas' closest friend among the writers, was ashamed of what had taken place before his eyes that Sunday. And he wrote as much in his well-read column:

> His name is John Unitas. You surely remember him.
>
> He's the man who made the franchise, contributed more than any player, coach or executive, living or dead or yet unborn.
>
> Unitas is suffering with a damaged arm, torn muscle fibers in his right elbow, yet he practices and goes to the games. He hasn't missed attending.
>
> If it hadn't been for him, the Colts would be just another football team. It's a sin to jeer Unitas.

Fighting for His Place

Too quickly Unitas was being forgotten. His name was mentioned less frequently. The fans' reminder of him was a huge billboard on the way to the stadium with a smiling Unitas proclaiming that he used Red Crown Gasoline for action. Unitas remained hidden almost in the shadows for the next two months of the season. Shula had no intentions of playing him. He didn't need him.

Morrall was doing a superlative job, better than anyone could have expected from a journeyman quarterback with a crewcut like Unitas, the legend he replaced. Going into the final week of the campaign, the Colts were on a seven-game winning streak following the Cleveland loss and had indeed raised eyebrows around the league with a 12–1 record behind Morrall. They were even better than the year before and never came close to losing during their hot streak. All that remained was a final game against the Rams in Los Angeles.

That's when Unitas appeared again for only the second time in what was a long season for him. With the playoffs approaching, Shula had to find out about Unitas, whether he could trust him anymore in getting to the Super Bowl in the third year of the big game's existence. He gave Unitas half of a game to show him, to remove any doubts in his mind.

94

After standing on the sidelines for two months, Unitas relished the opportunity. He wasn't used to watching and the inactivity gnawed at him. The Colts continued to streak, 28–24, and it would have been nice to say that Unitas won it to wring some hope from a season that consisted of two halves of football. In truth, he didn't. However, he did play better than he had against Cleveland, but in reality, he achieved nothing that would give him an encore. He was sagacious with his ball fakes, scrupulous in his play-calling, and his receivers rallied around him. The statistics declared that he was 10 of 21, with two touchdowns and an interception. But what they didn't show was that Unitas couldn't throw deep. He was half of a quarterback.

As such, the Colts didn't need anything from Unitas. They finished 13–1, and the nomadic Morrall was voted the NFL's Most Valuable Player, as well as the Comeback Player of the Year, even before the Colts defeated Minnesota in the playoffs and routed the Browns 34–0 in the championship game. Morrall experienced the greatest year of his career in throwing for 2,909 yards, 26 touchdowns, and 17 interceptions. Shula had himself a quarterback. It was a Unitas-type year and there was no question that Morrall had earned the right to start against the New York Jets in Super Bowl III two weeks later.

For Unitas, the season just got longer.

8

A Lonely Figure

T HE EXCITEMENT THAT SURROUNDED SUPER BOWL III LOFTED the NFL to another dimension. It had equaled or surpassed the hallowed World Series. The football league's propaganda artists had one game to pump and the benefit of two weeks to promote it, instead of the seven-game format that showcased baseball's championship. In the first two years of the Super Bowl, the popular Green Bay Packers and their charismatic coach, Vince Lombardi, made easy victims of two American Football League teams: the Kansas City Chiefs and the Oakland Raiders. Now there was to be a new championship team as the Baltimore Colts clashed with the New York Jets.

This Super Bowl was the biggest yet. It was a showdown of coaches. For openers, the Jets' Weeb Ewbank, who had gotten the Colts their only two championships and now was the first coach to win titles in both the NFL and the AFL, was going against the Colts' coach, Don Shula, who had replaced Ewbank after he was fired by the Colts' owner Carroll Rosenbloom in 1963. It was the old coach against the new one.

It was also a showdown of quarterbacks. Joe Namath, the brash Jets quarterback, would duel with Johnny Unitas if the latter was healthy. They were two guys from Pittsburgh, a healthy one and a frayed one, and the sparks from their battle would rival the neon lights of trendy Miami Beach if Unitas' arm would allow him to duel.

Laying the Odds

The nation's bookmakers made the Colts an 18-point favorite, which was unprecedented for a championship game. Why even bother to play the contest? When Namath learned of the one-sided odds at a team celebration dinner in New York, he exclaimed, "Eighteen points! How do they figure that?"

It was the biggest point spread in the Super Bowl's short history and wasn't equaled until 1995, when San Francisco covered the spread with a resounding 49–26 victory over San Diego.

Ewbank found himself in the same situation with the Jets as he had when he first got to Baltimore in 1954. Like the Colts, the Jets were laughed at for the first three years of their existence. They were survivors from the American Football League, when they were known as the Titans, and had labored for four years in the antiquated Polo Grounds before going bankrupt. Then David "Sonny" Werblin and his partners rescued them and brought them to Shea Stadium for the 1964 season with the new name they had adopted in 1963.

And he did so with a flourish never seen before. Werblin, the one-time guiding genius of the Music Corporation of America believed in star power. There were no owners in the NFL like him, and he shook the stodgy establishment by giving Alabama's Joe Namath a $400,000 contract. It was a contract previously unheard of in pro football annals. Werblin had extraordinary insight into the value that Namath represented and recouped his invested money in a Super Bowl dividend five years later. He had figured right.

"I believe in the star system," said Werblin. "That's what sells tickets. Namath is Joe DiMaggio. He's Gregory Peck, Clark Gable, and Frank Sinatra. When he walks into a room, you know he's there."

Anticipation Builds

The media knew where Namath was when the Jets arrived in Fort Lauderdale 10 days before the Super Bowl. The Colts weren't scheduled to arrive until Saturday, but Ewbank wanted the extra few days to get the Jets acclimated to the warm temperatures that made south Florida a winter mecca from the cold. As soon as Namath walked off the tarmac, a horde of newspeople was waiting.

"Hey, Joe, what do you think of Earl Morrall?" asked one television reporter.

"I can think of five quarterbacks in the AFL better than Morrall," said Namath. "Myself, John Hadl of San Diego, Bob Griese of Miami, Daryle Lamonica of Oakland, and Len Dawson of Kansas City."

There was no mention of Unitas. In any other year, it would have been Unitas' time. But he was nothing more than a spectator on the sidelines just waiting, hoping he would play on Sunday. He was unsure of it ever happening.

"It's a new experience after 12 years," he said. "You want to get in. Your muscles and body are willing, but your arm can't. You just can't do what you normally do."

Naturally, when the Colts finally arrived on Saturday, the press attempted to provoke a reaction from Morrall regarding Namath's statement of a few days before, which made headlines. But the veteran Morrall, a quiet individual, would not allow himself to become embroiled in any inflammatory controversy. "Joe Namath is entitled to his opinion," was all Morrall would say.

On Monday, word had gotten around that on Sunday night Namath and Lou Michaels, Baltimore's field-goal kicker and defensive end, had been involved in a heated exchange at Fazio's, one of the Italian restaurants in Fort Lauderdale. Cooler heads managed to prevail, and Namath picked up the check for everyone with a $100 bill. The night ended on a cordial note when Namath dropped off Michaels at his hotel.

Later in the week, Namath created more headlines. He was in Miami to receive the Touchdown Club's award as the player of the year. The dinner was held at the celebrated Miami Springs Villa and was sold out. Astronaut Gordon Cooper and Indianapolis 500 winner Jim Rathman were also present, but it was Namath's night. He punctuated it boldly by declaring, "The Jets will win Sunday, I guarantee it."

His statement definitely guaranteed more media frenzy. The stage that once belonged to Unitas was now occupied by Namath. He was the new generation of athlete, and he had an aura around him like the star-maker Sonny Werblin had wanted. Namath was photographed in New York wearing a full-length coat, did a panty hose commercial, and was known as a nighthawk around town—often with a pretty lady on his arm. For his celebrity behavior, he was dubbed "Broadway Joe." He was all the things Unitas was not. The only things they had in common were that they were two Catholic guys from Pittsburgh who could throw a football.

Namath was certainly the central figure. It was as if no other players mattered. He was creating more excitement than the first two Super Bowls combined and doing an excellent job of psyching out the Colts. Even Shula was affected. He was peeved about Namath's remark that five quarterbacks in the AFL could throw better than Morrall.

"How Namath can rap Earl is a thing I don't understand," said Shula. "How the hell can you rap a guy that's the National Football League's Player of the Year? Particularly when Earl's had the percentage of completions he's had, the touchdown passes he's had, and the big yardage he's accumulated for us. Namath can say whatever he wants to say, but I don't know how he can rap a guy who's accomplished the things Earl has for us all year."

Indeed, in the euphoria surrounding Namath, some facts were overlooked. Morrall had a much better year statistically than the New York heartthrob. He had completed 182 of 317 passes (57.4 percent) for 2,909 yards, 29 touchdowns, and 17 interceptions. Namath had thrown 380 passes and completed 187 (49.2 percent) for 15 touchdowns and 17 interceptions. Unitas, for one, appreciated Morrall's efforts.

"Earl did a tremendous job for us," praised Unitas. "I can't say enough about him. He took over the offense more and more with each game. Earl has been tremendous as long as he stays consistent."

The Quarterbacks

It was Unitas, not Morrall, whom the fans adored. He was still the idol and the adoration soothed him. One day at the Colts' hotel, they came at him from all directions in the lobby: kids and adults, holding books, scraps of paper, and ballpoint pens. Morrall realized the moment and graciously stepped away unrecognized. Patiently and politely, Unitas signed and signed, thanking each fan for thinking enough of him to ask for his autograph. When he had finished, Unitas gave a wave and went to his room with a good feeling. He sat back comfortably in an easy chair and savored the 15-minute interlude in the lobby below.

Unless he got to play significantly on Sunday, the scene in the lobby would be the highlight of his first Super Bowl, since fate had reduced him to an uncomfortable spectator's role for the biggest football game of the season. And, big games were what Unitas had thrived on. Knowing that he wouldn't get to do it again wasn't easy on him. He had competed all his life, but was being denied the moment. And at 35, with a damaged arm, there wouldn't be many moments left.

But Unitas was already looking to the next season, when months of rest would have brought his arm strength back. The orthopedic surgeon who examined Unitas in November gave him hope. He told the quarterback that his arm would be as good as new by the middle of summer. All he needed was rest. There was no doubt in Unitas' mind that he would be okay by then.

"What I'm going to try to do is give the arm complete rest in January and February," said Unitas, "and then throw the ball for two or three days the first week in March. If I have to, I can make adjustments."

If there was one thing that Unitas didn't want, it was pity. He didn't want any part of it. More than anything else, he hated being ministered to because of his fierce pride that had been with him all his life. But the next year, if there was to be a next year, he would need more than that. Confidence always had been his strongest ally—better than those strong Colts offensive lines, better than Raymond Berry catches. He never wavered in the great faith he had in himself. As he bluntly put it, "Confidence is one thing I don't lack."

"I'm not well enough to play right now," he said. "My arm is all right. That's no problem. The only thing is I haven't played much, so I'm not sharp and I might be slow picking up things out there. I haven't started all year, so it's no big deal. I'll be there Sunday and Shula knows where to find me."

The fire to play was burning inside of him. His chances of playing, however, were less than 50 percent. He would be ready if called upon, but if he was, then the Colts would be in trouble. No starter gets pulled unless he isn't playing well and the team is behind almost to the point of being desperate. Unitas had been in such situations before, but always as the starter.

"Earl should be starting because he has been playing all year," acknowledged Unitas. "He's an excellent quarterback and he deserves all the honors he's getting. Why shouldn't he start Sunday after all he's done?"

Unitas had no remorse. He knew that if he remained healthy and cured his arm, he'd be in the spotlight again. He felt it, and the way he talked about the next season made it seem like a reality—and not as a backup either. He wasn't anybody's number two man. He made that clear, too, and quite tersely: "I got confidence I can be number one and will be."

Namath also had confidence. He sneered at the odds that made his team 18-point underdogs. No championship team was ever that big of a predicted loser. Still, Unitas had a kind word for Namath. "He's an excellent thrower. Showboat? No, that's too strong. Make it flamboyant. That doesn't sound as bad."

The generous characterization was typical of Unitas. He was never known to badmouth anybody. He was a product of his upbringing by immigrant parents who taught him respect, and Unitas carried his early teachings all those years to the playing field. His whole life was playing football and coming home to his family, which now numbered five children. "I just love to play, really I do," he would often say. "I don't know of anything in the world

I enjoy more than playing football." And, to the fans, he was still their hero, one of the last athletes who was raised during the Great Depression. Those few Depression athletes came into the world of sports with a ferocious intensity. No one had more than Unitas. Someone was always rejecting him and nothing came easily. Then, with the supreme game of the NFL just a few days away, his arm cheated him out of more glory.

The Super Bowl game itself revolved around three quarterbacks: one who was about to experience more than he ever dreamed; one who was approaching the peak of a Cinderella year; and one with a crippled arm, who was standing not too deep in the wings. Only Unitas had been to a championship game before, and he knew that the flashy Namath wouldn't find it easy: "He's never faced anybody like he's going to face in our defense," said Unitas. "Our defensive football team has been spectacular all year. They shut out four teams and you just don't shut out National League teams. They've kept us in a lot of ball games. Our defense can stop a team cold, completely cold.

"From the films of games I've seen, the Jets haven't had much of a pass rush put on them. They haven't really been put under that much pressure. Our pass rush will be something I think Namath will remember a long time. Joe throws the ball extremely well and they do have good receivers. He's kept the Jets in the football games and they finally won a title. We'll just have to put a little pressure on Joe to make him throw the ball sooner than he wants."

The Orange Bowl

Sunday couldn't come soon enough for the players who had been waiting for two weeks, and when dawn did break, ominous low clouds moved swiftly in a northerly direction. There was still a chance for rain. It had rained heavily the night before, but now the sun was trying to struggle through the dark clouds. Johnny Unitas could only wonder if the sun would shine on him. Rain would favor the Colts. They had the heavy runners and a quarterback with two sound legs; Namath's tender right knee required heavy taping.

Just before noon, Namath answered a knock on the door of his suite at the Gault Ocean Mile Hotel. A bellhop entered the room holding a basket of flowers. He placed it on the table and smiled as he left the room with a five spot in his hand. Namath had received flowers before from friends and admirers. This was something different. They were a dozen red roses sent by Lou Michaels. Namath took that memory with him when he walked into the Orange Bowl for the 3:00 kickoff.

The sun would break through the clouds every now and then, and the threat of rain diminished. The Orange Bowl was colorfully manicured. The white chalk marks contrasted brilliantly against the green sod. In the middle of the field, against a blue background, was a silver replica of the Super Bowl trophy. The east end zone was sprayed a rich blue, with the words BALTIMORE COLTS and their helmet design emblazoned in white, along with the shield of the NFL. The west end zone was painted green, with the inscription NEW YORK JETS and their logo printed in white, together with the emblem of the AFL.

In less than an hour the field would be a battleground for crashing bodies. The players were completely unconcerned with the décor as they briskly went through their pregame warm-ups, the Jets at the east end of the field and the Colts at the west side. This was the first time the two champions had felt the ground of the Orange Bowl since they began preparations for their Super Bowl confrontation.

The Jets were designated as the visiting team. They were playing in an AFL stadium in a league city where only weeks before they had finished their regular-season play against the hometown Miami Dolphins. They were assigned the north side of the stadium, which was also the sideline used by the local team.

The Jets wore their road uniform of white trimmed with green, while the Colts were dressed in their traditional home jerseys of blue with white piping and white pants. After their allotted loosening-up drills, both squads returned to their dressing rooms for final instructions.

Some 10 minutes before the kickoff, the squads returned to the pit of battle. The Jets entered first, cheered in their underdog role by wildly

Two landmarks in the Unitases' Pittsburgh neighborhood: St. Justin's church (above) and high school (below), where Unitas' football career was launched.

Despite a successful two-year high school career at quarterback, the slender Unitas received little attention from college recruiters outside of Louisville's Frank Gitschier (top photo, at right), shown here inducting Unitas into the Cardinals' Hall of Fame. The school also erected a statue (right) bearing the likeness of their most famous gridiron star.

Unitas was drafted by the Pittsburgh Steelers but was given no playing time in training camp and was then unceremoniously cut from the team.

Unitas eventually signed a $7,000 contract with the Baltimore Colts prior to the 1956 season and was quickly thrown into the starting role due to another player's injury.

Unitas' first two plays as quarterback of the Colts were an interception and a fumbled snap, respectively. PHOTO COURTESY OF THE INDIANAPOLIS COLTS.

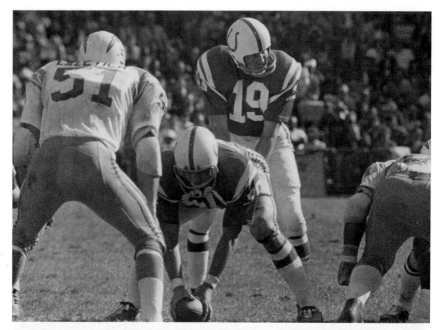

Fortunately his growing pains didn't last long, and he finished his first season with a rookie-record 55.6 completion percentage and—more important—established himself as a true on-field leader.   PHOTOS COURTESY OF THE INDIANAPOLIS COLTS.

In his third season, Unitas led the Colts to the 1958 championship game. Above, Unitas (center) is shown game-planning with coach Weeb Ewbank (left) and backup quarterback George Shaw three days before the contest, which has since come to be known as "the greatest game ever played." Below, Unitas hands off to Alan Ameche for the overtime score that beat the New York Giants at Yankee Stadium.

If he wasn't one already, the 1958 title game helped make Unitas a full-blown superstar. Here he shows off his new Corvette courtesy of *Sport* magazine in recognition of his outstanding performance. PHOTO COURTESY OF AP/WIDE WORLD PHOTOS.

screaming supporters who flashed hand-painted signs and waved New York Jets banners. One obvious banner read: BROADWAY JOE WE LOVE YOU. Namath had brought to the underdog role more color and glamour than ever in the history of sports. This was the hour in which all his taunts and candid remarks of the previous week might be stuffed down his throat. That is what the odds-makers figured, and a lot of people went along with them. When was the last time any bookmaker gave anything away?

The Colts trotted onto the field. The rabid Baltimore fans made their feelings known. This was a team that was considered one of the finest defensive machines of all time. Baltimore had won 15 of the 16 games it took to get them to the Super Bowl. In four of those games, Baltimore blanked the opposition. In two others, they prevented the opposition from scoring a touchdown, yielding only field goals. In five other games they surrendered only one touchdown. It was an awesome defensive combination that challenged its foe head-to-head. The defense wanted its rivals to come at them. The Colts thought nothing of putting a safety at the line of scrimmage, seemingly leaving themselves vulnerable to the pass. The Colts were known for their great ball pursuit. They would snuff out the ball carrier and bring him down to earth with a thud. They hit quickly and hard, from all sides. Sometimes the ends would crash; tackles would charge after a split second delay; linebackers were noted for the blitz; and even the safeties would penetrate to spill the quarterback behind the line of scrimmage.

The Colts were considered almost impregnable on defense. They possessed a blend of age and youth and a savage ferocity for attacking a ball carrier. Their indefatigable pressure again and again had forced their opponents into numerous errors throughout the season. Regularly they had provided their quarterback with excellent field position. Their game was to force the opposition into a mistake and go for a quick score. If a touchdown was unattainable, then the Colts had an excellent scoring weapon in field-goal kicker Lou Michaels, a powerful left-footed performer. Ordell Braase, a 6'4", 245-pound end and a 12-year veteran, was the oldest member of the defensive unit at 36. Next to him was tackle Fred Miller, a 6'3", 250-pounder who, at 28, was in his sixth season. Alongside of Miller was the other tackle, Billy Ray Smith, a 6'4", 250-pound All-Pro. Another veteran performer, the 33-year-old Smith was in his 10th campaign. The remaining end was big Charles "Bubba" Smith, a 6'7", 295-pound behemoth. Only in his second season, Smith had come into his own and made a big difference on Baltimore's defensive line. Any one of them could look down on Namath and come away laughing.

Baltimore's linebacking was greatly respected. Right linebacker Don Shinnick, 6', 228, was the leader. At the age of 33, he was in his 12th campaign. Dennis Gaubatz, at 28, was a 6'2", 232-pound, sixth-year veteran who operated in the middle, while All-Pro Mike Curtis, at 24, was a 6'2", 232-pound, fourth-year player who covered the left side.

The defensive secondary, which had intercepted 29 enemy passes, was supposed to provide additional trouble for Namath. If the front four or the linebackers didn't get to the Jets' quarterback, then the secondary would. The youngest member of the quartet was Rich Volk, a safety who was an All-Pro despite the fact that he was playing only his second season of professional football. The other safety was Jerry Logan, who was a six-year campaigner.

The cornerbacks, with the unenviable mission of guarding the swift pass receivers, the flanker, or the split end, were both hard-nosed veterans. One was Lenny Lyles, in his 11th season, and the other was Bobby Boyd, an All-Pro in past seasons, who was playing his ninth year in the NFL. They knew their assignments. In the manner in which the Jets attacked, Lyles would cover George Sauer, an All-Pro split end, while Boyd would cover Don Maynard, the deep receiver, who was also an All-Pro. These were two of the great individual battles that could determine the final outcome.

This very same defensive brigade had dealt the Cleveland Browns an ignominious 34–0 beating in the NFL championship game just two weeks before. So convincing was the Baltimore defense that they limited Leroy Kelly, pro football's leading runner, to a mere 28 yards. So cohesive was the Colts' defensive unit that they permitted the Browns to cross midfield only twice, with the deepest penetration being only the 35-yard line. It prompted Cleveland head coach Blanton Collier to remark after the game that the Colts' defensive team might be one of the best of all time. So complete was the Baltimore triumph that head coach Don Shula handed out a game ball to every member of his 40-man squad. It was an added piece of psychological warfare that Shula had employed, with the Super Bowl and Joe Namath waiting just two weeks away.

Going against Namath, the Colts were going against pro football's most explosive quarterback. He had it all: the arm, the release, the knowledge, and the guts. Yet the 18-point spread called by the betting parlors was the largest spread of any of the three Super Bowl encounters. That's how much respect the bookies had for the Baltimore defense. Everyone knows the name of the game is quarterback first and defense next, and despite the fact that the Colts were going against the best, they were the odds-on choice to make it a runaway.

Morrall was something of a Cinderella. He had been discarded by four other professional teams and, for years, was considered nothing more than a back-up man. Mechanically he was sound. But in leading a team to a championship, he never was considered able. The only time in his uneventful career that he had held a job was with the New York Giants three years before. That was the only time in his long career that he actually felt he belonged. He had sparked the beleaguered Giants for two years and brought them some measure of respectability. It was all short-lived. Morrall fractured his wrist, and the Giants quickly acquired Fran Tarkenton from the Minnesota Vikings. It was obvious that Morrall would never be a starter again, a role he had fought for throughout his frustrating career.

Finally, with his rag-arm reputation, he was traded to Baltimore in August 1968, and suddenly in one season, it was all rags to riches. It was ironic: an injury deprived him of his regular job with his Giants, and an injury to the great Johnny Unitas had opened up a job for him in Baltimore. He made the most of it, and despite the fact that Unitas was still a key figure, it was Morrall who earned the respect of his teammates and the right to start in the Super Bowl.

Johnny Unitas, a living legend in Baltimore, would be on the sidelines, while a quarterback from the trenches would lead the Colts. It didn't seem right. Baltimore's running attack wasn't overpowering. Not having a breakaway runner who could quickly change the course of a game, they chiefly depended on Tom Matte, a heavy-footed halfback. Matte's greatest distinction in eight professional seasons was the time three years earlier when he courageously played quarterback after injuries had struck down Unitas and his back-up, Gary Cuozzo. Matte earned plaudits for almost leading the Colts to a playoff victory over the vaunted Green Bay Packers in a sudden-death skirmish in Green Bay. Alex Karras, the outspoken Detroit Lions tackle, termed Matte "a garbage-can runner." Nonetheless, Matte was an effective runner. He got the hard yards inside and could also run well, although without any great speed, to the outside.

At fullback, Shula alternated Jerry Hill, a seven-year veteran, and Terry Cole, a fine rookie. Hill was regarded as the better blocker of the two, and in the Baltimore way of doing things, a blocking fullback is an important asset. Both could get the tough yards inside, while Cole could move better outside. Both were methodical workhorses, neither of whom could electrify a crowd. They hit away, for three or four yards at a clip, and from this attack approach the Colts could employ the pass to better advantage.

Baltimore's biggest threat was a Morrall pass to one of three excellent receivers, flanker Willie Richardson, split end Jimmy Orr, or tight end John Mackey. Richardson had the speed to burn a defender. He was expected to work on left cornerback Johnny Sample and beat him to the inside. This was the pattern employed by Oakland's Fred Biletnikoff in the AFL championship game against the Jets. Orr, a cagey 11-year veteran, was expected to teach the Jets' young Randy Beverly, only a second-year pro, a few lessons in the art of catching a football. Mackey, the Colts' leading pass receiver, was one of the game's most dangerous receivers. In the open field, Mackey moved with speed and power. He would operate against safety Jim Hudson, a give-nothing performer, who was one of the hardest tacklers in either league.

The Jets' game plan was not expected to deviate from the successful plans they had employed during the final 10 weeks of the campaign. They were primed to set up the running game and then revert to the passing game. Namath had two fine runners to work with: fullback Matt Snell and halfback Emerson Boozer. Snell, an excellent blocker, was most effective on a draw play. He was also a threat as a secondary receiver coming out of the backfield. Boozer, although bothered by a troublesome knee most of the campaign, was the club's outside running threat. He, too, could be employed as a secondary receiver on a flare-pass pattern.

Namath's primary receivers were three of the finest in the AFL. George Sauer, who led the league's receivers in total number of receptions in 1967, finished second to San Diego's Lance Alworth by just two catches. Don Maynard, the deep receiver, finished fifth in receptions but second in total yardage, despite being handicapped by a painful hamstring pull. Maynard and Namath had perfected their timing on long passes down the sidelines. Pete Lammons, the tight end, had good hands. Namath looked to him in the middle when Sauer and Maynard were covered. At times Namath would keep the defense off balance by throwing a quick one, down and in, to Lammons.

The New York defense, although not as distinguished as Baltimore's, nevertheless established itself during the year's campaign. There weren't many teams that generated a successful running attack against them. They took pride in allowing the fewest yards rushing when the season was over. They did it on the final day of the season, when they contained Miami's ground game. They weren't expected to encounter any great difficulty with Baltimore's minimal ground attack. Only the Jets' secondary remained a bit suspect, and if Morrall got time to throw, he could pierce the defense.

Namath had to have generous protection. His offensive wall had provided him ample time, except for a couple of contests, all season long. This game would be their biggest challenge, against the most-talked-about defense in pro football. They also were aware that if anything happened to Namath, they would quickly lose any chances of earning the lion's share of $15,000 each for their day's work. It was as simple as that, and no game plan could spell out how to protect the passer. It had to be done by individual effort in the predetermined match-ups. Could Dave Herman hold back Bubba Smith? Could Randy Rasmussen handle Billy Ray Smith? How successful could Bob Talamini be against Fred Miller? And could Winston Hill hold his own against Ordell Braase, while center John Schmitt formed the point on the protective pocket? A game is won in the trenches, with one-on-one, hand-to-hand combat. The offensive linemen are the unsung heroes in the violent world of professional football.

At five minutes until kickoff, the officials signaled both benches for the respective captains to meet at midfield. Unitas, Lenny Lyles, and Preston Pearson trotted onto the field first to represent the Colts. Unitas, protecting his right arm, carried his helmet in his left hand, still displaying the boyish crew cut he had maintained for 13 years. Namath and Sample completed the meeting a few seconds later. It was somewhat of a memorable occasion for the two Jets. Namath, as a youngster in high school in Beaver Falls, had always admired Unitas. And Unitas, like Namath, was from a small town outside of Pittsburgh. For Sample, it was the sweet taste of revenge. It was the closest he had gotten to a Colts uniform since Baltimore released him as a player eight years ago. He was branded as a troublemaker, and Sample could never quite forgive them for the rap. Like Namath, he too was an open target for Baltimore. He was the one defensive player the Colts figured to beat.

Although the toss of the coin was held an hour before, referee Tom Bell had to go through with the ritual for the benefit of the 75,377 fans in the stadium and the countless millions watching on television. He indicated that the Jets had won the toss and had elected to receive, while Baltimore chose to defend the west goal, which was at the closed end of the stadium. The temperature was recorded at 73, with the wind blowing north at 18 miles per hour.

Because of the number of highly distinguished guests, the game was delayed for almost 10 minutes. Sitting in the north stands were President-elect Richard Nixon; Vice President–elect Spiro Agnew; Governor Claude Kirk of Florida; Governor James Rhodes of Ohio; astronauts Frank Borman, Bill Anders, and Jim Lovell; and comedian Bob Hope. Another familiar comedian, Jackie Gleason, sat on the Jets' side in the south stands as a guest of the Dolphins' managing partner, Joe Robbie.

The moment was at hand. Lou Michaels signaled to the referee that he was ready, and he approached the ball in his customary manner. Boom! He got off a good kick that Earl Christy caught on the fly two yards deep in the end zone. He began his ascent upfield looking for a convoy of blockers. He managed to extract a little running room before he was tackled by Alex Hawkins at the 23. That was the first sound of contact, the one that's supposed to ease all the tensions of the players. The fearsome Baltimore defensive legion trotted onto the field, as did the New York offensive unit. It was time for the first test.

The Jets broke the huddle fast. Namath barked the signals. Baltimore's defense focused on Namath. The Jets quarterback took the snap, turned, and cleanly handed the ball to Matt Snell, who picked up three yards on the right side of Baltimore's defense. Everyone made contact, which is why games are often opened with a running play.

New York again came out of the huddle quickly. Namath again gave the ball to Snell, who this time tested Baltimore's left side. The crowd's roar indicated that Snell had found some running room. He maneuvered nine yards for a first down before being stopped by Rich Volk on the 35.

Now it was Emerson Boozer's turn. The lithe halfback tried to go outside but was repelled by Shinnick for a four-yard loss. This was Baltimore's defense in a familiar presence.

On the fourth play of the game, Namath elected to pass. He hit Snell coming out of the backfield for a nine-yard gain. Satisfied with the result, Namath slapped the part of the shoulder pad that protected him around his chest. On third down and five, Namath designated a draw, with Snell carrying. It was the same thing Fred Miller figured, and he dropped the New York fullback for a two-yard loss.

A Curley Johnson punt gave the Colts their first opportunity on offense from their own 27-yard line. Morrall also broke the huddle quickly. He received the snap from center Bill Curry, quickly dropped back to pass, and hit Mackey for a first down on the 46. On the next play, Morrall sent Tom Matte around the right side for a 10-yard advance to the New York 44. Two plays, two first downs. The people who laid the 18-point spread were happy.

Now it was Jerry Hill's turn. He made his way around the left side for seven yards before Jim Hudson came up to drop him. Matte then went inside for only one yard. Hill again carried, this time inside the right tackle for five yards and got a first down on the Jets' 31. In five plays the Colts had produced three first downs. They appeared to be going in for a score.

Hill tried to go outside but was upended by the Jets' Gerry Philbin three yards behind the line of scrimmage. In a passing situation, Morrall tried to hit Jimmy Orr but threw the ball short. However, on the third down, Morrall went back again to throw and connected with Tom Mitchell for another first down on the New York 19.

Morrall, in eight plays, had accounted for four first downs and brought the Colts to within a shadow of the goalposts. He decided to go for the quick kill while he had the Jets on the run. On first down he looked for Willie Richardson and hit him in the hands, only to see him drop the ball.

Burning with the desire to produce a fast touchdown, Morrall faded back to throw for the fifth consecutive time. Finding no one open, he was forced to run and made it back to the line of scrimmage, where the Jets' middle linebacker Al Atkinson met him head on. The situation now dictated a field goal attempt from the 27-yard line, almost automatic for the pros. However, Michaels' kick sailed wide to the left, and the Colts, who seemingly were headed for seven points but were willing to settle for three, suddenly had nothing.

Namath went to work on his own 20 and went for a pass play before the Colts defense could assert itself. He hit Snell in the open, only to have his fullback drop the ball when he heard the footsteps of the fast-closing Dennis Gaubatz. On a quick move, Namath deposited the ball in Pete Lammons' hands for a short two-yard gain. He then requested a half-back pass to Bill Mathis, who made his way for 13 yards before being stopped by Gaubatz. Then, in rapid succession, Namath called for three pass plays. On the first, he sent Maynard deep downfield, and although the swift flanker had Jerry Logan beaten by several steps, Namath over-shot him, as the crowd moaned. Next he hit Sauer for a six-yard gain, but when he went to his split end again on the same pattern, he over-threw him.

Again the Jets were forced to punt. Timmy Brown gave the Colts excel-lent field position by returning Johnson's punt 21 yards to the Baltimore 42. Morrall seized the opportunity to move quickly and threw a pass into the arms of Mackey, who dropped the ball in the open. After Hill made three yards, Morrall positioned Richardson on Sample. It was their first confrontation of the game, and Sample emerged the victor by breaking up the play.

David Lee's first punt of the afternoon for Baltimore was a beauty. The ball rolled dead on the Jets' 4-yard line, where Baltimore's vaunted defense moved in to take advantage of the situation. Snell almost got the Jets out of the hole by carrying for nine yards on two trips. With a third-and-1, Namath called a smart play. Detecting the linebackers in close to stop the impending one-yard run for a first down, he sent Sauer break-ing into the middle. He connected, for an apparent first down, only to have Sauer fumble when he was brought to earth by Lyles. Ron Porter, a linebacker, recovered the loose ball on the Jets' 12-yard line, and the Colts got their first break of the game.

Matte took a pitchout and stepped his way around the left side for a seven-yard gain as the second period opened. With a third-and-4 on the New York 6, Morrall slipped back to pass. He located Mitchell in the end zone and threw on target. However, the ball bounced high off Mitchell's left shoulder. It ricocheted so high that Randy Beverly caught it in the manner of a baseball player settling under a high fly ball. Once again

Baltimore blew a scoring opportunity, and the Jets' defensive team came off the gridiron elated and fired up. Twice Baltimore had penetrated dangerously deep into New York territory, and both times they had come away empty-handed.

The Jets put the ball in play on their own 20. Namath gave Snell the ball three consecutive times, and he moved for one, seven, and finally six yards and a first down. Checking off at the line, Namath signaled for a draw play, which meant that Snell again was designated as the ball carrier. He responded with a 12-yard advance and another first down on the New York 46. The Jets, who managed only two first downs the entire first period, quickly got two the last two times they put the ball in motion.

Then Namath went to his aerial game for four consecutive passes. Don Shinnick broke up the first one, which had been intended for Sauer. Namath hit Bill Mathis for six yards and then reverted to Sauer for fourteen more and a first down on the Baltimore 34. Again he dispatched Sauer on the left side, and he rifled one that accounted for 11 yards and still another first down on the 23.

The fans in the north stands were on their feet. They sensed a Jets touchdown or at least a Jim Turner field goal. Boozer got only two yards as Namath switched to the run. Returning to the pass, Namath zeroed in on Snell, who found an opening in the middle, for 12 yards and another first down on the 9. Namath asked Snell to carry, and the hard-working fullback bullied his way over the right side for five yards. One more time Namath called Snell's number in the huddle, and this time the gritty fullback went all the way in from the left side.

The Jets were on the board.

Following the kickoff, Morrall tried to mount an attack from Baltimore's 28. On a first-down pass, he threw over the head of Richardson. However, on the next down, he found a connection to Matte with a 30-yard pass that provided the Colts with a first down on the Jets' 42. Hill managed to bang his way for four yards up the middle. Morrall tried to send Matte wide around the right side, but Verlon Biggs turned him in for no gain. Then Morrall tried to complete a pass to John Mackey, but it was foiled by Sample. On the fourth down, Michaels, who had missed a 27-yarder in the first quarter, tried to boot a field goal from the 46. Like the previous one, it was wide, and a third Baltimore scoring chance was wasted.

On the next series of downs, Namath directed the Jets from their 20 to a field-goal situation from the Baltimore 41. However, Jim Turner's try was wide, and the Colts took over on their own 20, with 4:13 remaining to play in the first half. Sample yielded a short run of six yards to Richardson. Matte then electrified the huge throng by breaking away behind some beautiful blocking around right end for 58 yards before being cut down by Billy Baird on the New York 16. After Hill made only a yard, Morrall again isolated Richardson on Sample. Richardson broke down the sidelines and then cut inside on a spot pattern that was supposed to embarrass Sample. However, the wily veteran defender reached in front of Richardson and intercepted the ball with a picture-book catch.

Sample had it figured all the way: "I moved a step to the outside, but I played him to the inside," he explained later. That one play made up for his poor performance two weeks before against Oakland, which had almost cost the Jets the championship.

Johnson had to punt from his end zone to get New York out of danger. There were only 43 seconds remaining when Baltimore took over on the Jets' 42. Morrall collected only one yard on a safety-valve pass to Hill. Then, in a key play that brought the crowd to its feet, Morrall handed the ball to Matte, who appeared as if he was going to run around his own right end. However, Matte suddenly stopped and threw the ball back to Morrall on the left side with nobody near him. Morrall had four receivers downfield. Orr was wide open, frantically waving his arms in the end zone. Morrall never saw him.

The confused Jets secondary was trying to collect itself when Morrall threw the ball in the direction of Hill. From out of nowhere, Hudson picked the ball off on the 12 and fell down on the 21, clutching the ball as the half ended.

"I don't know what happened," confessed Hudson. "I fell down, and when I got up, I picked out the first blue shirt I saw. Man, I'm winded."

The first half ended in bitter frustration for the Colts. On four occasions they saw scoring opportunities evaporate. No one would mention the Jets' defense in the same breath with Baltimore, and yet the Colts were held scoreless. New York had gotten on the scoreboard first. Their defense had risen to the occasion. Holding the Colts without a point was a bonus. The offense revealed that they could move the ball and the defense showed they were equal to the challenge.

The Colts were in trouble. Morrall did not have a good first half. His passes were erratic, some overthrown, others off the mark, and he had difficulty finding receivers who were open. In all, he was 5 of 15 for only 71 yards and embarrassed by 3 interceptions. Shula had a decision to make at halftime. Does he stay with Morrall or turn to Unitas? When the Colts returned to the field, Morrall was still the quarterback. Disappointed, Unitas once more took his place on the sideline. The sun was shining brightly, but it had not found Unitas.

The teams lined up for the second-half kickoff. Baltimore received, and they knew they had to move quickly. On the first play of the half, Matte fumbled, and Ralph Baker recovered the ball for New York on the Colts' 33. Namath worked his way down to the 11 with two first downs. However, the Colts defense met the challenge. They spilled Boozer for a five-yard loss. And then, for the first time, Baltimore got to Namath. Bubba Smith charged like a bull and dropped Namath like a broken doll for a nine-yard loss. Namath's third-down pass fell incomplete, but Turner made good on a field goal for a 10–0 New York lead.

After the kickoff, the Colts bogged down. They failed to produce a first down, and a Baltimore punt presented the Jets with the ball on the New York 32. Once again Namath moved the club. He engineered three first downs, which brought the ball to the Colts' 24. Mathis could extract only a yard from the middle, and Namath stepped back to pass on second down. He tried to hit Maynard deep in the end zone, but Maynard caught the ball over the base line. Namath jammed his thumb and came off the field for a play. Vito "Babe" Parilli replaced him, and when he threw an incompletion, Turner booted a 30-yard field goal to push the Jets into a 13–0 lead.

There were only four minutes remaining in the quarter. Shula had seen enough. He called to the solitary figure on his right. He wanted Unitas. Unitas threw off the rain cape that rested loosely on his shoulders, talked for a few seconds with Shula, and dashed onto the field like a frisky colt in an open meadow. The loud cheer from the stands was inspiring. Unitas, who maintained that he was 75 percent healthy, was called upon to create another one of his miracles.

Namath watched as Unitas took over for the Colts. "Johnny's here," Namath told his teammates. "We better hang on to the ball." There was his boyhood idol, and they were going to meet on the field in the final half, or what was left of it. The anticipation of a pass instead resulted in a five-yard run by Matte. Unitas' pass to the halfback barely gained a half yard. On third down, he threw accurately to Orr, only to see the usually reliable receiver drop the ball. Once more the Colts were forced to punt, and the Jets were in possession on their 37-yard line with only 2:24 remaining in the period.

Time was increasingly becoming a factor, and when the third quarter was nearing its end, Namath had the Jets moving. Sensing the kill, he wanted to get some more points on the scoreboard. After Snell gained three yards, Namath tried to reach Sauer with a pass but threw the ball a little too high. Apparently he and Sauer detected something. Lyles was playing Sauer too deep, playing him loosely for fear the clever end might slip behind him. Namath came right back to his wide receiver the next two times, once for 11 yards and the next for 39, and suddenly the Jets were on Baltimore's 10-yard line. Snell picked his way for four yards to the 6 as the quarter came to a conclusion. It was obvious the Jets were ready for more points. Three running plays failed to get the touchdown, and the Jets had to settle for a Turner field goal nine yards away from the goalposts. Their lead was now 16–0, and Unitas had only 13:10 left to rally the Colts.

Unitas tried hard. He was out there with an arm shot full of medicine trying to produce a Garrison finish, as he had done many times in the past.

Putting the ball in play on his own 27, Unitas brought the Colts to the Jets' 25. He threw over Richardson's reach on the first down, and then turning to Orr, one of his favorite targets over the years, he threw a bit short, and the ball was intercepted by Beverly in the end zone. From the 20, Namath wisely stayed on the ground as he moved his club upfield, while at the same time running out the clock. Two first downs and a penalty brought the Jets to within field-goal range from the 42. This time, however, Turner couldn't deliver. Nevertheless, Namath used up almost five minutes on the drive, and when the Colts put the ball in action on their 20, only 6:34 showed on the clock as the shadows grew long and the Orange Bowl lights were turned on.

Baltimore had one last gasp. Unitas inspired them for an 80-yard march despite the fact that he completed only three of the ten passes he attempted. On the fourth down from the New York 1, Hill finally reached the end zone to give Baltimore its first touchdown with just 3:20 left to play.

The Colts were successful with an onside kick that Mitchell recovered on the New York 44. Unitas jumped into the breach, trying to effect a miracle. He connected on his first three passes, which carried the ball to the Jets' 19, where it was second-and-5 for an all-important first down. Unitas tried Richardson, and Sample once again broke up the play. Third-and-5. He looked for Orr and threw short. Now it was fourth-and-5, and it seemed likely that the Colts would go for the field goal from 26 yards away and then try another onside kick, the reasoning being that you take three points whenever you can get them. The Colts would still need a field goal, along with the necessary touchdown, if they expected to win. Shula decided to go for the touchdown, and the last hope rested on Unitas' erratic arm. He went to Orr again, but threw behind him, as the ball and Baltimore's hopes fell to the ground.

Namath succeeded in running down the clock. Baltimore finally gained possession of the football on their own 34, with just eight seconds left. For the records, Unitas tried two more passes and completed just one. But no one ever remembers that. The moment they remember is when the gun sounded to end the game. The crowds spilled onto the field, pouring out their joy and congratulations to any Jets players that ran by. An 18-point underdog completely outplayed the favorite.

The attendant at the Jets' dressing-room door was almost crushed under the force of hundreds of bodies. Finally some calm settled, and the attendant managed to pull open the door and let the jubilant players inside. One by one the players made their way through the pulling and tugging multitude. As soon as the players, coaches, and club official assembled, the team meditated in prayer for a moment. Then shouts of joy broke the silence. Sample jumped on top of a large table and announced that it was decided to award the game ball to the American Football League. It was a great honor.

Namath was ready to talk. He was calm, and whenever a particular question rankled him, he would snap back, "What are you, an NFL writer?" Some of the writers tried to goad him, but Joe wouldn't be trapped.

"A whole lot of people were wrong," Namath replied when asked about the game. "Eighteen-point underdog, gee whiz," he said, shaking his head. Then he continued talking while cutting the tape from his sore right knee. "Baltimore is a damn good football team. They didn't give me any mouth out there, and they didn't take any cheap shots. They're a good, hard-nosed club. Our team did everything well. We didn't have one offensive penalty. I felt I wasn't throwing good to my left, and I told Sauer so. I can't say enough about our defense. Ordinarily, 16 points isn't enough to win, so that should tell you something. Now, if you'll excuse me, fellows, I want to take a shower."

Baltimore's dressing room was ghostly solemn. The players dressed silently and quickly and were in no mood to talk. There was no reason to linger. The story was in the winner's locker room, where almost all of the entire horde of media assembled. Yet, there was a bit of twisted irony to it all, once the game had ended. In 1958, Unitas had established the NFL, and, 10 years later, Namath had done the same thing for the AFL. Two guys from Pittsburgh had created a piece of pro football history.

"How good was Namath?" a writer asked Unitas.

"Sixteen to seven," answered Unitas succinctly.

119

He wanted to play more, and if he had, maybe he would have given the Colts another championship. All he needed was a touchdown and a field goal. Some 30 years later, after he had retired as coach of the Miami Dolphins, Shula indicated as much.

"Maybe I should have put him in the game sooner," admitted pro football's winningest coach.

That said it all.

9

Still the Best

WHEN THE 1970 SEASON DAWNED, JOHNNY UNITAS WAS FACED with still another challenge: how much would the switch to the American Football Conference and its wide-open style of play affect the Colts as a team, and him in particular? In the AFC, defensive backs were schooled in the bump-and-run style of pass protection.

This time Unitas' arm appeared as strong as ever, and he demonstrated as much by throwing 327 times during the 1969 campaign. The Colts finished second that year with an 8–5–1 record. And if it weren't for a pair of three-point losses to San Francisco, Baltimore may well have won another Coastal Division championship.

The Colts' Coach Bolts

The second-place finish rankled owner Carroll Rosenbloom, who still had not forgiven Don Shula for the embarrassing loss in Super Bowl III. Their relationship was strained, which left Shula uncomfortable. Interested in talking with Shula about a coaching position, the Miami Dolphins approached Steve Rosenbloom, the owner's son, about opening up a dialogue with Shula. While his father was away on a business trip to Japan, the younger Rosenbloom gave the Dolphins his permission for them to talk to Shula. In a quick move, Shula bolted from the Colts' corral and signed a three-year contract with Miami. Not only were the Rosenblooms caught by surprise, but so were the players. The only balm that soothed the Colt's irate owner was Commissioner Pete Rozelle's decision to award Miami's number one draft pick to the Colts as compensation.

Unitas first learned about the Miami caper when he was there. A sportswriter telephoned Unitas and asked him if he was a candidate for the Baltimore coaching job. The question stunned Unitas.

"What are you talking about? We've got a coach," said Unitas, somewhat perplexed.

"You mean you had a coach," the writer informed him. "Shula resigned to go with Miami. Are you a candidate?"

Unitas gave him a quick, firm, "No."

Unitas' relationship with Shula had grown cool with every passing week of the 1969 season. The acridness had started when Unitas didn't get to play more in the Super Bowl. He had produced the Colts' only touchdown and was confident that he could have gotten more if Shula had not waited until the end of the third quarter to send him on the field to relieve a struggling Morrall.

A story had appeared in a New York newspaper at one point during the season that Unitas, feisty and proud, offered the ball to Shula and snapped, "Here, you want to be the quarterback?" Unitas refused to comment on it. He preferred that anything negative that happened around the team stayed in the clubhouse. Yet those close to the situation knew that Shula had taken much of the game away from Unitas—and nobody did that.

Unitas, the ultimate team player, remained tight-lipped to avoid an open rift with his coach. "We had a game plan," he would only say. "I followed that game plan. Let's let it go at that. There's nothing I want to add."

Don McCafferty, the Colts' new coach, was a total opposite from the intense Shula. Although he had been in the NFL for 12 years as an assistant coach, he was probably the least well-known among the league's head coaches. He was a quiet type who portrayed a fatherly image to his players. Most of them had known him as an assistant coach with the team for 10 years. They felt comfortable with him. "I'm the patient type," said McCafferty.

Making Adjustments

Unitas needed a patient coach. He was 37 now, and although his arm showed life in the 1969 season, he still had to exercise it to improve it even more. He did so three times a week during the spring under the watchful eye of Bill Neill, the head of physical therapy at Kernan Hospital. Neill had him lift weights to strengthen both his arm and his legs. Unitas also threw about one hundred balls per day to Neill, and when John Mackey and Willie Richardson came by, Unitas had two willing collaborators.

Unitas was philosophical at that juncture of his career, with a training regimen that was all new to him. "An athlete has to have good legs. When they begin to go, that's it," he said.

"This year we did what I'd call a maintenance-type training, different from last year," said Neill. "You wouldn't believe how weak he was in the right arm when we started working last year to build his strength. We have various tests to measure muscle and strength development. Now, of course, his arm is just as strong as ever, maybe a little stronger. We worked a lot on building up the upper extremities. John didn't run as much this year as he had in the past. He figured he could do that when he goes to camp. I know that he is pleased by his arm and has confidence in it."

It wasn't the first time Neill had worked with Unitas. He had done so in other years, but not as intensely. This year was more important, however, with age and an arm injury factored in. Neill also got Unitas to spend time with a punching bag as if he were a fighter training for a match. Neill made use of three different types of bags, and even had Unitas set up a speed bag in his garage at home. Punching the bag was a hand-to-eye coordinating exercise that boxers of all weights heavily rely on. "I'm a great believer in punching the bag and there aren't many boxers who can rat-a-tat-tat better than Unitas," said Neill. It was as if Unitas were a heavyweight fighter working on a comeback, only without the roadwork and sparring partners. In reality, Unitas was training for a comeback, except on the gridiron instead of inside a ring.

Neill also saw another side to Unitas. He was not just an athlete pushing his body to produce more in the few years he had left. There was a private side to the great quarterback that very few knew, and Unitas wanted it that way. In his private time, John always had a soft spot for children, and what Neill witnessed made him appreciate his patient that much more.

"For as long as he's been coming to Kernan, John always finds time to visit with the kids," said Neill. "You can't imagine how much it means to them. They know him and when he comes to see them, well, he's just great with the kids. With John, visiting the kids isn't just once in a while. It's part of his day."

And Unitas had a deep appreciation for Neill. On the final day of his training session, before he got ready to report to summer camp, he left Neill with a kind word: "Bill, I'll keep playing as long as you keep holding me together." Neill never forgot those words.

A Comeback and a Change

Unlike most athletes, Unitas enjoyed training camp. And unlike 1968, he didn't baby his arm in 1970. Instead, he threw with intensity just like in all the summer camps before his arm gave out. Unitas felt whole again. The only thing that was different was that he didn't get much of an opportunity to throw during practice to get his timing down, a part of the game that was most important to him. There were too many other quarterbacks around, and the coaches wanted to evaluate every one of them before letting any of them go just in case Unitas' arm failed him again. Berry wasn't around anymore, and Unitas asked any of the veteran receivers to stay after practice and get in some extra work like the old days.

"Raymond and I used to do that a lot," remembered Unitas fondly. "Raymond was a fanatic for work. He was always trying to improve, and we used to work on all kinds of situations, like the sideline pass that Raymond was so good at catching and keeping his feet in bounds."

Those were the times Unitas missed most. But times were changing. It was a different day and the Colts were playing in a different conference in 1970. After being one of the glamour teams of the NFL during the Unitas years, the Colts and two others, the Cleveland Browns and the Pittsburgh Steelers, were moved to the American Conference. The addition provided great balance and strength to an already strong conference.

The switch didn't make a difference to Unitas. "It's the same game, right?" he asked. "If they want to move some teams around, there's nothing I can say about it. I'm paid to play and I'll play in any league where they want to pay me. The new arrangement will be more interesting for the fans. It'll give them a chance to see some teams and players they haven't looked at before. But for me, it's all the same football."

Unitas didn't do anything different to prepare for his new challenge. What he concentrated on most was reviewing films on some of the teams he would face. He wanted to familiarize himself with the different personnel and pick up patterns the teams had, the way they handled given situations at given times on the field. Watching films told him all that.

"From what I've seen of most of these American Conference teams, they play it a little differently on defense than some of the older teams in the NFL do," said Unitas. "For example, they have their defensive backs playing a lot more bump-and-run, where they hit the receiver as soon as he comes off the line to try and slow him up. They like to play the receiver a little tighter. A lot of those defensive backs are quick and fast, real hay burners.

"You know, I always thought the way to play Berry was bump-and-run. Not many of the teams did that against Raymond. I think they'd have done better to come up tight on him because Raymond didn't have good speed. Of course, I never mentioned it to any of them. Besides, Raymond would have found a way to get open."

Unitas was more than anxious for the 1970 season to begin. He felt as good as he ever had, and he wanted to eliminate people's doubts. He always had his pride to prove himself, and now he had an arm that was healthy and strong. He even surprised everyone early in the summer when he appeared at the rookies' one-day session—perhaps looking for another Raymond Berry. He dressed with the first-year players and went on the field and threw as much as anyone that day. He simply loved to play. And he was feeling happy after he was voted the Pro Football Athlete of the Decade by the Associated Press. For someone who had gained 20 miles in the air with his passes after starting his career as a $6-per-game quarterback, Unitas anticipated making his mark during the 1970s.

Unitas joked about his years in football—and his age: "I enjoy camp and had the same room in the dorm for 13 years," he said. "Then last year they moved me from the third floor to the second. Guess they figured I was getting too old to walk up the steps."

Unitas didn't look his age when the preseason action got underway. Baltimore defeated Oakland in its opening game, then made Kansas City its second victim, and Unitas didn't have a modicum of pain. It was the Colts' 10th consecutive victory during the hectic summer (when 85 player squads tried to make the roster), and it was the 27th of 29 exhibitions, which was an impressive showing. Unitas only played the first quarter and one sequence into the second in the 17–3 win over the Chiefs. He tried 12 passes and completed half of them for 94 yards. Although he didn't have a touchdown pass, he also didn't have an interception, and took the Colts on a 63-yard drive to produce a field goal. Unitas' work left an impression on the Kansas City coach, Hank Stram. "John Unitas is a great artist, there's no question about that," said Stram. "To me, he looks as good as ever."

Unitas was ready to open the regular season against San Diego. And he did so without a contract. He wasn't the least bit perturbed by it either. "I went an entire season without signing," he said. But this was different. At his age, a serious injury—any injury for that matter—would diminish his value.

He incurred an injury after leading the Colts to a 16–14 win over the Chargers. Unitas limped off the field with a swollen knee. He had been under pressure almost the entire game because of a poor performance by his offensive line. Countless times Unitas was driven into the ground after getting off a pass, and he wasn't throwing deep. He would have had to hold the ball a split second longer.

Somehow, Unitas returned to practice that week with a bandaged knee to prepare for a Monday night game against Kansas City in Baltimore. But this time against the Chiefs he struggled pitifully. Before the end of the second quarter, Morrall relieved him. The score was 24–0 at that point, and the Chiefs continued on to a 44–24 victory.

For the third game of the season, against the Boston Patriots, Morrall was named the starter. "Unitas isn't physically ready and the only solution is to get him healthy again," said a concerned McCafferty with a new revelation: "He's been bothered by a back problem which restricted his follow-through on passes."

The pride and the intestinal fortitude that ex-teammate Bobby Boyd ascribed to Unitas surfaced during the Boston game. Hobbled by his knee and a sore back, Unitas came off the bench in the fourth period and partnered a 55-yard scoring pass with the speedy Roy Jefferson. There were less than three minutes left when he did it, and the touchdown insured a 14–6 win. The pass, a soft one to Jefferson across the line of scrimmage, caught the Patriots by surprise, as the speedy wide receiver ran virtually untouched for the defining touchdown.

After the game, Unitas caught hell from McCafferty. "I gave him a good chewing out," said McCafferty. It was something that had never happened before to Unitas. "I told him to run three plays and then punt. It could have cost us the game. I didn't want to take any chances leading 7–6." Unitas' reaction was clear and poignant: "That's not the first time I've called a play nor will it be the last time."

The quarterback's precarious pass was a headline in *The New York Times*. Unitas just wanted to show that he could still make the big play and silence the rumors about what his arm could do. McCafferty, a mild-mannered individual, also had something to prove. Even though he was easy-going by nature, he needed to demonstrate that although he was in only his first year as a head coach, he was the boss. Nothing more was made about it, and if there was any trouble causing a rift between McCafferty and

Unitas, it wasn't evident after that one outburst. Besides, the Colts had won two of their first three games, and the Kansas City debacle was behind them. Winning cures egos.

Whatever It Takes

Unitas also had to cure his thinking. His once strong right arm, which could propel a football as far as 70 yards, was now deflated by about 15 yards. He also had to adjust his approach because of the speed of his two wideouts, Willie Richardson and Roy Jefferson. He had to deliver the ball quickly to them, faster than at any time in his career. The precise patterns with Berry were a thing of the past. Unitas stood back in the pocket back then and knew the exact moment to throw his pass a split second before Berry broke. It was an art form. And the crowds loved it. But now pro football's passing theory was customized for speedy receivers.

A consummate pro, Unitas made adjustments, and the Colts kept winning. They were 5–1, and he was eagerly looking forward to his next start against Miami, which was the Colts' biggest challenger to the Eastern Conference title. Miami meant Shula, who was bringing the Dolphins to Baltimore for the first time since he fled the Colts after the 1969 season. Colts fans felt betrayed by the abandonment and were aroused enough to yell their disapproval at their former coach that Sunday.

Unitas let it be known that it wasn't the first game in which he had gone against Shula: "I played against him when he was a defensive back at Washington and he was very good," said Unitas.

According to the statistics released weekly by the league, Unitas, alarmingly, wasn't very good. He ranked 14th among the 15 quarterbacks who were on the list, and, glaringly, his pass-completion percentage was under .500. Unitas did not care much for statistics. He preferred wins over perfect afternoons. Winning always came first, and he still had a little magic left in him. During the preceding three weeks, Unitas pulled out two victories in the last minute or two. That was the Unitas everyone knew and his way of shunning the statistics.

He had to keep his arm supple and did so with frequent massages and dips in the whirlpool, along with three 15-minute sessions each week with the weights. "Just enough to keep the strength," he explained.

Still in the Game

One day after practice the week of the Miami game, Unitas sat in front of his locker and talked about retiring. His age and his physical ailments suggested it, although it was a subject he didn't like to address. His outlook was quite a bit different than it had been two years prior: "I once said I'd like to play until I'm 40," said Unitas. "That's a nice age to retire. But it is something you have to look at week to week, game to game, day to day. I could quit next year. I could quit next week. The arm feels good. The legs feel good. That's what counts. When I start feeling bad and can't get the ball where it is supposed to be, I'll quit."

The 35–0 rout of Miami didn't make him want to quit and was quite satisfying to Unitas and the Baltimore faithful who booed Shula. It was the Colts' fifth straight win, and their chances for the Eastern Division crown were brightened considerably.

With the offense operating effectively, the defense took on a personality of its own with Charles "Bubba" Smith and Billy Ray Smith up front, Mike Curtis and Ted Hendricks behind them, and Jerry Logan and Rick Volk in the secondary. The colorful Hendricks, who was basketball tall at 6'7" and was appropriately nicknamed "the Stork," explained the surge of the defense: "Let's face it," he said, "the defense is spoiled. The offense has been the team here for so long that we expect the offense to score while we coast the rest of the game."

Baltimore's next game was a Monday night build-up of Johnny Unitas against Bart Starr in Green Bay. Unfortunately, much to ABC's chagrin, the showdown never materialized. Starr, who had announced his retirement at the end of the previous season and could commiserate with Unitas about that, had a sore shoulder and couldn't play. And while Starr had made his retirement known, it was far from Unitas' mind. Every now and then when he was asked, Unitas repeated that he could play until he was 40. Two weeks after the Packers game, he put it in writing when he signed a three-year contract that took him to his 40th birthday.

Unitas said that the game against the Packers was on the worst field he ever played on. It was a beast of a night, cold and windy, and it rained throughout most of the game, which accounted for the low-score Baltimore win, 13–10. Unitas secured the win in the final quarter. With 10 minutes remaining, Unitas faced a difficult challenge with a third-and-8 on his own 5-yard line. If the Colts couldn't produce a vital first down, Baltimore would be forced into a precarious punting situation from its end zone, which would undoubtedly give Green Bay valuable possession on the Colts' side of the field.

On the second-down play, Unitas sent flanker Ray Perkins as a decoy up the right sideline, but instead turned and handed the ball to Norm Bulaich for a run up the middle. Unitas was like a chess master. In the third-down huddle, he told Perkins, "Do it again and on your third step, start looking for the ball. I'm just going to put it up there for you." Unitas did so perfectly. The floater dropped softly over Perkins' shoulder and he reached the 26-yard line for the needed first down before he was stopped.

McCafferty knew the importance of the play. "John calls them all," he said. "I sent one in and it was a flop, so I left the rest up to him."

Unitas was pleased with his new and final contract as a Colt. He negotiated it by himself, which made it more rewarding. Although the dollar amount wasn't made known, it was probably more than his last three-year contract that paid him $100,000 per year. He never had salary problems with Rosenbloom, who considered Unitas a treasure. In fact, Rosenbloom even tacked on 10 more years to the contact to guarantee Unitas employment in an undecided capacity, one of those to-be-agreed-upon-later things, but definitely not as a coach. Unitas expressed to Rosenbloom that he would prefer to work in the front office and was willing to learn the business from the ground up. "The new contract called for three more years of playing, or if for some reason I get hurt or don't want to play, then I'm free to retire," said Unitas gleefully.

In the closing weeks of the season, Unitas brought the Colts closer to a title. Before facing Buffalo and the New York Jets, the division's two tail-enders in the final two weeks, the Colts had to take on an Eagles team that was 2–1–1 in its last four games after opening the season with seven straight losses. The Eagles were a team that liked to blitz, and with an aging Unitas, they were expected to do it more. Philly's twin-terror blitzers were Gary Pettigrew and Tim Rossovich, who came after quarterbacks from both ends of the line. The complete blitz package would include a defensive back, someone like safety Ron Medved.

With a freezing gale at his back, the doughty Unitas conquered the elements with a vintage opening drive. In 11 plays, he maneuvered the Colts on a 71-yard journey for a touchdown, the keynote to Baltimore's 29–10 victory. After an incomplete pass to Eddie Hinton, Unitas threw only three more passes, but was perfection in converting all third-down throws into first downs: third-and-8 on his 31 resulted in an 11-yard strike to Jefferson, third-and-5 on his 47 turned into a quick eight-yard strike to Mackey, and third-and-10 on the Eagles' 14-yard line, with a smart, swift three-yarder to Mackey, resulted in the touchdown.

"People may say he's old and all that shit, but he can still beat you," said Eagle linebacker Ron Porter. "Some days, there's no one who could beat you better."

The Colts closed out their season with two division rival victories and won the East with an 11–2–1 record—a game and a half better than Miami. Unfortunately, in the final game against the Jets, Unitas, in obvious distress with a sore back, had to leave in the first quarter. It was discouraging because the playoffs began the following week. The one consolation was Morrall: he showed that he could be depended upon if necessary. He threw four touchdown passes in the 35–20 defeat of the Jets.

Yet it was still Unitas' season, and he was named the NFL Man of the Year for it.

However, for all the games that he heroically pulled out during the 1970 season, Unitas had never brought himself back to the ultimate feats of the earlier years, before his arm trouble in 1968. The hallmark of his glory years, the touchdown pass, was noticeably missing from his arsenal. In his first 12 seasons, he averaged two touchdown passes per game. In 1969 and 1970, his touchdown passes decreased to fewer than one per game.

Despite the danger signs, four days before the playoff game against Cincinnati, McCafferty, remembering the incomparable Unitas of those 12 years, named him as the starter. Unitas didn't disappoint him or the sellout crowd. Toward the conclusion of the first period, he got Baltimore in front on another big third-down play, reminiscent of his game against Philadelphia, with a 45-yard connection to Jefferson. On the Colts' first possession in the next quarter, he got them a field goal. Once more it was aided by a key third-down play. A 21-yard pass to Bulaich positioned Jim O'Brien's 44-yard field goal that supplied the Colts with a 10–0 halftime margin. Hendricks noted that Baltimore's defense was brilliant in allowing the Bengals only 35 total yards.

The aging warrior looked anything but old in the third quarter. He converted another important third down, only this time with his own legs. Finding no open receivers, Unitas pulled the ball down, tucked it into his side and took off like a two-year-old colt on a 17-yard run. The crowd loved that. However, Unitas' gallant efforts didn't result in any points when several minutes later, O'Brien was wide on a 44-yard field goal try.

Halfway through the final period, Unitas produced the clinching touchdown. His magic was mystifying. It was another third-down play. This time he looked to Hinton for a 53-yard beauty that again brought the local fans to their feet: it was the Johnny Unitas of 1958 and 1959 all over again—and more. Unitas had thrown two touchdown passes and run 17 yards to set up a field goal. The Colts would play for the AFC championship against the dangerous Oakland Raiders team.

Still a Legend

If Unitas wanted to play at age 40, then he certainly could draw inspiration from Oakland's George Blanda, another Pittsburgh athlete, who was still kicking field goals at the Geritol age of 44. Blanda was also still good enough to play quarterback and was the backup to strong-armed Daryle Lamonica. Before the game was over, Blanda played three quarters of football and came close to pulling an upset on the Colts. His actions accounted for all his team's points, which included a mammoth 48-yard field goal to get the Raiders on the board in the closing minutes of the first half.

Baltimore was developing a pattern of scoring first, which was always the way Unitas wanted it. Once more he contributed with a third-down, 12-yard pass to Richardson, which enabled O'Brien to boot a 16-yard field goal six minutes into the first quarter. Following another patented third-down, 12-yard pass, this time to Hinton, who was instrumental in getting to the Oakland 27, Unitas dropped back to pass on third down again. He sent Richardson deep and delivered a throw into the end zone, which was perfect, but unfortunately dropped. With a chance to add a field goal, O'Brien's 35-yard attempt was wide. The next time Unitas was on the field, the Colts scored. His 43-yard pass to Hinton enabled Bulaich to cross the goal line from two yards out for a 10–0 lead, which Blanda reduced with his field goal right before halftime.

It was only the beginning for the gray-haired Blanda. On the opening drive of the third period, he tied the game with a 38-yard touchdown pass to Fred Biletnikoff. Unitas came back quickly and would have had another touchdown if Richardson hadn't dropped his second pass in the end zone. Baltimore had to settle for O'Brien's 23-yard field goal to reclaim a 13–10 lead. Unitas wasn't through and he didn't give up on Richardson. On the inevitable third-down call, he passed to him for 11 yards and a first down. He called his number again for a resulting 13-yard completion to the Oakland 11. Unitas called for the old "Statue of Liberty" play, something he brought with him from the sandlots, in which he faked a pass while the running back took the ball from his hand. It fooled the Raiders, and Bulaich scored to push the Colts' advantage to 20–10.

The seemingly indomitable Blanda wouldn't go away. Before the fourth quarter was two minutes old, he got the Raiders a touchdown with a 15-yard strike to Warren Wells that brought Oakland to within a field goal of the Colts with almost an entire period of playing time remaining.

Unitas viewed a potentially dangerous scenario and didn't wait long to defuse it the next time he got the ball. On the third down, he connected with Perkins on a 68-yard pass for a clinching touchdown. The Asylum on Thirty-third Street was bedlam. Unitas was 27 years old again—at least he felt that way. His play selection throughout the game was excellent. He delivered the points, including the final touchdown to Perkins. Unitas had guts and the confidence that went with them.

"He's still the best," said Blanda.

Maybe, just maybe, Unitas would still play at 40 like Blanda had. He sure looked like he could that day.

10

One Long Pass

I N AN IDEAL WORLD, JOHNNY UNITAS WAS YOUNG, 25 OR 26 YEARS old, and he was healthy: no ailing arm, no sore back, and no tender knee. But the reality was that Unitas carried those ailments into Super Bowl V against a rugged Dallas defense.

This was his Super Bowl. Two years prior, it had been Joe Namath's, when Unitas couldn't play in a season that belonged to Earl Morrall. Unitas was almost a forgotten figure at Super Bowl III as the media sought out the flamboyant Namath and the Cinderella Morrall, who was summarily put down by the Jets quarterback. The stoic Unitas was an afterthought.

Speaking Out

But it was different this time in Miami. Unitas was restored to prominence on the team and was the *coup de théâtre*, once more the cherished hero in the fickle world of sports. It could very well have been his last hurrah, because at 37, Unitas would be the oldest player on the Orange Bowl turf, and he would be 38 before the next season came around.

For three days hundreds of media types continually came looking for Unitas. Everyone wanted to talk with him just like before. Unitas, who wasn't exactly one for interviews, politely sat in the hotel's media salon day after day and answered a barrage of questions about his injuries and his retirement plans. He admitted to soreness in his shoulder and said he could throw, but not with the speed he used to have or as long as he once could throw.

"I'm doing the same thing I always have," said Unitas, "throwing interceptions. I'm going to continue to throw the ball even if I have six interceptions. Just because I overthrew a few people doesn't mean I'm not going to come back to the same receivers. If I don't do that I'm making it easy for the defense."

It was a relaxed Unitas, and he was as candid as he always was with his remarks. Usually he gave short, quick answers, but on that particular day he took time to be more detailed with his explanations. It was a priceless treasure for an audience of writers who had been accustomed to a more sphinx-like Unitas for the past 15 years. He sat slouched behind a table, his face relaxed by a frequent, easy grin. He made his points for almost an hour. Maybe, just maybe, he knew there wouldn't be many more days like that, and he gave the media an earful.

"I can't put as much speed on the ball as I did but it doesn't prevent me from doing the same things," said Unitas. "Instead of trying to line the ball from the right hash mark to the left sideline, I might pick a better time to do it. I might wait until the ball is positioned in the middle of the field."

"Ten years ago, if I saw a five-foot hole, I could throw hard enough to get it through. Now, I might have to wait until I have a better hole. I don't have any difficult parts in passing. It's just a matter of knowing when and how to do it. When I have to throw the ball out of bounds, one of those 30-yard passes that gains 10 yards, notice that I don't have the zip I once had. I used to try and fire the ball through open holes. But I don't do that anymore either. Getting older has just forced me to think and it hurts."

It was quite an admission for the proud quarterback, who was never one to dwell on the past. But he was dealing with the reality of his age. He was banged up and sore, but he still could play the game of football— just maybe not at the level that brought him his greatness. He was smart enough to make adjustments and savvy enough to fool opposing defenses. Unitas realized he was not the Unitas of the fifties and sixties; his arm, shoulder, and knee were all reminders. He remained dangerous because of his grit, and he was driven by an inexhaustible pride that he had taken with him on the field for all those 15 years of Sundays that brought him legendary status. He was asked if he had any difficulty living up to the legend he had become, and Unitas didn't hesitate to answer: "I don't think of myself that way."

But others did view him as such. He was essentially a private individual, but he was looked upon as an animated folk figure. His walk, his sloped shoulders, his crew cut, and his jersey number were instantly recognizable to millions of people across America.

In the twilight of his football career, he would have another Sunday in the biggest game of them all to add to his lore. Through it all, he remained calm and confident. He said, "I never had a sleepless night before a ball game, I have no trouble relaxing before a game, and, as a matter of fact, I'll lay down and take a 10-minute to 12-minute nap before we go on the field Sunday."

Preparations for the Game

Super Bowl V was against Dallas, and Unitas knew his opponent well. He and Morrall studied films not only in the classroom, but well into the night in the room they shared. Morrall, too, had to be prepared, should he be needed to relieve Unitas if any of his ailments hampered him to the point where he couldn't be effective.

With simple candor, Unitas revealed how he was going to attack the Dallas defense: "They're vulnerable if you can get them out of position," he said. "Their linebackers are probably the best as a group in football. They are changing their pass coverage all the time, making you read along with them.

"I'll try to get a tendency. Get keys from certain personnel and find out what they like to do in a certain situation, down yardage, a passing situation, and the side of the field. It's just a matter of picking up their tendencies as the game goes along. You try to set up one play with another. You try to get individuals in one-on-one coverages, and then you try to beat them."

In his candor with the press, Unitas didn't disclose everything about his ailments. He had come out of a game against Cincinnati suffering severe headaches. Doctors found nothing of a serious nature and he was cleared to play in the championship game against Oakland. Unitas described his discomfort as a "dull pain" on the left side of his head, and the doctors conceded that it was close to being a mild concussion from his head hitting the ground. "I got up and saw a few stars," he admitted, "and I didn't want anything mentioned about the trouble." His vision was clear and his balance normal, and he played the following week against the Raiders without anyone knowing about his condition. However, medication didn't give him any relief in the three weeks leading up to the Super Bowl. "I have the pain all the time and I guess all I can do is wait it out," he said.

When the season began, the Dallas Cowboys head coach Tom Landry had been certain of one thing: his defense. They were a seasoned bunch, who had earned the reputation as a "Doomsday Defense." However, his offense was a question mark. His regular quarterback, Craig Morton, was coming off shoulder surgery, and his reserve, Roger Staubach, was playing in only his second season in the league after a tour of duty following his graduation from the Naval Academy.

But after the ninth game of the year, Landry hadn't been sure of anything. In an embarrassing display of ineptitude before millions of viewers on Monday Night Football, the Cowboys had been soundly beaten by the St. Louis Cardinals, 38–0! That loss left Dallas with a 5–4 record. A great many people bet that they would never play in the Super Bowl that January. The defeat was the second thrashing the Cowboys had absorbed in a short period of time. Only four weeks before, they had been routed by the Minnesota Vikings, 54–13, in a demonstration of even greater futility. Hardly championship play.

Then the Cowboys pulled themselves together and won five straight games to finish with a 10–4 record. The defense clearly asserted itself; in the last four games, it yielded only 15 points, allowing only one touchdown in the final game of the season. In the playoff games, Dallas shut out Detroit 5–0 and then handled San Francisco in the championship contest, 17–10.

"After the St. Louis game, most people wrote us off," said Landry. "It was up to us. We were either going to collapse or come back. If the players weren't doubting me, they were the only ones. I felt the team had to become closer together in attitude. We weren't getting much outside support at that point, so we had to generate it among ourselves. It was a 40-man pickup."

The success of the Cowboys centered around their running attack and defense. Morton's arm miseries were only part of the reason for the defused Dallas air game. Lance Rentzel, one of the team's primary wide receivers, was suspended for the remainder of the season because of personal problems resulting from a morals charge. The club's other wide receiver, Bob Hayes, was not only a deluxe pass catcher, but a dangerous punt returner as well. However, the speedy Hayes, whose total of 34 pass receptions was the lowest of his career, nevertheless led the Cowboys in touchdowns with 10. Part of his mediocre performance was the result of being benched for two full games and part of three others.

That was why the Dallas running game took on ever more significance. Morton was looked upon by many as the least impressive quarterback ever to play in the Super Bowl. But while he had his problems, so did his counterpart, Johnny Unitas. Many felt that the veteran 37-year-old couldn't throw the long ball effectively any more, but he was also beset by personal problems. A week after the game Unitas' wife filed for divorce.

Still, Unitas led the Colts to an 11–2–1 record. He completed 166 of 321 passes for 2,213 yards and 14 touchdowns. But the most glaring statistic was that he had 18 interceptions. The year before, when Baltimore had finished with an 8–5–1 record, people had started to whisper that

Unitas was finished. He had completed 178 of 327 passes, had only 12 touchdowns, and 20 interceptions.

"I can't throw as far, and I can't run as fast," said Unitas in response to the criticism. "Quarterbacks can't permit themselves to think of injuries, or they'll leave their game in the locker room. The Cowboys linebacking unit is a great one. They are not as big as some, but they are strong and they have great speed and mobility.

"Probably the biggest thing they have going for them is they have been playing together for a long time. With all that experience, they know exactly what they are doing and the best way to do it. Up front, I think the Cowboy rush is better than most we've played against this year. If you want to beat the Dallas defense, you've got to figure out some way to beat them."

Two years later, Super Bowl III was a lingering nightmare for Morrall. "Sure, I think about the game," confided Morrall. "I still get flashbacks. I keep seeing Johnny Sample reaching around Willie Richardson to make an interception. I keep seeing Jimmy Orr wide open on the flea-flicker play. I keep seeing the ball bounce off Tom Mitchell's shoulder pads, and Randy Beverly's interception. All my flashbacks are bad.

"You always remember the mistakes, not the good things. I'll be on the phones on the sidelines Sunday. I'm sure if I get a chance to go in, it'll mean we are losing, and I don't want it to go bad for John. But that doesn't mean I wouldn't want to play. I'm ready to go in any time."

"Everybody knocked our team this year. But it got progressively better as the season went on. We had new players; we were in a new league; we had new defensive alignments to face. It was an adjustment for the veterans as much as for the rookies. Early in the season we had to think. Now we don't have to think."

Super Bowl V

In breezy, 70-degree weather, it was Unitas' time. When Dallas couldn't make a first down upon receiving the kickoff, Unitas appeared. He, too, was unsuccessful with only a 5-yard pass to John Mackey for his efforts. Again the erratic Dallas offense failed to generate anything, and Unitas had advantageous field position on the Colts' 42-yard line. Unitas wanted to pass—only this time deeper—to Norm Bulaich. However, linebacker Chuck Howley intercepted the ball on the Dallas 32 and returned it to the Baltimore 46 to give the Cowboys roping room as the offense hurried back on the field. Still, they couldn't do anything. However, when Ron Widby punted, Dallas got a big break. Ron Gardin fumbled the kick on his own 9-yard line, and the loose ball was recovered by Dallas' Cliff Harris. The Cowboys were presented with an opportunity to score the game's first touchdown. However, the Colts defense rejected any further advance from the 7-yard line, and the Cowboys had to be content with Mike Clark's 14-yard field goal and a 3–0 lead.

There were only five minutes left when Unitas took over the offense for the third time. Although a strong proponent of the pass, Unitas turned his back on it completely. He called three straight running plays, which only netted eight yards and didn't come close to getting the Colts their only first down. Was he hurting? Was it the arm? The back? Or was his head throbbing with pain that may have affected his vision?

When the first period ended, Morton had taken the Cowboys to the Baltimore 7-yard line with a 41-yard pass to Hayes, the type of throw crowds expected from Unitas. The result was another field goal in the opening minutes of the second quarter.

Unitas returned but still didn't look right. He kept trying and threw two more passes, one that was incomplete and another that was short. The defensive backs were faster than years ago, and Unitas' arm wasn't as strong. He had now attempted four passes, completed only one for five yards, and had another interception. But he wouldn't quit, he was too proud for that. On third down, he tried again from his 25-yard line and he knew the rush would be coming. The pass was one he'd always remember, the most bizarre in his career.

The grim-faced Unitas tried to hit wide receiver Eddie Hinton, but the pass sailed over Hinton's head. Hinton leaped as high as he could. However, the ball tipped off his fingers toward Dallas cornerback Mel Renfro. He, too, couldn't control the ball, and it landed in the arms of

Mackey, who ran the rest of the way for the game's first touchdown. The peculiar play tied the score at 6–6. The impending conversion, which would have given Baltimore a 7–6 lead, never materialized as Jim O'Brien's kick was blocked.

Midway into the quarter, Dallas got its second break. Attempting to pass on third down from his own 21-yard line, Unitas, finding no one open, began to run. He was hit hard by linebacker Lee Roy Jordan, and fumbled. Jethro Pugh recovered the ball for Dallas on the 28. Three plays later Morton hit Duane Thomas with a seven-yard touchdown pass to give Dallas the edge, 13–6.

Unitas tried to get the Colts going on the next series but failed. On third down, he was hit hard by defensive end George Andrie. His wobbly pass was intercepted by Renfro, and Unitas trotted off the field holding his side. He was hurt. It was an all-too-familiar scene. The next time Baltimore got the ball before the half ended, Morrall took over.

When the third period began, Jim Duncan fumbled the kickoff and Richmond Flowers recovered the ball for Dallas on the Baltimore 31. Keeping the ball on the ground, the Cowboys moved for a first down on the Colts' 2-yard line. But Thomas fumbled, and Duncan redeemed himself by recovering the ball on the 1-yard line. No one seriously threatened the score after that, and the quarter ended with Dallas still in front.

On the first play of the fourth period, Morrall's third-down pass was intercepted in the end zone by Howley, which killed another threat. However, after a Dallas punt, Morrall had the Colts moving again. On a first-down play on the Dallas 39, Morrall lateraled the ball to Sam Havrilak, who passed to Hinton on the 5-yard line. Hinton fumbled, and the ball rolled out of the end zone for the touchback. It was the *seventh* Baltimore turnover.

Just as quickly, Dallas gave the Colts the ball back. On third down from his own 23-yard line, Morton's pass was deflected by Duncan and intercepted by Volk, who ran it back to the three. Two plays later, Tom Nowatzke went over for the tying touchdown.

It appeared that the game would end in a 13–13 tie and go into over-time. With just over a minute to play, Morton tried to pass from his own 27-yard line. His pass bounced off halfback Dan Reeves' hands and into the arms of Curtis, who brought it back to the 28. Morrall was thinking field goal. Two runs advanced the ball to the 25. On third down, Jim O'Brien was sent in to attempt a game-winning 32-yard field goal. With only five seconds showing on the clock, Jim O'Brien came through.

The Colts prevailed in an error-filled game, 16–13. So frustrated was Dallas' All-Pro Tackle Bob Lilly that he threw his helmet about 40 feet into the air.

O'Brien, the game's hero, appeared calm in the Baltimore dressing room. He told about a dream he had a week before the game.

"Right after we got down here, I had a dream that a long field goal was going to win this game," said O'Brien. "I didn't know who was going to kick it or how far or when it would happen, but now I know. All the guys had confidence in me and that was the big thing. When we went out there, Earl just told me to kick it straight through, that there was no wind, just to kick it. I hurt my knee on the kickoff before the field goal, and I was concerned that it would get stiff. But I didn't think about it when I made the kick."

The winning kick made Don McCafferty the first rookie coach to win a Super Bowl. Naturally, he was happy when the players handed him a game ball along with O'Brien.

"The turning point had to be Curtis' interception," said McCafferty. "That set it up for us. We had a lot of bad breaks in the first half, but we hung in there. I kept Morrall in the game although the doctor said Unitas could return because I thought Earl was doing a real fine job and I saw no reason to make a change."

But change was coming and sooner than Unitas could ever imagine.

11

One More Chance

WITHOUT ACKNOWLEDGING IT IN WORDS, UNITAS HAD TO ACCEPT the fact that his aging body no longer permitted him to do the things on a football field that he had been so good at doing. He had been incomparable, the exalted king among the quarterbacks. That was then. At one time he had the fastest setup and delivery in the game. But he had become just above average. At one time he was a threat to carry the ball with reckless abandon. But that had become rare. And at one time he could throw the 60–70 yard pass and hit a receiver in stride, which was textbook form. But even the 40-yarders had become hard. He was still Johnny Unitas, though, and nobody was going to tell him when to quit.

He was 38, and his 15 pro seasons had spanned a couple of eras. He had led Baltimore to five titles and three world championships, was the NFL's Most Valuable Player three times, and was named the Pro Football Player of the Decade for the sixties. He had been named the league's best quarterback of the first 50 years—and there had been other good ones like Sammy Baugh, Sid Luckman, Norm Van Brocklin, and Otto Graham on the list. It was Luckman who praised Unitas "as the greatest quarterback ever to play the game."

Yet Unitas remained unimpressed by his past achievements because he expected such things of himself. It is somewhat of a paradox that the most exciting quarterback in pro football history was a person of so little visible emotion. But perhaps his stoicism enabled him to remain calm under pressure while exuding fervent tenacity to overcome all the injuries his body had absorbed.

Another Serious Injury

Unitas wanted more than the 1971 season. "I'm not ready to quit yet," he declared. He pushed his body harder to be ready for his 16th year with the Colts. Maybe too hard. He had been training hard for weeks under the watchful eye of Bill Neill, lifting weights, and punching the speed bags just like in other years. His weight was almost perfect, just two pounds more than the 196 at which he played.

During the first week in April, Unitas had a date with Tom Matte to play paddleball at the Towson YMCA a month before his 38th birthday. Paddleball is a fast-paced game and Unitas could easily melt off the two pounds playing it. Unexpectedly, tragedy raised its ugly head. Positioning himself for a forehand shot with his left foot forward, Unitas pushed off on his right foot, swung, and without any warning whatsoever, dropped in pain on the hard wooden floor. "Who kicked me?" he asked Matte and laughed about it.

A moment later, Unitas surmised what had happened and it wasn't good. "I tore my Achilles tendon," he said with the calmness of someone who had broken a fingernail. "I guess I must look kind of funny folded up there on the floor." He got up and limped into the locker room without any concern about the severity of the injury. He later admitted that "it was one of the sharpest [pains] I've ever felt in my life. I was in agony."

So was McCafferty when Matte phoned him from Union Memorial Hospital to relate what had happened: "Don, you need to get down to Memorial Hospital. I think John tore his Achilles tendon." McCafferty thought it was a joke. "Matte, I don't want to hear those gosh darn jokes," said McCafferty. Matte reassured him it wasn't. "Mac, it's not a joke. I just took John to Union Memorial."

McCafferty got more bad news several hours later. Matte had doubled up in pain on the floor of a restaurant in the suburbs. He was rushed to a local hospital and given Demerol. Then he was shipped to Union Memorial, where he began coughing up blood. Matte informed the doctors that he had ulcers and waited for the Demerol to wear off before an evaluation could be made. Matte phoned McCafferty and told him he was in the hospital too. McCafferty again thought it was a joke. "Matte, the first one was bad enough," said McCafferty. When the Demerol wore off, Matte was diagnosed with acute appendicitis.

At 6:00 P.M., Unitas was wheeled into the operating room for what resulted in 90 minutes of surgery. His tendon was separated two inches above the heel. The doctors were optimistic about the surgery and expressed their belief that Unitas would be in a cast for only six weeks. Unitas had learned to live with pain and the discomfort of his ailments. Since he started with the Colts, the seemingly indestructible Unitas had suffered broken ribs, a punctured lung, dislocated fingers, torn knee cartilage, broken vertebrae, tendonitis of the elbow, and now this. The Achilles injury was the most serious of all, and doubts were expressed that someone of Unitas' age could play pro football.

"I feel fine," said Unitas from his hospital bed the next day. "This has been some year. First I was hurt in the Super Bowl, then my wife sued for separation, and now this. I'll play again. I'm counting on being there this season like nothing ever happened."

Unitas' cast was scheduled to be removed sometime during the Memorial Day weekend. That was too long for Unitas to wait. Two weeks early, he was sitting on the training table in Eddie Block's office without a cast on his leg, flexing his ankle, twisting it as far as he could to one side and then back to the other side. When Block entered the room, he immediately screamed at Unitas to stop.

"It's not going to hurt anything," said Unitas. "I've been doing it for three hours."

"Don't," pleaded Block. "Please don't. I have a bad heart."

Working His Way Back

Persistence had always been a part of Unitas' psyche, from his high school days to the five-year journey that took him to college and the Pittsburgh sandlots before he landed with the Colts. "You take what you see and make the most out of it," believed Unitas. Persistence was needed more than ever to bring him back from a debilitating injury, one that could be the death knell for someone at age 38.

But he was recovering from the serious injury with remarkable speed. The original estimate was that Unitas would be off crutches by June 15. Unitas surprised everyone again. A week before he was supposed to be off crutches, he was at Lake Tahoe playing golf and undoubtedly would have walked the course if a golf cart had not been available. Still, the skeptics in Baltimore were of the opinion that Unitas would embarrass himself before he relented and admitted personal defeat. Unitas had an answer for them. "I could care less how I play my last game," he said. "What does it matter if I go out on top or on my butt? The only thing that concerns me is whether we win or lose, not what the writers say."

Unitas had circled September as the target date for his return. He looked at mid-August to start running in training camp and then hopefully to play in the final preseason game on September 10, 1971, in Jacksonville. It was an extremely optimistic outlook, but to Unitas it wasn't impossible. "If there is anybody who can come back from this, it's John," said end coach Dick Bielski. Unitas was relentless in his rehabilitation, making light of the four-inch scar when he put on his socks and laced up his cleats. He didn't miss an hour of training with Bill Neill, the physiotherapist who had watched over Unitas for years and contributed so much to his well-being. Neill had to control Unitas' tenacity, which could become a deterrent and prolong his recovery.

"We have been very lucky with John," said O'Neill. "No complications from the operation and excellent healing so far. We had to take off John's cast. He kept playing golf and the thing was falling off, but he is progressing well."

Keeping His Word and Fighting for His Place

On Sunday, July 11, Unitas was on the practice field at the Colts' training camp in Westminster. And he wasn't just standing around that first day. He was on the field with the rest of the players doing calisthenics as if nothing had ever happened, just like he had said he would. It was an inspiring sight to the 25 rookies and the 19 veterans, especially to the newcomers who were seeing Unitas, the legend, before their very eyes. The businesslike Unitas was impressing everybody again with a mind-over-matter transformation in record recovery time. Unitas' recovery was in sharp contrast with Alan Ameche's, who had the same Achilles injury in 1960 but preferred to call it a career at the age of 27. "I'll be ready in September," Unitas had vowed.

Although there may have been some question, no one seriously doubted that Unitas would be there for the season opener against the New York Jets on September 19. He wouldn't start—that would be expecting too much—but he was dressed in full gear on the sidelines with an arm he claimed "felt stronger than it has ever been." The Colts won their opener 22–0, and then following a one-point loss to Cleveland, won their next three games for a promising 4–1 start in defense of their world championship. And it was their defense that excelled, allowing only a miniscule total of 24 points in five games.

Despite the win cycle, Unitas wasn't happy. He had played in parts of the first five games. He had replaced Morrall with 10:39 to play at Minnesota when the Colts needed a touchdown to tie the game at 10–10. He didn't deliver, just missing on the tying touchdown throw in the end zone near the end of the game. His frustration surfaced in the dressing room as he finished dressing. A Minneapolis writer wanted to know why Unitas wasn't playing much and asked him if there was a reason for it that nobody knew. Unitas gave him a cold stare. "Ask the coach," he snarled, nodding his head toward McCafferty. "There's not a damn thing wrong with me. If they keep playing me the way they are playing me, I might retire tomorrow. It might be a kind of game to someone else, but I don't like to sit down."

McCafferty answered Unitas' inflammatory remarks calmly and avoided any open rift with his quarterback. "I've been going with Earl and we've been winning," he pointed out, refusing to discuss the issue any further.

Morrall remained the starter and took the Colts to a 7–2 record after a battle with Miami for first place in the Eastern Division. In the last four games, Unitas had come off the bench in a mop-up role, something that he had declared he would never do, which added to his frustration. All he had to show for his token appearances were 22 completions in 50 tries. Worse, there were four interceptions and no touchdowns. The whispers criticized that maybe he should quit, which gnawed at him. It was hurtful to someone who had done so much and led the Colts all those years. But Unitas did not beg or solicit sympathy. He had never been one to deceive himself, and he felt that he could play more and wanted the chance. He was stubborn and determined to make his critics look bad.

Unitas still had a feel for the game, a quality that only the great ones have. In the win over Pittsburgh, he was sent in to give the backfield reserves a chance to run with the ball. But there was one thing that nobody knew except Unitas: Eddie Hinton was having an off year. Unitas wanted to help him by completing a couple of passes to lift the receiver's confidence. Unitas kept throwing to Hinton and did so once too often. In admittedly trying to force the ball, Unitas threw an interception that drew comments that it wasn't the same Unitas and maybe his time had come.

Only Unitas would decide that. And he wasn't ready to go. Rather, he insisted that he wanted to play, but he still refused to criticize McCafferty's decision to stick with Morrall. He even denied reports that there was friction between himself and the coach. Unitas acknowledged that Morrall was doing a fine job and didn't see how McCafferty could change quarterbacks in midstream. He emphasized, as he always had, that the only thing that mattered was that the team continued to win. Through it all, he felt that the media had misinterpreted some of his comments. He cleared the air somewhat but made his feelings known in doing so.

"I'll go along with what they want to do, even though I don't like it," said Unitas. "I'm not going to cause any trouble. It's hard enough to play the game without creating problems. Yet, when someone asks me if I want to play, of course I'm going to say I do. If they ask me why I don't, I tell them to ask the coach. I just mean it's his decision.

"I've never told Mac I wanted to play. He knows that. Anyway, if there was a problem between us, it would be up to him to come to me, not for me to go to him. I'm not the run-the-clock-out quarterback either. If and when I get in there, I want to throw the ball and do what I think is best. That's the way I came in and I may as well go out the same way."

Baltimore's Hero

McCafferty believed in Unitas and gave him back his starter's role the week after the Colts defeated the Rams. The Colts won three of the four games Unitas started and improved their record to 9-3 with a first place showdown with the Dolphins in Baltimore. After that game, Shula was still hated in Baltimore, and Unitas, because of the way he was playing, was once again revered. It was a special day: Unitas' magic reappeared. He gave a fantastic performance that left Colts fans euphoric over the 14–3 triumph. Unitas was everything he had been during his peak, and he impeccably delivered two touchdown drives to lift the Colts into first place.

He had not waited to conduct his virtuoso performance either. On the first drive of the opening period, he led the Colts 81 yards in 18 plays for a touchdown. He was superb in hitting on seven of eight passes for 48 yards, while masterfully consuming 9 minutes and 53 seconds to frustrate Miami's defense. And he repeated his ploy in the second quarter. That time Unitas took the Colts 87 yards in 16 plays and used up another 9 minutes and 26 seconds as Matte scored his second touchdown. Even Shula looked at what Unitas had done with awe. "Unitas had a great game," he said later. "He looked like he did in the fifties and sixties."

Unitas was unemotional as he stood in front of his locker. He was overly modest in saying that he didn't see anything different about his performance as compared to previous games. Of the three passes on which he missed, one was overthrown and the other two were dropped by Matte and Bulaich. When Matte had returned to the huddle, Unitas glared at him. "Catch the ball Matte," he said. Significantly, none of Unitas' next 10 passes were dropped. He was indeed the master again.

"I just took what was available," he said matter-of-factly. "They just dropped so deep, I took the short stuff. They had nine guys back there deep. Where else could I put it? I looked for the deep stuff, read the defenses, and just took what they gave us."

Matte realized it and marveled at what Unitas had done. "John called the finest game I've seen him call in a long time," he said.

But Unitas couldn't give Baltimore the Eastern Championship. The following week against New England, they lost a tough 21–17 game to the lowly Patriots, while Miami disposed of Green Bay, 27–6, to win the East by a half game. Unitas had thrown for only 942 yards, the lowest yardage of his career (the 1968 injury season notwithstanding), but he proved that he still knew how to win, which was all that ever mattered to him. And he was assured that he would start in the playoff game against Cleveland, which was just a week away.

Unitas had to do what Morrall couldn't, and that was to beat the Browns. In the second game of the season played in Baltimore, Cleveland had won 14–13, and Morrall had not been very good. The Browns had finished the season strong, winning their last five games to grab the Central crown with a 9–5 record. Even though the Colts were better at 10–4, the playoff battle was to be played in Cleveland.

The cold and icy winds off Lake Erie could get nasty at the end of December, but Baltimore enjoyed a break; it was 47 degrees and misty, a relief from any chilling snow. As long as Unitas wasn't ailing, he couldn't care less about the weather. He wanted to play a full game in the Super Bowl and Cleveland was the first step.

The Colts were without Bulaich in the backfield. He had suffered an ankle sprain during the Miami game, which made his appearance extremely doubtful in the playoffs if the Colts advanced. Don Nottingham, a chunky 5'9" running back who was nicknamed the "Bowling Ball" because of his stature, replaced Bulaich and lined up alongside Matte. A rookie out of

Kent State, Nottingham was playing in front of his hometown fans, and before the day was over, he would make them proud. He had shown some promise during his first year with the Colts, lugging the ball 95 times and averaging 4.1 yards per run. He also scored five touchdowns. In a scoreless first quarter, Nottingham showed that he could be a factor in the biggest game in which he ever played. Unitas handed him the ball five times, and Nottingham responded with 26 yards and also caught a pass for five more.

Unitas, too, looked sharp. He had the same accuracy he had demonstrated in the Miami game two weeks prior. Against Cleveland he threw eight times and completed seven passes for 44 yards. And when the second-quarter action began, he was like General Patton on the battlefield. On a drive that began on his own 8-yard line with 3:36 of the first period remaining, Unitas never flinched as he took the Colts 92 yards in 17 plays using 8:09 minutes of clock with Nottingham providing the touchdown.

Safety Rich Volk set up Baltimore's second touchdown five minutes later. He intercepted Bill Nelsen's pass at the Colts' 48 and ran the ball back to Cleveland's 15-yard line. A pass interference penalty moved the ball to the 7, and Unitas turned to Nottingham again. And just like that, the hometown rookie crossed the goal line for his second touchdown and a 14–0 lead as the first half came to a close. It had been a productive half for both Nottingham, who carried 12 times for 54 yards, and Unitas, who was 8 of 12 for 68 yards. Unitas and the Colts were in control.

With five minutes left in the third quarter, the Browns finally scored. Don Cockroft booted a 14-yard field goal to give the Browns some hope with a 14–3 score. But Unitas wouldn't allow them any more than that. He worked fast and it took him only four and a half minutes to get the points back. He did so with another admirable drive: 71 yards in 10 plays with O'Brien kicking a 42-yard field goal to restore Baltimore's 14-point margin, 17–3.

The Colts defense kept it that way. Cleveland did not score again. The remaining points—and the only ones in the final period—came off the leg of O'Brien, who added a 15-yard field goal for Baltimore's 20–3 win. Unitas was solid with 13 of 21 passes for 143 yards, and Colts fans had a new hero in Nottingham, who carried 23 times for 92 yards and scored the game's only touchdowns.

Baltimore was going to Miami, and Unitas couldn't have been any happier.

12

Not Enough

JOHNNY UNITAS DIDN'T KNOW IT AT THE TIME, BUT HE WOULD play his last meaningful game in the NFL against the Miami Dolphins in the 1971 AFC Championship game. It was not just another game for Unitas. He wanted to win this one more than some of the others. This one was personal.

Bad Blood

Unitas still harbored ill feelings toward Don Shula because he did not get to play in Super Bowl III against the Jets until it was too late. He had provided the Colts with their only touchdown in the ignominious 16–7 defeat and felt if he had played more, the result would have been different.

Carroll Rosenbloom felt very much the same way. He never forgave Shula for the humiliating loss, and there were stories around that the Colts' owner had lost quite a sum of money on the outcome. He made Shula the victim of his anger with bitter tirades the final two years. He went as far as to eliminate any mention of Shula in the program of the Dolphins-Colts game program in Baltimore during his last season. The personal feud even reached the desk of NFL Commissioner Pete Rozelle, who tried to broker a peace between the two personalities. Unsuccessful, Rozelle, in a show of strength of his office, fined Rosenbloom $5,000 for his disparaging remarks, which he felt were detrimental to the league as a whole. "I think Carroll is wrong in prolonging this thing," said Rozelle. The acrid Rosenbloom-Shula controversy was paramount in creating a natural rivalry between the two teams.

The weather, or maybe the Orange Bowl itself, had been a challenge to the Colts. Although they barely won Super Bowl V, they had lost Super Bowl III and then suffered two other losses when they appeared in the Orange Bowl. In the last one, they had complained about the heat and the humidity. The weather was on Baltimore's mind, so the Colts arrived in Tampa on Tuesday and did not travel to Miami until Saturday, the day before the big game. "The heat is a home-field advantage in the same category with the way the cold used to be for Green Bay when the Packers were playing all those late-season games," said Rosenbloom.

Shula had some misgivings about the condition of the field, instead of the weather, which he had grown to love during the two years he had spent in Miami molding the Dolphins into champions. College football's Orange Bowl classic was to be played on Saturday night and less than 24 hours later was his big game. Shula always looked for an edge, and he claimed that the problem was that the synthetic fibers in the surface were starting to break off. He maintained that a slippage problem was caused by the fibers standing up instead of matting, sounding ever so much like a certified groundskeeper. Apparently, Shula was worried that his dynamic running back duo of Larry Csonka and Jim Kiick, a big part of his offense, wouldn't have proper footing. "I think something has to be done after this year, either replacing the surface or going to some other surface," said Shula. However, Al Rubio, the stadium's manager, wasn't concerned in the least. He had a labor force of one hundred to work through the night to prepare the field. "The Super Bowl has become a routine to us," he said. "Do you think this is bigger than the Super Bowl?"

Young Versus Old

It was indeed a big game for Dolphins cornerback Tim Foley. He vividly remembered December of 1958 when Unitas led the Colts to the overtime win against the Giants in the NFL's championship game in New York. Foley was an eight-year-old youngster in Wilmette, Illinois, and a fourth-grader at St. Francis Xavier grade school. He grew up wanting to be like Unitas when he played quarterback at Loyola Academy 10 years later. He never forgot the Colts-Giants game, and now he had to play against Unitas 13 years later.

"You know what? When that game was over I went outside with my brother, Mike, who was 10, and we took turns pretending we were Johnny Unitas," said the good-looking Foley. "I had a hard time all last week just thinking about playing against him. I first played against Unitas in a pre-season game last year. It was like a dream. I looked across the line and there he was. I watched him throw to guys like Raymond Berry and they just destroyed defensive backs. I tried to tell myself that it's been all those years, that he can't be as good now as he was back then, but it was hard to make myself believe it."

In the preseason game, Foley came up with an interception against his idol, but later in the game, he broke his foot, which sidelined him for the rest of the season. "So, the first time I really faced him was here in Miami, this year," said Foley. "I was fortunate to get another interception and we won." However, for the rematch in Baltimore, Unitas took the Colts on two nine-minute drives for a 14–3 victory, which awed Foley. "The old master was perfect in those drives and he'd make first downs by inches," he said.

The old master was 38 now and a generation removed from Miami's 26-year-old quarterback Bob Griese. Yet they were alike in their personalities: quiet, cool, efficient, and almost standoffish with their conservative attitudes. Like Unitas, Griese could read defenses, which contributed to his being the leading quarterback in the AFC for the regular season. They both respected one another too. "Unitas showed what a quarterback should and can do," said Griese. Unitas was every bit as complimentary: "Griese, as I said before, is the best young quarterback in the game." On Sunday, they would face each other for the third time in seven weeks, but this was the one that counted the most, and Unitas wanted it.

The Contenders

Shula was looked upon as a miracle worker in Miami. He had finished second in the east with a 10–4 record during his first year and won the division with a 10–3–1 record for the 1971 season, a half game ahead of Baltimore. Miami's exhausting 27–24 overtime playoff win over Kansas City, which had consumed 82 minutes and 40 seconds, had excited South Florida and was a television highlight for a week all over the country. Amazingly, the only ones who didn't see the spectacle were the Colts. They were on a plane to Cleveland. When they arrived at their hotel, they just missed seeing Garo Yepremian's game-winning 37-yard field goal. "All of a sudden—you're out there for 82 minutes and suddenly it's over," said Nick Buoniconti, Miami's clever middle linebacker. "It's hard for you to realize you've been out there so long."

Buoniconti was hoping that he wouldn't spend a long day against Unitas. After facing him four times, he felt that mystery was the secret to Unitas' game. "His coaching staff might draw up a game plan, but once the game starts I don't think they know any more about what John's going to do than us," said Buoniconti. "I don't think he tells his teammates either. He just goes out and does it. Maybe he doesn't even know himself until the game starts. With Unitas, it's scary. He seems to know what you're going to do before you do."

Unitas did realize the importance of Buoniconti's presence in the Dolphins' defense, which was the strongest in the league against the run. Buoniconti had been snubbed by the NFL 10 years earlier for being too short and too small. "Buoniconti is the key to the Dolphins' defense," said Unitas. "If you block him, then you should be able to run on them."

However, Baltimore's running game was suspect. Five days before the game, Tom Matte had a swollen knee and couldn't do more than jog at practice. Norm Bulaich was also nursing a serious injury, one he sustained against New England in the last game of the season. When trainer Eddie Block, who had used a mile of tape during the year on Bulaich's assorted leg ailments, first saw the injury, he said, "Well, let's hope he'll be back for the Super Bowl." The Colts were already looking that far ahead.

Buoniconti and the rest of the Dolphins players took a long time getting over their win over Kansas City. None of them had ever been in a situation like that before, neither the players nor the coaches. And no one could predict how much the game had physically taken out of them.

"Guys were exhausted on the sidelines," said Buoniconti. "Everyone was getting cramps in his legs, and our center, Bob DeMarco, had cramps in his hands so bad he couldn't hardly snap the ball. Tuesday's practice this week was a tired, ragged thing. We couldn't do much running. Just a lot of game plan stuff, head work."

There was headwork of a different kind awaiting the teams at the kickoff. It involved three principals: Shula who wanted to quiet Rosenbloom, and Unitas who wanted to show Shula. There was also a fourth that Unitas didn't know about. Joe Thomas, Miami's director of scouting, was sitting in the press box studying him. Thomas would arrive in Baltimore six months later and change Unitas' life forever.

The Colts Versus the Dolphins

Unitas couldn't have asked for better weather, and the 4:00 start actually provided him with three extra hours of rest for whatever the 74-degree weather presented. Baltimore's defense rejected Miami's opening drive. Unitas appeared ready for it and got the Colts to the 45-yard line with a 16-yard, third-down pass to McCauley. Surprisingly though, he reverted to the Colts' running game, which only advanced them eight yards on three plays and created a punting situation.

Unitas no sooner got to the sidelines when Griese stirred Unitas' memory of his own past accuracy as a passer. On the second down, Griese delivered a 25-yard dart to Paul Warfield at midfield, and the smooth, long-striding wide receiver outraced both Colts safeties to the goal line. It was a perfectly executed 75-yard play, such as those that had once been so natural to Unitas. Halfway through the quarter, Miami had jumped into a 7–0 lead.

Unitas moved quickly. His first two passes accounted for 41 yards and Baltimore was on the Miami 39 poised to strike. After Don McCauley was stuffed, Unitas called two pass plays. He overthrew McCauley and, under pressure, threw short to Don Nottingham. The Colts were left with a 46-yard field goal attempt, which Jim O'Brien missed.

But Baltimore got the ball right back and Unitas got the Colts moving again. He started the series with a first down that got the Colts to the

Dolphins' 43. When McCauley couldn't get more than three yards, Unitas returned to the air. His two passes, however, were unsuccessful; one was overthrown and the other rejected by cornerback Tim Foley. With five seconds remaining in the first quarter, O'Brien missed again, this time from 48 yards out. After positioning two field-goal attempts, Unitas was wondering what it would take to score a point.

The Baltimore defense stopped Miami's opening series in the second period. Unitas came back strong with one of his signature drives. There was fire in his steel gray eyes, which could have stared down a lion. He took the Colts 71 yards in 13 plays starting from his 19-yard line and unwound the clock for 7:06 minutes only to encounter frustration. On fourth down from the Miami 7, Nottingham got only one of the two yards needed for a crucial first down.

Unitas had been at his youthful best. He had produced four first downs and the only two passes he threw collected 31 of the 72 yards. But strangely, as in the first quarter, he didn't throw any more, which created some doubt. The last six plays were given to the running backs. For someone who loved to throw, the choice of plays seemed odd.

Once again the Colts defense made short work of Miami's attack. In three plays, Unitas had the ball back in his hands with 3:24 left until halftime. It was ample time for Unitas to operate from the Baltimore 41. After he endured a sack, he bounced up with a 20-yard completion to Eddie Hinton. McCauley got four yards and Unitas turned them into a first down with an eight-yard pass to him on the 31-yard line with two minutes lit up on the clock. Unitas set up the pass with a four-yard run by McCauley. However, his next two passes to tight end Tom Mitchell fell harmlessly incomplete. O'Brien was dispatched to convert a 35-yard field goal try, but it was blocked. The Colts left the field disheartened by the missed field goals of a 7–0 struggle in which they had 19 more plays than Miami, yet couldn't score.

The Colts needed another Unitas comeback in the second half like the ones that were his trademark during his NFL career. The defense had performed extremely well, but it was up to the offense to score. Unitas' first opportunity came after the Colts received the second half kickoff. On a third-down play, he hooked up with Hinton for a 20-yard completion for a first down. That was all. Unitas was sacked again and his third-down, nine-yard pass to Hinton left the Colts three yards short of a first down. Baltimore's defense continued its strong play, and after allowing two first downs, succeeded in getting the ball back for the offense.

Unitas had poor field position to work whatever sorcery he had left. His first-down pass to Nottingham fell short, and after McCauley gained four yards, Unitas broke the huddle from the 17. He didn't think twice about going to Hinton, his hot receiver. But Miami cornerback Curtis Johnson played Hinton tight and deflected the ball, which ricocheted into the open arms of Miami safety Dick Anderson. Anderson never stopped running until he had covered 62 yards for a Dolphins touchdown and a 14–0 edge. "My eyes were popping as I ran," Anderson said afterward. The Unitas magic was slowly disappearing.

In the closing minutes of the quarter, Unitas had 4:33 to effect another comeback attempt from the Baltimore 20. He had faced similar challenges dozens of times and prevailed. But this time, he had to see if there was anything left in his once-magnificent arm. Driven by his pride, he dropped back to throw eight times. Like a gladiator, he held his ground, took his hits, and connected on five passes, although one resulted in an uncharacteristic six-yard loss. His last throw was once more to Hinton. This time Jake Scott picked it off as the period ended.

It was Griese who did what Unitas wanted to do as the final-quarter action began. On a third-down play, he rifled a 50-yard pass to Warfield to set up the Dolphins' third touchdown from the 5-yard line. Csonka, Miami's bruising runner, got it all on one run for a 21–0 Miami bulge with only half of a quarter left in the game.

The odds for the older Unitas were insurmountable, yet he wouldn't quit. He threw all six times he took the ball from center and managed to complete half of them to reach the Miami 25 with 5:30 left. However, it ended there on the soft turf of the Orange Bowl. His final pass, intended for McCauley, was intercepted by linebacker Mike Kolen on the 19.

Unitas' durable arm had held up 36 times for the most passes he had thrown in a long time. He gained 224 yards with his 20 completions, but with the three interceptions, he failed to get even one touchdown. The Colts had not been held scoreless for seven seasons. Baltimore had dominated offensively by executing 68 plays to Miami's 45 but still couldn't even get a field goal. Amazingly, Griese threw only eight passes and completed four of them. But the two to Warfield were game breakers. They contained 125 of Griese's 158 passing yards. Unitas had maintained that Griese was a more accurate passer than Namath, and Griese showed it with those two throws—the kind Unitas used to make with surety.

The defeat galled Unitas. He was dispirited because he had not accounted for a single point. He had quarterbacked more wins than anyone in pro football, and yet he came up empty. He was asked about what many observers considered to be a key play in the second quarter. With his team trailing 7–0, Baltimore had reached the Miami 9-yard line, needing two yards for a first down. Instead of kicking a field goal on fourth down, the Colts decided to run for it. Buoniconti read the formation, charged into a gap, and stuffed Don Nottingham after he picked up a yard. Unitas would have preferred to throw the ball instead. He was asked about not kicking the easy field goal.

"It was not my decision," he quickly answered and changed what could have been a volatile debate. "If you want to run on the Miami Dolphins, you have to be able to block Buoniconti. Today we couldn't block him. He had an excellent game. Because of him we just couldn't run the ball. Our game plan was to run the football at them but we couldn't do it. Maybe we waited too long to start passing. Maybe we should have come out throwing right away."

That had always been Unitas' game. He had no idea it would be taken away from him the following season.

13

The Last Year in Baltimore

T HE 1971 SEASON HAD ENDED ON AN ACRID NOTE FOR UNITAS, but things got worse for him when the 1972 campaign dawned. The aging warrior had been blindsided countless times on the playing field, but the biggest hit he was to take happened off the gridiron. In an unprecedented, historic transaction, Robert Irsay purchased the Los Angeles Rams from the Dan Reeves estate and immediately transferred ownership to Carroll Rosenbloom in exchange for the Baltimore Colts, which raised eyebrows at training camp. The opportunistic Rosenbloom and the affable Commissioner Pete Rozelle were close friends, and if Rosenbloom needed a favor, he got a big one.

Changes in the Colts Camp

Unitas lost a friend in the shrewd Rosenbloom, who got the best of Irsay, a chunky 49-year-old millionaire. Rosenbloom winked after the deal, and why not? In the biggest heist in sports history, Rosenbloom acquired a heavily populated metropolis, which was the nation's number two television market. Rosenbloom's purchase immediately went up in value by at least 50 percent.

Nobody in training camp knew who Irsay was or had even heard his name. Amazingly, he didn't appear before the coaches and players until the third week of camp. He brought Joe Thomas, his new general manager with him. Thomas was at least known to some extent because he had some football background as a defensive line coach with the Colts before Unitas had arrived. Since that time, Thomas, a keen judge of player talent, had built the Minnesota Vikings and most recently the Miami Dolphins into Super Bowl contenders with good drafts and good trades. Thomas made his presence known by announcing that he intended to do things his way with the Colts. Irsay was going around calling everyone he met "Tiger" because he couldn't remember names. It was a strange new look to Baltimore's management.

Thomas' credo was that he built teams in two areas: the draft and trades. He also said that he built from within, using younger players who would be around to serve longer and to constitute the heart of the club. If there were any problem areas, he would rectify them by trades. When he first joined the expansion Vikings as their director of player personnel, he was the first employee on the payroll, which was the same distinction he had with the expansion Dolphins. "I honestly thought I'd be the Vikings' first head coach," he said. Thomas made it clear that the future of the Colts was in younger players—and he convinced Irsay of the same. That theory certainly didn't bode well for the popular Unitas.

An Aging Hero

The quarterback without compare was 39 years old. He had passed a football for nearly 23 miles during his career with the Colts, a tribute to his abilities at the position. His confidence had always been supreme. "There is a great difference between confidence and conceit," was how he looked at it. Yet all great quarterbacks are egotists. Although Unitas was never one to flaunt it, in his quiet way, he remained sure of himself once he put his head down in a huddle with 10 others. Four years prior, when Morrall replaced the sore-armed Unitas and led the Colts to the NFL title, Unitas' ego also got sore: "I'm still the quarterback of this club," he said. Then when he came back from a torn Achilles tendon less than two years prior, he was told that he could be the comeback story of the year. "Comeback, hell," he said. "I ain't been away."

But Unitas soon would be gone—only he didn't expect it. It almost happened during a preseason game against Kansas City. He was unceremoniously driven to the ground on his head by Chiefs defensive tackle Wilbur Young on the second play from scrimmage, and Unitas had to be helped off the field. "For a moment I had no feeling in my arms, but I do have a stiff neck and I'll be all right in a couple of days," Unitas assured everyone.

That contest turned out to be a big break for 25-year-old Marty Domres, who replaced Unitas in his first game as a Colt and engineered a 23–17 victory. Although he didn't do anything spectacular, he showed poise for someone who hadn't played much. It didn't matter that he matriculated from Columbia, an Ivy League school where academia and not football was the pinnacle. He was young, which met with Thomas' approval.

Unitas did open the season as the starter, but without success. Playing with a number of his regulars sidelined, Unitas couldn't operate effectively and lost 10–3 to St. Louis. However, the following week against the Jets, Unitas was spectacular. He dueled with Joe Namath. When the almost four-hour shootout ended, Namath won. But not before the two combatants put on an aerial show that made it seem like the Fourth of July in September. Unitas completed 26 of 45 passes for 376 yards and two touchdowns, with no interceptions in the 44–34 loss. Namath was better. He threw for 496 yards and six touchdowns. Namath and Unitas set an NFL combined record for passing yardage: 872. It was Unitas' kind of game, and even he had to admire the six touchdown aerials Namath fired. He always believed in the touchdown pass and would take it over any statistic. "I'd rather go for six any time," he said.

The Changing of the Guard

When the Colts lost two of their next three games, the impetuous Thomas wanted Unitas benched. He was looking to the future with his youth movement and ordered McCafferty to start Domres. "Big Mac" McCafferty refused, and within 24 hours he was fired and replaced by a subordinate, John Sandusky, the team's line coach. There would be no Unitas-Namath duel six days later in New York, although Jets fans were anxiously awaiting a repeat of their exciting first meeting.

Unitas just shrugged his shoulders at the unsavory benching. "Thomas phoned me Monday the day of the change," said Unitas. "He told me, 'We're making a coaching change and we're going with younger fellows. That means that Marty will be playing more. But I don't want you take this as a slap in the face.' It seemed kind of funny. But what the hell is it but a slap in the face? There's no reason for me to be in this position. I've been playing well. That's the hard thing to swallow. And now I'm not even in their plans for the rest of the season."

Unitas was having a good season. And he was doing so with some of his best runners and receivers unavailable. His statistics showed that he completed 56 percent of his passes for 1,044 yards and three touchdowns. But Baltimore lost four of its first five games and Thomas decided to give up on the present. He was an empire builder before he came to the city, and he wanted to move into the future overnight with Unitas losing his throne to an untested newcomer.

At least Thomas had the courtesy to inform Unitas of the change before he heard it from anyone else. That would have been execrable to someone of Unitas' stature. He was owed that much. Thomas had first informed him that he had made a change in the coaching staff, which meant that Unitas would be playing for his fourth coach in Baltimore. Ewbank, Shula, and now McCafferty were all gone, and Unitas was the only one left. He had to wonder for how long.

The media quite naturally saw through the situation. McCafferty was fired because he wouldn't play Domres ahead of Unitas. So Thomas turned to Sandusky, who would acquiesce to Thomas' desire to start the younger quarterback.

Sandusky was asked if the decision to bench Unitas was his or Thomas', and he took the fifth like a mafioso at a grand jury hearing. "I have no comment on that," said Sandusky. "I sat down and talked with John about it. We talked about the McCafferty situation too, and he showed no bitterness. He didn't show his feelings, which is typical of John Unitas."

But Unitas thought about things and later approached Sandusky. He wanted a complete clarification of his status. He had assumed that Domres would start against the Jets as an experiment because he had completed only one game during his three previous years in San Diego. Sandusky informed him otherwise. Unitas wasn't going to be part of it. His time was over.

"I asked him about it, and he told me that Marty was going to play for the rest of the season, that he wasn't going to pull him out if he had a bad series, that barring injury, Marty was the quarterback," said Unitas. "The thing that bothers me is that I want to play another season after this and then probably retire."

The stigma that retirement represented had hung over Unitas for the past two years like a murky cloud, and it was a rare moment when he acknowledged it. He intended to play another year and hoped that he had another season left in him. He faced difficulty with the zone defense that was now in vogue, and said of it, "It should be outlawed because it has taken away the big play." So Unitas, whose throws once went through defenders, had to try to skirt by them. His once remarkable consistency was under scrutiny week after week and revealed good games and poor ones. No one had to tell Unitas how he played. He knew that better than anybody. "I know I can't throw the ball as hard as I used to," he confessed. "It doesn't get there as fast as it once did. But my arm isn't that weak. I can still throw the long pass and I can still read defenses and coverages better than anyone."

But even before the 1972 season began, Alex Karras, the outspoken ex-defensive tackle of the Detroit Lions, said that Unitas should retire. It was one player talking about another player, someone from the trenches and not a portly coach who watched from the sidelines and hadn't played the game in a decade or two. Karras spared no negative opinion in his assessment of Unitas, but he also praised him. "Unitas to me is probably the greatest quarterback to play the game of football and why he keeps trying to go on like he's going baffles me," said Karras. "He just belittles himself. He's not an average quarterback anymore. In his prime, there was nothing like Unitas. He was blessed not only with a gifted arm but had great ability to pick a team apart immediately and find a flaw in the defense. He just can't throw like he used to."

By November, a fading season in which the Colts only won five games, rumors were rampant in Baltimore that Unitas would be traded. The Colts were 1–6 at the time, and losing gives birth to rumors. The Los Angeles Rams, who were in a title drive out west, were desperate for quarterback help and considered acquiring Unitas. Like Unitas two years ago, Rams quarterback Roman Gabriel had a lame arm, which was alarmingly evident during a game against the Oakland Raiders. He completed only 3 of 16 passes and had 4 interceptions. Because Rosenbloom, an old friend who owned the Rams, and Rams general manager Don Klosterman knew Unitas from Baltimore, there was some degree of validity to the rumors. However, Klosterman was quick to squelch the stories, insisting that there was no way for him to make a deal for a frontline quarterback at waiver time. Besides, Klosterman asserted that he was satisfied with Gabriel and his backup, Pete Beathard. There were reports, too, that Washington, three thousand miles closer to Baltimore, was interested in Unitas. Through it all, Thomas was adamant that Unitas would remain with the Colts.

"How could I make a deal?" Thomas said. "Nobody has talked to me about a deal. You get this all the time on a player of Unitas' stature, except the one person who can trade him—me. I want Johnny Unitas here the rest of the year. After that, we'll sit down and talk. I want it understood that there are no untouchables on the team, and as long as I'm the general manager, there won't be."

Unitas' frustration over his undecided future boiled over in the locker room after the Colts won their second game of the season over the New England Patriots in a Monday night game in Boston in which Unitas didn't play one down. He kicked his jersey and vented in front of Hubert Mizell of the Associated Press: "There's no use in staying around here, not the way they're treating me. There's nothing I can do about it either. It was their decision not to play me anymore."

The next day, Unitas said he didn't remember saying anything like that. He acknowledged kicking the jersey, but pointed out that he did so toward the pile of dirty clothes and that it wasn't unusual to do so.

Neither Sandusky nor Thomas could comment on the incident or Unitas' remarks because they claimed they didn't hear him say it. But Thomas, who had a hot temper, was caustic nevertheless in his remarks and added to the fire. "I found an aging, rotting ballclub when I came here," he said. "It began skidding at the end of last season. I had to look to the future, and the quarterback who's almost 40 doesn't have a lot of future. It's not popular to bench an immortal like John Unitas, but you can't afford a team to dry up on you. Baltimore was a great team, the Super Bowl champions only two years ago, but they can forget that era, it's gone. You can't keep going with a quarterback who'll be 40 years old next May."

The End of an Era

The end for Unitas was hard for his legions of fans to take, but Unitas had said he didn't want to play any more. "Why should I?" he had asked. After replacing the injured George Shaw in 1956, the indestructible Unitas went on to complete more passes for more yardage and more touchdowns than any other player in NFL history. But Unitas always maintained that he had no regard for records, and he once became angry when a game was stopped in Minnesota so that he could be presented with the ball for setting another mark. "This is a game of winning, not records," he said. "What good is a record if you don't win?" When it was brought to his attention that now he would not be able to get 299 more yards to reach a career total of forty thousand, he snapped, "What he hell do I need forty thousand yards for?"

The Colts could have done things differently with Johnny Unitas; management could have been kind. They could have let him finish his final season with the Baltimore Colts with the No. 19 on his back visible on the playing field. They didn't have to shove him aside. He deserved better. Much better. Unitas was the symbol of Baltimore. The truly great ones don't accept the aging process gracefully in any sport. The San Francisco Giants clumsily had done the same thing to the great Willie Mays, and two months later it happened to Unitas. Like Mays, Unitas was an athlete without compare.

Unitas did get to play in his final home game. The Colts were playing an inept Buffalo team. Near the close of the fourth quarter, Domres pulled up grabbing his thigh after he ran 15 yards to score Baltimore's fourth touchdown for a 28–0 bulge. After the Bills scored their only touchdown, Sandusky sent in Unitas. The faithful cheered just as a yellow single-engine plane flew over the stadium trailing a banner that read, "Unitas We Stand." And the great quarterback seized the moment. Almost on cue, he promptly threw a 23-yard pass to Hinton, who raced the rest of the way for a 63-yard touchdown. No one who was there that December day will ever forget the 287th touchdown pass of Unitas' glorious career.

Unitas carried that memory with him into the final game of the season in Miami. He stood on the sidelines watching and waiting for the game to end, and with its conclusion, his career with the Colts would come to its close. Then Domres got hurt again near the conclusion of the first half. Who but Unitas would replace him? Unitas came onto the field, and the Dolphins fans stood to applaud him just like they had during the pregame warm-ups. He still was a glimmer man. It didn't matter that the second pass Unitas threw of the four plays he called was intercepted. They saw him in action and not as a lonely figure on the sidelines.

In the dressing room, Unitas wasn't as emotional as the Dolphins fans, but he acknowledged them: "I was very nice to them. I threw the interception," said Unitas. "But that was very nice of them."

In many ways, Unitas was glad that the season had ended. Football had not been fun for him in 1972. "It was the worst year I've gone through in professional football," he said. "I haven't made up my mind yet about next year."

Three weeks later he was no longer a Colt.

14

Exile

SIX MONTHS AFTER UNITAS WAS TRADED TO A TEAM ACROSS THE country from his former home in Baltimore, he was still hurt and angry with the Colts' general manager, Joe Thomas. Unitas and Thomas had met before the trade, and in response to Unitas' wish to play for an additional two years as a Colt, Thomas had said that his quarterback had three options in the National Football League: play for the Colts at a renegotiated salary, be traded, or retire. He said, "We are willing to listen to any trade offers for [Unitas]. If the right thing comes along for us and for him, the chances are fifty-fifty he'll be traded."

Unitas' response was bitter: "They've embarrassed me and I would never play for Baltimore again. I started the season well and I finished high in passing in our division, but Thomas made a bad mistake in replacing me with Marty Domres, an inexperienced quarterback, too early in the season. I don't think the Colts handled it well at all. They could have broken Domres in gradually. But instead, they put their whole season on him and virtually said, 'We're throwing in the towel [on Unitas].'

"The thing is, the whole thing could have been avoided. When I was benched, we still had a shot at winning the division or at least making the playoffs. What they should have done was call me in, tell me what they hoped to do, and let me play until they had no chance of making the playoffs. Then I would have said, 'Fine, if that's what you want to do, I'll sit down and work with the young quarterback and then I'll retire.'"

Thomas did not respond to Unitas' acerbic remarks. Instead, within five days, he had made the deal with San Diego—without consulting Unitas. Unitas learned of the trade when he was awakened by a reporter: "Well, that's news to me," he said. "I imagine [Thomas] wanted to get me as far away as possible."

After the deal had been made, Thomas refused to discuss it. All he would say was, "You can fry an egg too long. The deal is done, and that's it."

In his one request of the Colts' management, Unitas asked to be traded to a winning team close to home. He would have preferred Philadelphia or New York, or maybe to finish his career in Pittsburgh. Instead, he was sent to the San Diego Chargers, who were 4–9–1 in 1972 with their quarterback John Hadl, who wanted out of San Diego.

The Chargers were looked upon as the Rouge's Regiment of the NFL, with such controversial players as Tim Rossovich, Duane Thomas, Deacon Jones, and Mike Garrett, among others. They weren't Unitas' kind of teammates: "Just because I've been traded doesn't mean I'm going there. I don't know if it's legal," he said.

Unitas particularly minded the loss of his 10-year contract with Baltimore, which had guaranteed him $300,000 and a front-office job when he retired from playing. He would be making double his Colts salary by playing for two years for the Chargers, however.

Johnny Unitas Day

To bid their hero farewell, Baltimore fans arranged to honor Unitas at Pimlico Race Track on May 19, 1973, on "Johnny Unitas Day." The Preakness was run that day, and a race was named for the beloved quarterback: the John Unitas Purse. In a ceremony honoring Unitas, his jersey No. 19 was retired and then presented to Dick Gallagher, the director of the Pro Football Hall of Fame. Five years later, Unitas was honored by an induction to the Hall himself. All proceeds from the event went to charity.

Commissioner Pete Rozelle recognized the occasion and sent a telegram to Unitas. The affable commissioner was witty as usual in his message:

> Except for causing half the male youngsters in the country to adopt your posture, I can think of no one who contributed more positively to the growth of professional football with your remarkable performances since 1956. Best personal wishes and I regret I cannot join those honoring you in person today.
> Regards,
> Pete Rozelle

The Baltimore fans continued to honor their idol and later named a street after him. Appropriately, it was dubbed Unitas Pass.

The San Diego Chargers' flamboyant owner, Gene Klein, was a big admirer of Unitas. He paid Baltimore $150,000 for the right to negotiate with him, which was unheard of back in 1973. Klein also gave Unitas a two-year contract worth $500,000, which was more than even NFL commissioner Pete Rozelle made. Nobody in football made that much money—especially at an age when the average player was long retired. That's how much Klein worshipped Unitas. In Klein's eyes, Unitas was royalty; he treated him as such and paid him accordingly.

New Environs

But Unitas, a blue-collar guy from Pittsburgh and Baltimore, felt out of place in tropical San Diego. He was a stranger in a town of surfboarders and beach bums on the other side of the continent without friends. The lush, verdant grass was too plush. The Pacific Ocean was too blue and too big, nothing like the tranquil waters of Chesapeake Bay. The Pacific waves were hostile, large, and noisy, which only surfers found rewarding. Unitas just didn't look right in a helmet adorned by lightning bolts; he was out of character playing for an original AFL team with glitzy uniforms. And San Diego blue wasn't Baltimore blue.

He had played for 17 years in the enchanted glen of Memorial Stadium, with all the crazy fans that caused it to be known as "the world's largest outdoor insane asylum." He was used to the summer rains and the winter cold. San Diego, with its palm trees, was a foreign land. People knew about him in San Francisco and up the road in Los Angeles because he had played there. In San Diego, he was only a name from the past from another league. Yet no other player of his time had performed miracles so casually, and the Chargers brain trust was gambling that he had a few more left.

The crewcut was out of place now and so were his high-top shoes. But he wanted to play, and San Diego gave him the chance; for that he was grateful. But the end was near and Unitas had to suspect as much. His body had absorbed a tremendous amount of punishment over the years, but he kept pushing himself, asking his body to give him one more year.

Unitas asked for no favors, no special treatment when he reported to the Chargers' training camp in its picturesque setting in Irvine. He participated in the two-a-day drills with all the rest of the players, who were new to him. He ran with them more than he had ever done in Baltimore, and he did so in his trademark high-top shoes, the black ones, just like Sammy Baugh wore in another era. The running was a challenge to Unitas' 40-year-old legs. After 10 days of double practices, Unitas' knees ached, but he never asked out. "They do a lot more running here to get in shape than we did in Baltimore, and I've paid a price for it," was all that he would say while icing his knees one day after practice. "All of that pounding has made my right knee sore. A couple days ago, because I was favoring the knee, I pulled a muscle. The hurts take longer to go away."

But he wanted to play. He put his 40-year-old body through its most vigorous training camp in 17 years. The sandlots in Pittsburgh, where it all began, were a distant memory now. Unitas was fighting for his football life 20 years after he conquered the hard dirt, the rocks, and the broken glass on that sandlot field. Only now he was proving that he could play on the manicured fields of professional football. Unitas could never rest on his achievements, even though as recently as the previous year he had had one of his better seasons, finishing as the number four quarterback in the AFC passing statistics—even while failing to start the last nine games.

"People don't even ask what have you done for us lately," said Unitas. "They ask what have you done for us five minutes from now." To regain respect, Unitas would have to replicate his own greatness.

But it wouldn't be easy. Unitas did not mesh well with his new teammates. One day after practice, some of the players were in a closed room and Unitas knocked on the door. He had heard some noise, but his knock created deathly silence. Finally, a player opened the door. "Do you have a beer?" asked Unitas. The players continued shooting the breeze, just innocuous football chatter, then Unitas saw something strange. Unitas remembered, "One guy lit up a cigarette, and all of a sudden the cigarette starts coming down the line. 'You just got one cigarette? Oh, excuse me guys, I'm in the wrong room.'"

Unitas began to wonder if San Diego was his purgatory. It wasn't what he had expected, from the organization itself to the players. Unitas had too much pride for such an environment. "That was a very poor football team," said Unitas. "Poor organization. Terrible. Some of 'em were smoking dope or taking pills. They had all the malcontents and that's what I walked into. I mean, it was really spooky. I had never been involved or confronted or seen anyone take pills or smoke grass, and those guys used to do it going into the dressing room. There were a lot of good guys there, but some people were completely obliterated all the time."

Unfailingly Determined

Yet he was as driven as ever before. He could have remained in Baltimore, in his home, drunk an occasional beer with some of the guys at the Golden Arm, and become wealthier with the number of business enterprises he had going. But first Unitas had to have one more year of football, even though he had nothing left to prove in his Hall-of-Fame career. "There's only one reason he's decided to play," said a member of the Colts' organization who requested anonymity. "He's got to prove them [Thomas and Irsay] wrong. It's almost an obsession with him. His pride is at stake. And if you know Unitas, you realize that's more important to him than money or records or anything."

Chargers head coach Harland Svare was convinced that Unitas had enough left in him to help turn around the Chargers after three years of losing. He had marveled at Unitas when, as a Giants linebacker, he had faced him twice in the 1958 and 1959 championship games. Svare didn't forget that Unitas beat him with a key third-down pass. Svare had been a teammate of quarterback Charlie Conerly's, who played at age 42, so that coach concluded that Unitas had another year or two of magic in his right arm.

"What we're looking at is the best in the business," said Svare. "The best quarterback that's ever been. I honestly think the game is more suited to him than 10 years ago. He doesn't pretend his arm is what it used to be. But he can make up for it in a lot of little ways. He's a strong leader and will keep the team together. Unitas is very much in control of the game."

Getting Settled

Svare treated Unitas regally by giving him a private room from day one in training camp, something he never got with the Colts. It was the residence advisor's room at Cal Irvine, with a bedroom and small anteroom in front. Svare couldn't do enough for the quarterback he worshipped. When the rigors of camp caused Unitas back spasms, Svare ordered a waterbed for Unitas' room to help ease his quarterback's pain. Unitas was grateful. "I didn't ask for this room," Unitas made it known. "I guess they figure a 40-year-old needs a lot of sleep."

At his age, calling plays was Unitas' strength. He'd done it for so long and no one was better. He didn't delude himself into thinking that he could carry a team on the strength of his arm alone—which he felt was the best it had been in years. San Diego's offensive philosophy was a good fit for him, even though it wasn't his preference. The Chargers built their offense on the run. In many ways, that was a relief to Unitas. He had an arthritic knee and an arm that had more mileage than a used Goodyear tire. If Unitas was going to win for Svare, it would be with his guile and wisdom of 17 years. Unitas was comfortable with Svare's approach.

"I know they like to run the ball here," said Unitas. "I knew when I came I wouldn't be throwing the ball as much as I did in Baltimore. No matter what you do, it's usually dictated by the way the defense plays you. In Baltimore we passed first and ran second. Here, if the run goes well, we'll stay with it."

He was still thinking like a passer, but instead of going long, he would be throwing to his running back more. Unitas understood: "When you've been around as long as I have, you learn to do other things with your skills. I can still throw long, but that's not the idea of effective and winning football." He began to sound like a coach because of his years of experience. His intangibles were perhaps stronger now than his physical or mechanical abilities and he would need everything he had left to play another season.

He was in a new environment, and although football was always football to him and came so naturally, he still had to learn a new playbook and terminology. On the practice field one day in his red shirt, white shorts, and black high-tops, Unitas barked the signals: "Yellow 25. Yellow 25." No one moved. His running backs looked at him at about the same time his linemen turned around. Then, almost in unison, everyone burst out in laughter. Unitas had called a Colts formation. "This was a complete change for me," he said. "The holes are the same, but the number of backs are different."

With an entirely new group of receivers, Unitas' prime mission was establishing a rapport with them. It wasn't like the golden years he had with Raymond Berry when they worked every day after practice on patterns and timing to hone their precision. No one came to Unitas and volunteered to do extra work. He had to ask them and not always with positive results. Unitas was still old school, one who had to work to achieve greatness. "I have to get my timing down with the receivers," he kept saying. He needed the extra time to do it because he wasn't getting enough reps in practice. The passing drills were limited to only 20 minutes, and Unitas and the two other quarterbacks, rookie Dan Fouts and Wayne Clark, had to split the time. "I was averaging throwing seven to ten passes a day," said Unitas. "You don't get much work that way."

Unitas missed the old camaraderie of his former teammates; he didn't have that anymore, not in San Diego. Unitas said, "There's nothing I can do about it so I'll just learn to accept it. I just got to realize it's different out here."

Unitas started slowly in camp with his bum knee and sore back. Yet it pained him more that he wasn't throwing enough—hardly at all, in fact. A great many of his passes that were incomplete fell short. There weren't long ones either because the Chargers' offensive philosophy had shrunk the passing game to less than 40 yards.

But, two weeks into camp, Unitas looked like his old self, with strong, sharp passes that had Bob Schnelker, the old Giants tight end who was in charge of the offense, smiling: "He was really throwing them in there today, wasn't he? Some of the receivers were so surprised he almost knocked them over a couple of times."

Unitas had some unfinished business with the Colts. In mid-August he filed a $725,000 lawsuit, charging them with a "malicious breach" of his 10-year contract with them. The suit alleged that starting from October 15, 1972, Thomas had "engaged in a course of conduct which was designed to and did, in fact, embarrass and humiliate Unitas and otherwise make it impossible for Unitas to carry out his obligation under the agreement." The suit also claimed that "Thomas directed the coach not to allow Unitas to play football except in an emergency or as a substitute player although Unitas was in excellent physical condition and possessed sufficient skill and capacity to play on a regular basis." Unitas was seeking $225,000 in compensatory damages and $500,000 in punitive damages. Finally, it was charged that the owner of the Colts "no longer wanted Unitas to be associated with the team and caused Unitas to be traded to the San Diego Chargers without prior consultation or notification."

Unitas' legal battles were far away in Baltimore. On the field in San Diego, Unitas worked hard to do what he did best, and slowly it all came back to him. Although the Chargers dropped their first three preseason games to the Giants, Cardinals, and 49ers, Unitas put up good stats in the five quarters he played. He was 17 of 29, had a 69 percent completion percentage, threw for 218 yards, and had a touchdown and three interceptions. Unitas was still adjusting to moving the ball by running and not passing, which he still preferred.

His tender knee, which was still puffy and discolored, nevertheless felt better. Yet Unitas insisted that like his tender arm in 1968, the knee needed only rest. Unitas didn't have time to sit. The regular season was three weeks away and he wasn't where he wanted to be with the new offense. There was even some concern about his physical condition. Unitas just shrugged. "My arm feels fine, but my right knee is giving me some trouble. It's been sore. I don't know if my legs will hold up through this year," he said.

The big test for Unitas and his value to the Chargers for the 1973 season came in the team's fifth exhibition game against the Rams in Los Angeles. Unitas was scheduled to play for the entire game. "My arm is the best it's been in four years," Unitas assured the coaches. But his back was causing him discomfort. He endured spasms one day in practice and painfully left the field. He attributed the condition to favoring his right knee. Svare was asked what he would do if Unitas' back went into spasms on September 16 when the Chargers were to open the season against the Redskins in Washington. "Punt," he joked. That's when Svare ordered the waterbed to be placed in Unitas' room.

Playing with Heart

Unitas knew how much the Rams game meant. He had played in the Coliseum before, and the Rams were no strangers to him. So Unitas faced their "Fearsome Four" defense and earned its respect. Despite a 30–17 defeat, Unitas nevertheless left the Chargers breathless with one of his efficacious performances that rekindled memories for Svare, who saw the same Unitas of the 1958 overtime thriller. In the dwindling minutes of the second quarter, Unitas took the Chargers 87 yards for a touchdown in a brilliant one minute and eight seconds of artistry, passing on every down and laughing at the clock. Then, in the final minutes of the game, he almost duplicated his masterpiece—only to see Dave Williams fumble after catching his pass on the Rams' 14-yard line.

It was showtime for Unitas and he unveiled every pass in his repertoire: short and long, hard and soft. His first touchdown was drilled to Williams, cutting across the middle for a 28-yard reception. The other came out of a massive rush from the Rams defense. Unitas recognized it, calculatingly moved up into the collapsing pocket, and found running back Bob Thomas for a 44-yard touchdown. In all, he threw 31 times and completed 18 for 286 yards. Sadly, five of his passes were dropped. For one night, Unitas lit up the Los Angeles sky. Unitas felt young again and Svare couldn't have been happier.

"He knows more about football than anyone I've ever met," said Svare. "I've been associated with some great quarterbacks as a player and a coach—Charlie Conerly, Y. A. Tittle, a lot of them. But no one could touch him. Aside from everything else, the arm, the head, the leadership, he's the smoothest ball handler I ever saw. He never makes a mistake."

In the final exhibition game against the Minnesota Vikings, fans were looking for a sign of hope from last year's losing season. Unitas gave it to them. He was 16 of 24 for 231 yards and had two touchdowns and a ringing endorsement of his work in the preseason. He completed more than 60 percent of his passes, but there was one unexpected call in the Viking game that further thrilled Svare. Needing a yard on fourth down on the Minnesota 30 for a first down, Unitas disdained calling an automatic run. He had noticed that the Viking cornerback, Nate Wright, had come up quick on wide receiver Jerry LeVias on an earlier play. Unitas instructed LeVias to go deep, but he just missed him in the end zone by an arm's length. Svare and the crowd appreciated the call nonetheless. "It was as unexpected as anyone could imagine," said Svare.

Still, the critics weren't convinced. Some scouts claimed he couldn't throw passes with any strength anymore. Others felt that he wouldn't hold up for an entire season without his back, legs, or arm giving out. But Unitas showed his grit when he threw his body at cornerback Bobby Bryant, when Bryant came up to the line of scrimmage to tackle running back Mike Garrett. At 40, there was no fear in him. "They say he doesn't have the arm, but I've never seen him better than the last two weeks," said Unitas' teammate Deacon Jones, who had chased after Unitas when Jones played defensive end for the Rams. Even Unitas, who was never one for statistics, had to feel satisfied with what he had accomplished. He was Cervantes' Don Quixote in a helmet, with the odds, like the windmills, stacked against him.

Unfortunately, at the regular season opener a week later in Washington, where family, friends, and fans came to see Unitas' debut as a Charger, the windmills were too high. In the worst defeat of his professional life, Unitas was embarrassed by a 38–0 Redskins massacre. His offensive line betrayed him the entire game. It frustrated Unitas so much that he screamed at them: "Dammit, I have to have more protection than this!"

Unitas received more help in the next game as the Chargers had an easy time with Buffalo, 34–7. However, the Chargers couldn't extend their momentum and dropped a tough 20–13 game to Cincinnati the following week. The Chargers, with a 1–2 record, next headed to Pittsburgh, Unitas' hometown, where he had never played a game in all his years with Baltimore. No one had to tell the players how much the game meant to Unitas. Not only did they have to win, but Unitas had to look good doing so. It was only the second time that Unitas had actually appeared in Pittsburgh. He had been there in 1968, but Earl Morrall started as the Colts' quarterback while Unitas rested an ailing right arm on the sidelines and hardly played at all that season. Now he would start and the game was that much more meaningful to him.

Yet neither team expected the result: it was Washington all over again—only worse. After three quarters Unitas was benched, his pride singed by a 35–0 whipping. The rookie, Dan Fouts, finished up for him and looked sharp with 11 pass completions in the fourth quarter that led to three touchdowns in the 38–21 loss. After four games, Unitas wasn't the starter any more, just as he had ceased to be after five games during the 1972 season with Baltimore. The team that was supposed to be built around Unitas had undermined him with a slumping offensive line that had been the strongest single unit of the team the previous year. Unitas couldn't control the offense the way Svare expected. He didn't always have the blocking. Or the same two running backs in the backfield for more than one game at a time. Or the timing with his receivers wasn't there. Not only had Unitas thrown seven interceptions, but he had been sacked 22 times! Even the younger, bigger Fouts would have crumpled from the physical onslaught.

A couple of weeks later, as he watched Fouts from the sidelines, Unitas never doubted his ability: "I could never figure out why they traded for me in the first place," he said. "My legs are a little sore, but I can still play."

But could he? Obviously the Chargers didn't think so. It was Fouts' season after four games—the same number as when Unitas took over for George Shaw during Unitas' rookie season with the Colts in 1956. Unitas got another chance against Kansas City, but he came up empty in the 19–0 loss and walked off the field with a sore shoulder. The talk that quickly followed was that it might have been the last of Johnny Unitas. One week later, in the first week of November, pro football's most renowned player was placed on the inactive list. A disappointed Svare stepped down as head coach of a 1–6–1 team and sat in his office as a full-time manager.

That same week the Chargers tried to trade Unitas to his hometown Steelers. Terry Bradshaw had suffered a partial separation of his throwing shoulder in a game against Cincinnati and was expected to be sidelined for four to six weeks. His replacement, Terry Hanratty, left the same game with sore ribs on his right side and couldn't raise his arm over his head when he took off his uniform to get dressed. It would have been poetic justice if the team that had rejected him in 1955 endorsed his return 18 years later, but Pittsburgh still didn't want him.

Unitas had played the 1973 season out of pride rather than for money. He became a victim of a team that played poorly in a 2–11–1 season. Unitas was a stranger to such futility. Unitas himself, a stranger to San Diego, returned to Baltimore a disillusioned quarterback. "Just having the opportunity to play professional football has been everything to me," said Unitas.

He sounded like he wasn't going to play anymore.

15

The Decision

S AN DIEGO WAS A CULTURAL CONVERSION FOR UNITAS, AND HE WAS not really ready for it. He felt that the players weren't dedicated enough, not working and sacrificing the way he always did. There weren't any more hour-long sessions after practice, and he didn't have the patience for anyone who didn't make an effort. "They don't have the dedication and the concentration that they should have," said Unitas. "This has probably made it more miserable than anything else, knowing that you are playing with guys who probably have quite a bit of ability but they just don't give a damn." Unitas had quite a bit of serious thinking to do about the 1974 season.

Wishes and Reality

Time was Unitas' enemy as he approached his 41st birthday in May. Did he want to play one more season? Would he be physically able to play? The thought filled his mind: "The lucky ones are the ones who quit on their own, who never let themselves be talked into one last training camp too many." He said, "If I wish for anything out of football more than I've had, is that I will know enough to quit that way."

Unitas had to know what the statistics told him about the 1973 season. He threw for his lowest total of yards (except for his injury-plagued

1968 season), 471, in completing only 44 percent of his passes. There were only three touchdowns and seven interceptions—inferior numbers in any quarterback's dossier, but especially debasing for Unitas. He couldn't care less about records, however; what he needed now was another healthy year because he wanted to play. But was he still able? He made a trip to San Diego two weeks after his birthday to find out. The Chargers had a new coach, Tommy Prothro, who did a good job at UCLA. Prothro was the team's third coach in a year, after the short-lived Svare and his replacement Ron Waller, which meant that Unitas had to learn another new system. In a talkative mood with Jack Murphy, the sports editor of the *San Diego Union,* Unitas shared the future of the ball club as he saw it.

"I don't have the slightest idea whether the team will be improved," said Unitas. "I know they brought in a new coach and that means they'll be putting in a whole new system. It's going to take them a year or two to get the system down pat. They've got to be thinking three, four, five years ahead rather than worrying about this year. I don't think they can be worrying about winning a championship or division title in this particular season. But I've told them I will do whatever they want. I'll try to help. If they want me to play, I'll be more than happy to do that. I have a contract to fulfill and I will fill it under what obligations the contract specifies.

"You know, it's not just me. You've got to take into consideration the whole football team. I'm a little bit concerned about myself. You have to have some people to work with, people who want to win. I really don't know what they're expecting. The only thing I can tell them is that I'll come to camp in shape and whatever they want me to do after that is entirely up to them.

"Basically, I'm a competitive-type individual. I like the competition. I love the game. I enjoy playing. The thing that keeps you wanting to stay in the game is that this is a job you do well and enjoy doing it. The game is different than it was five or six years ago and it gets to where you don't know which end is up, what the hell their thinking is. The guys just don't have the dedication I would like them to have. You can't get them to do the things they should be doing. They don't seem to care whether they play football or not, as long as they make the team and get their checks. It's the general attitude around the league and that's the thing that irks me more than anything else. The camaraderie you get with the players, coaches, and sometimes owners is probably something you couldn't find in business. In my earlier years in Baltimore we had such a close unit."

His Way

Unitas had a contract, certainly his last, to fulfill, and he intended to do so. It was a commitment in his eyes. Yet it would have been more poetic if he could have finished his career in Baltimore, where he started it. He would have been a Colt for 19 years, which, significantly, would have matched his jersey number. After all those golden years in which Unitas achieved glory as the greatest quarterback on the planet, it all fell apart after a disappointing season with a new owner and chaotic management. Unitas had an amiable association with the Chargers' management but experienced unhappiness of a different kind with that team.

"I appreciated them calling me in and asking me to work with the kids," said Unitas. "It was something that never happened with the Colts. When they do things like that, it's not a hard situation to take." So, Unitas was resigned to work with Dan Fouts, who would one day enter the Hall of Fame, and rookie Jesse Freitas. Unitas was ready to accept the fact that he would never be a starter again in his final season and would play little, if at all. But he wanted to suit up and step on the field for one more season even if doing so meant standing on the sidelines. Then he would retire his way.

Unitas got an offer from the Washington franchise of the newly formed World Football League, which was scheduled to launch that summer. They wanted Unitas to become the team's head coach and general manager, something that Unitas had expressed he would do after he retired—but only if he had complete control. That was what Washington offered. However, Unitas informed them that he had another year remaining on his Chargers contract, which he would honor despite his reduced role.

Unitas was always a man of his word, and to him a contract was written in stone.

In Canton, Ohio, where he would be inducted into the Hall of Fame five years later, Unitas, in a shirt and tie, participated in the opening of a hotel. He was still a star and he was there working the room, shaking hands with everyone and saying how wonderful it was to be at the opening. He moved around freely and spoke candidly, not so much about his career, a topic he modestly avoided, but about the attitudes of the new generation of players.

"I just don't think players today have dedication," he said. "They don't want to take the time and the effort to work before or after practice. There's only so much time during practice and mostly that's to work on coordination and timing. Their primary concern is money, how many days off, what kind of pension will they get. This is something I think is hurting the game. I don't blame the kids for trying to get money because if they don't look out for themselves, no one will volunteer. But the attitude of some is not conducive to good football.

"I still enjoy the game. I even enjoy practice, which, I suppose, is kinda funny. But sometimes it's frustrating to see people with ability who don't want to use it. Once that whistle blows to end practice, they're gone. I had to go into the locker room a couple of times last year and pull people out to work with."

The Right Time

There was an empty locker room when Unitas arrived in San Diego in mid-July for the last training camp of his career. The NFL Players Association had issued a strike edict, and the players, like all good union members, picketed outside the training facility. Unitas didn't think twice about crossing the picket line. He was the first veteran to do so. "They know this is my last year as a player and my career is basically finished for all intents and purposes," he explained. There was no forecasting how long the strike would last and Unitas didn't have time to wait. He had to find out what he had left, if anything, for his 19th year of football.

It didn't take long for Unitas to learn that he had reached the end. It took him about 10 days to admit that his body couldn't do the things he asked of it anymore. He had always said that when it was time to retire, he, and only he, would decide—a quarterback to the end, calling his own play.

On a Sunday morning he limped off the field, saying to himself that the day had arrived. His legs didn't respond the way he expected them to. He was too slow, and his knees were sore and swollen. In his younger days, a young limping Johnny Unitas was still dangerous. But not anymore. He had to tell Prothro. It would be quick and simple.

"Tommy, I think I'm gonna retire," Unitas said, coming right to the point, typically not mincing his words. "I just can't do the things I like to do out there. I stepped in a hole and sprained the left knee and ankle slightly. I was getting a message."

"That might be the best John," agreed Prothro.

"I hate to quit playing football."

"It must be embarrassing to someone like yourself who has been able to do the things you've done to find that it has become an effort."

"No, it's not embarrassing, it's just that I can't do them."

He had become the greatest quarterback the NFL had ever known. He had owned half of the fifties and practically all of the sixties, and he was America's quarterback. But it all ended on a lonely practice field in San Diego.

16

Looking Back

IDEALLY, JOHNNY UNITAS' PRESS CONFERENCE TO ANNOUNCE HIS retirement as a player should have taken place in Baltimore, where he had been a Colt for 17 years. Instead, there was a meager local press turnout in San Diego, where, in reality, he was a stranger. But Unitas preferred the quiet way out. He had no prepared statement and answered questions off the cuff. After 18 years he was done. Chargers owner Gene Klein put it best by describing Unitas as "a living work of art."

Unitas left the game without ceremony, the same way he came into it in 1956 when he arrived in Baltimore as a nobody in an old Oldsmobile that clanked and spewed smoke from a faulty exhaust pipe. What he did during those Colts years impacted pro football like no other player's actions had before. He brought romance into the game. He was easily pro football's last hero. Nobody can play forever, but Unitas left a big void when he retired. He had completed more passes, gained more yards, and thrown for more touchdowns than anyone else in the sport, which assured him a unanimous first-ballot acceptance into the Hall of Fame.

Parting Words

Unitas was obviously disturbed by the changing face of pro football, especially the drug culture. Months later, in an interview with Mickey

Herskowitz of the *Houston Chronicle,* Unitas made his feelings known. "That's what disturbs me about so much of what is written today, the derogatory things. I know the newspaper people say, 'We've got to print it like it is.' But I'd hate for my kids to idolize someone who is into drugs, who treats others with contempt, who thinks his talent is a license to behave any way he wishes. I've busted my ass all my life to watch where I go, what I do, with whom I'm seen. I've spent 19 years in it, and a few guys make headlines for smoking pot and now the public thinks all pro football players are potheads.

"Some of the fun has gone out of the game. The thing that is so irritating is that the players coming into the league today won't take the time or put forth the effort of those 10 and 12 years back. They were more concerned then with the game and the team. Little else mattered. You don't have that now. They don't want to spend the time.

"The game has gone back to running and as far as I am concerned, it's ridiculous. But there are a lot of coaches out there who don't teach and there are a lot of quarterbacks who don't know how to read defenses. They've become leery of throwing the ball. It's not exciting football. In fact, it's boring. The abilities of the players haven't changed that much, but expansion has watered down the talent. When I started out, you had 10 or 12 teams. Today there are 26 with more to come. The quarterbacks today have better passing percentages than we used to have, but check the leading receivers. They're throwing primarily to the running backs. It takes talent to throw the ball downfield.

"Today's players don't seem to have as much fun as we did as a team. There was much more closeness between players when I started, much more closeness between management and fans. That's all missing today. Today's players want to get money, money, money. They don't want to perform as much. They won't sacrifice. They refuse extra time on the field, time they need. They've gotten much more lenient in their performance. They think they're the best and they're on a lark.

"That's one reason I wouldn't want to coach. I couldn't put up with a lot of the horse manure the coaches do now from some of the players. I wouldn't have any patience with the phoniness of some of 'em and the lack of dedication. I'd probably end up with a squad of 25. There are too many factions on the teams now. You got everything from temperance guys to women's lib. I came into the league without any fuss and I'd just as soon leave it that way. There's no difference that I can see in retiring from pro football or quitting a job at the Pennsy Railroad. I did something I wanted to do and went out as far as I could go."

An Honored Man

Unitas' new routine after Sunday mass was to hang around the house instead of playing football. He had a five-bedroom manse of white stucco graced by two tall front pillars. He had seven acres of land to groom, and he did the chores of mowing the grass and pulling the weeds himself, just like any other guy with a Sunday off. It was hot in August in the Maryland countryside, and instead of training camp, Unitas was doing his sweating on his own field, without a football. It was the first training camp he had missed in 19 years. "It's no big deal. I got enough things to keep me busy," he said.

There was some thought of honoring Unitas at the home opener against Green Bay with a public salute from the countless fans who idolized him. But he didn't want it; the way he was treated by the Colts' new-order management hurt more than any tackle he ever absorbed. No, not as long as Bob Irsay and Joe Thomas were still in charge. How could he thank them in front of a microphone before a sold-out stadium? "No, it's a nice thought," he politely declined. "I appreciate it, but it is not necessary. I'd rather not do it because I don't like the whole fuss and bother."

Unitas was still sought after. The New England Patriots wanted him to become part of their announcing talent for six televised exhibition games. CBS offered him a job as a broadcaster. He didn't seek any opportunities to coach because he had clearly expressed his feelings about doing so: "No, I'm not interested. The way things are with the players today and their change in attitudes would be difficult for me to accept."

An Example for All

The memories of the past were precious to Unitas. He recalled how it was with Raymond Berry, with whom he spent the most time. "I remember one night when the ground crew had put down the tarpaulin when our workout was over. But Raymond wanted to do some more things. So we pulled back the edge of the canvas cover until we could see the hash mark and ran patterns on that little part of the field. It was pitch black when we quit, maybe 8:00 in the evening, but we got things done that helped us win. Then in the game, if he was going to run a step-out pattern for five steps, I knew where he was going to pivot, make his break, and where he had to have the ball."

Unitas also remembered the camaraderie of his era in the game. He said, "When we were coming along, guys like Gino Marchetti, Artie Donovan, Dick Szymanski, Jimmy Mutscheller, those kind of guys, we used to do more together. I'm talking about off the field now. Football was the main thing. Now everyone more or less goes his own way. I've been fortunate in that we've had a lot of great guys over the years play for the Colts, guys you'd want to be with. I wouldn't say that I've been really close with anyone, but there have been a lot of guys I've liked and got along with real well. I still see them. Football has given me every opportunity I've ever had. No one else I know from a section of Pittsburgh from a poor family has been able to sit down with three or four presidents of the United States."

Carroll Rosenbloom was one of the first to express his sorrow at Unitas' retirement. "I would have liked to see him go out on one more great year," said the Rams owner, who always had a special feeling for Unitas.

Unitas had wanted another season as well. He had been with the Chargers for only one year, not even long enough to know his teammates. The end of his playing career was so unexceptional even though Unitas had always been associated with drama. He had persevered for all those 18 years with confidence and courage and an unimaginably high threshold for pain—all of which set him apart from the others. "The thing that makes Johnny Unitas the greatest of all time isn't his arm or even his football sense," said Merlin Olsen. "It's his courage."

The courage and confidence was discernible in the very first game he played as a rookie in 1956. In a contest in Chicago, the Bears beat the Colts 58–27. Jim Mutscheller, the tight end who became one of Unitas' most dependable receivers in the six years they played together, clearly remembered the game: "George Shaw, our regular quarterback, got racked up. There was no choice but to go with the young Unitas. The first pass he threw was intercepted and returned for a touchdown by J. C. Caroline. I remember seeing him after the game in the dressing room and being struck by the sheer amount of confidence he still had in himself. He was talking to the writers, and he had no question at all in his ability after that beating. I was amazed."

Remembering the Greatest Game Ever Played

It was Mutscheller who was involved in one of the most controversial passes in the NFL annals during the historical championship overtime game against the New York Giants. The Colts were in field-goal range to secure the victory, yet Unitas threw a seven-yard, completed pass that carried Mutscheller out of bounds on the 1-yard line. The gutsy call shocked everyone except Unitas and Mutscheller, and it was strongly challenged later after Alan Ameche scored the winning touchdown of the 23–17 thriller.

"I never thought twice about the call being dangerous," said Mutscheller. "To me, it was just another play. That was how confident the team was in Unitas' ability. He felt there was just as much error in his handing the ball off as there was in passing it. He transmitted that feeling to the rest of us and his courage was unquestioned. The way he could keep his concentration while taking violent shots from the defense will forever stick out in my mind."

The Bears' brute of a tackle, Doug Atkins, also admired Unitas for his toughness, and there was no tougher lineman around. He was a mountainous man from Tennessee at 6'7", 280 pounds, and he pounded quarterbacks and running backs with his massive arms until they moaned with pain. Atkins, more than any other player, inflicted a great deal of physical damage to Unitas' body. But Unitas always got up without complaining, except to say, "The Bears hurt me more than any other team."

Atkins remembered Unitas' perseverance. He said, "Johnny was an all-time great among a lot of them who were great in that period. He was the best I ever played against, and that was because he was so tough. You could beat him for 59 minutes, but that last one he would find some way to beat you. I remember one time, it was at the end of a game, and Bill George went in and got Johnny by the ankles, but he was still standing up. I finally got by Parker and somehow my shoulder pad got up under Johnny's helmet and ripped his nose. It was an accident, of course, but we were all jumping around. We thought for sure we had him this time."

Atkins got Unitas good. Blood was pouring profusely from Unitas' nose. It was an ugly sight, but he wouldn't come out of the game. His teammate Szymanski reached down, picked up some mud, and packed it on Unitas' nose. Unitas told the trainer, "If you take me out I'll kill you." The referee came over and told Unitas to take as much time as he needed. John waved him away. "Get the hell out of here so I can call the play," snapped Unitas. The play went for a touchdown.

"Damned if they didn't take time out and he went over and got some tape and came back and threw a ball that nobody could have caught, except that Lenny Moore dove over Caroline and did catch it and beat us," said Atkins. "I still remember how tough it was to beat him. You had to beat him the whole 60 minutes."

The Colts' Jim Parker also fondly remembered playing with Unitas. He said, "Johnny was the best, no doubt about it. I came out of Ohio State in 1957 and Johnny was just stepping in as the regular quarterback. We went through a lot together. The thing that always impressed me about him was that he never passed the buck, never bitched, never complained, and he beat 'em all.

"All I know is that he could win for you and I had the utmost confidence in him. It was funny that way. Johnny would get hurt or something and they'd put in a back-up and I just couldn't make my legs work for the new guy. They just wouldn't do it."

Unitas will indelibly be remembered for the December 28, 1958, championship game by the millions who saw it. Over the decades, it has been recognized as "the greatest game every played," and probably will be throughout time. More important, it was the most significant for the league. It was the defining moment that brokered a marriage between professional football and television. At the same time, it made Unitas a hero to every underdog in America in all walks of life. Unitas described that fateful game: "I've always felt that it wasn't a real good football game until the last two minutes and then the overtime. We played pretty well, but we should have blown New York out of the stadium and we didn't. Then we had to come from behind in order to tie and then go on to win it. Just the fact that it was the first overtime in championship play, that was enough to make people feel they had seen something fantastic.

"On the pass to Mutscheller, everybody kept saying, 'What if it had been intercepted?' Well, I don't call pass plays expecting it to fail. I thought this pass was there because they were jammed up right on the line. It was a quick pattern and if Jim had been covered, I would have thrown the ball out of bounds. We still could have kicked a field goal. So I figured what we had was a free shot at a touchdown, and I'd rather win by a touchdown than a field goal in a game like that.

"They always forgot that the month before, in the game that clinched the division championship and put us into the playoff, San Francisco had us down 27–7 at the half and we came back to beat 'em 35–27. That was a much better game. Our defense shut out Y. A. Tittle in the second half and that was quite an accomplishment."

That championship game still gave Giants linebacker Sam Huff nightmares decades later. In awe, Huff recalled Unitas and Berry's precision together. "He was the master," said Huff. "Several times we thought we had him. But he always came up with a big play. On the field-goal drive, I think he hit Berry nine straight times. We couldn't stop him. He always did the unexpected. And, for this reason, you could never get a pattern on him no matter how many computers you might use. He had it all."

A Giant Among Men

Unitas and Berry were like Fred Astaire and Ginger Rogers. Their intricate timing on pass patterns was impeccable. They worked and worked like a dance team at being the best. Few denied that they were the top passing combination in league history. Berry wasn't the fastest receiver, and Unitas wasn't exactly the most artistic quarterback, but together they dominated games with their own style. Over the years, Huff kept hearing the voice of Bob Sheppard over the stadium loudspeaker during that 1958 game, "Unitas to Berry, Unitas to Berry." That phrase haunted him.

All the additional hours of practice made the plays possible, especially for the slow-footed Berry. "When I came to camp my second year in 1956, the word was already out," he said. "They said some young quarterback looked really good. It wasn't long until Weeb Ewbank told me to work all I could with him. Even then, he knew Unitas was going to be superb. What Johnny had going for him most was belief in his own ability. For the type of attack that was in vogue at that time, Johnny's qualities were perfect.

"Weeb did a fine job of using the physical tools of his players. He encouraged Johnny to throw the football. We had good teams then, but there was never any question who was the boss. His arm never got tired. He could do it all physically back then and he cashed in on his durability. In those early days, his arm was something special."

Earl Morrall, who took over for Unitas during the 1968 season when Unitas' valuable right arm was injured, was effusive in his admiration for him. He also had a crew cut and was often mistaken for Unitas. His praise for Unitas, from one quarterback to another, was the ultimate compliment. "He can read defenses the way most people read a calendar," said Morrall. "I don't believe I know another quarterback who comes close to him in this skill. He is probably the most dangerous quarterback the game has ever known."

Even linemen, who were never the recipients of a Unitas pass, were in awe of Unitas' work. One in particular was Colts guard Dan Sullivan, who never made an All-Pro team but was nevertheless considered by Unitas to be "the most valuable player on our team." Sullivan was impressed by Unitas' gutsy plays. "He was the leader, analogous to a general in war," said Sullivan, who had to effectively block for Unitas to give him the necessary time to throw. "I saw him do impossible things in the 10 or 11 years I was with him. I admire him still. His brand of ball was the style I wanted to play, not stereotyped in any way. Offensive linemen are not supposed to be smart anyway and he always kept us off-guard. There never was a dull moment. Anybody who tried to guess with him would be wrong."

Perhaps no one appreciated Unitas more than Shula. They were two headstrong personalities and, at times, differed in their philosophy on offensive football, but Shula was cognizant of Unitas' ability the first time he played with him in 1956 as a defensive back with the Colts. "What Johnny meant to me in my coaching career is difficult to describe," said Shula. "There are so many memories. Johnny typified toughness in a quarterback. His willingness to take whatever punishment there was was remarkable. He's the greatest two-minute quarterback ever. I used to drive home from the stadium in Baltimore thinking about what he had done and I'd still be amazed."

He might not have been the most graceful athlete to watch as he sauntered out of the huddle in his high-topped shoes and stooped shoulders, but he produced the ultimate in performance. The ability was obvious, but it was his mind and spirit that dominated any game in which he ever played. He was born to be a quarterback, and he was the epitome for all who followed him.

17

The Hall of Fame

THERE IS NO BETTER WAY TO DESCRIBE JOHNNY UNITAS THAN TO say he was a natural. However, he was almost unnatural in his achievements during the 18 years he played the game. He excelled against the odds as a sandlot player and fought to become a professional football player. Unitas was a born leader, and he made the NFL popular while he resurrected an obsolescent Baltimore franchise that was scornfully mocked around the league. In the years he played there, the Colts won more games than anyone else and never once finished under .500 in the 1960s.

No one could have imagined that the fragile-looking youngster, looked upon with dismay by many of his teammates, would be the one to lead them to glory. "He was a total mystery," said running back Alex Hawkins, remembering the first time he saw Unitas. "He was from Pennsylvania, but he looked so much like a Mississippi farmhand that I looked around for a mule. He had stooped shoulders; a chicken breast; thin bowed legs; and long, dangling arms with crooked, mangled fingers."

Johnny Unitas would have played in a leather helmet. He was a throwback to another era, when legends like Harold "Red" Grange, Bronko Nagurski, Jim Thorpe, Sid Luckman, and Sammy Baugh would have welcomed him with open arms. He was that good and that tough.

Unitas as Broadcaster

Retirement placed Unitas in a different world. He became a shirt-and-tie guy and wore a headset to do television for CBS at its Sunday games. It looked foreign for someone who had been framed by a helmet with a single-bar face mask most of his life to be wearing an announcer's headset. If he hadn't looked right in a San Diego uniform, he certainly didn't look any better in a business suit. Nevertheless, he didn't change his demeanor for the cameras. He remained confident and honest and didn't follow the party line about not criticizing players. If Unitas saw something wrong, he didn't hesitate to say so. He was just being Unitas. Of his commentary style, he said, "Well, I believe in looking at the game like a coach. If a guy blows one, I'm going to say so. I'm not going to pull punches just because I know some guy who is involved. That's my opinion on how this job should be done."

Broadcasting was a new experience for him, one for which he hadn't trained. But he had fun and worked at first with Bart Starr. Unitas had to adjust to concentrating on the whole game instead of one or two players. "Yeah, I was a little nervous in my rookie game," he confessed. But each week he became more comfortable with a microphone in his face. He became more relaxed, which brought out some of his humor between plays. During an Atlanta game in Denver, the Falcons defense was doing a number on Bronco quarterback Charlie Johnson. Unitas quipped, "A couple of more hits like that and old Charlie will be up here in the booth with us instead of in the huddle." Later, Unitas offered another jibe when Atlanta quarterback Bob Lee was victimized by a sack. "I've never seen a quarterback yet who can throw from the seat of his pants." After five years, Unitas didn't want to be a broadcaster anymore. Unitas never wanted to talk football; he wanted only to play it.

Unitas as Businessman

Instead he got more involved with his business interests. He had quite a few promising ones: a Sheraton hotel; the Golden Arm restaurants in Baltimore and Orlando; the Lobo Golf Club in Orlando; Threeshore Shore

Land Development Company in Deltona, Florida; the St. John Crab Company in Welaka, Florida; and a 600-acre panel of land in central Florida all put together by his attorney, Dario "Ike" Icardi.

Icardi, who had known Unitas from high school, was impressed with Unitas' "intelligence and remarkable depth." Icardi said, "I make proposals, and we make decisions. I have to temper my ambitions with what John wants me to achieve. I've learned a lot from John. He's a remarkable businessman. There is no profit to this point, only investments."

It appeared to be the ideal setup for Unitas. His widowed mother spent quite a bit of time in Florida, and he was also involved with his brother, Leonard, in a Firestone Tire dealership there. More ideally, Unitas did not have to relocate to Florida and could look after business from Baltimore, which was special to him. "I have a good working and personal relationship with Icardi," said Unitas. "When I'm not meeting with him in either Orlando or Baltimore, then we are back and forth checking on problems and seeing how much progress we're making. We have a lot of work to do."

Initially the Unitas-Icardi relationship seemed to be a winning combination. However, as time passed, Unitas' trust of Icardi cost him. He paid the attorney a monthly stipend for handling his business and tax situations. Unfortunately, years later, like Cinderella, the clock struck 12:00 and with it took away the fortunes Unitas deserved but never enjoyed. In 1991, he filed for bankruptcy.

Despite Unitas' business setbacks, he did have one stroke of luck: he rejoined the Colts. After Joe Thomas was fired in January 1977, Unitas signed on as a "special consultant" to the team. Although his official duties were not defined, Unitas was happy to be a part of the organization that had meant so much to him. He said, "I'll make public appearances for the Colts whenever they want me and my schedule permits. And I'll take special scouting assignments on the same basis. When you play for a team for 17 years, it becomes part of your life and you become attached to it. I had always hoped that after I quit playing I could remain with the Colts in a front-office job. Until now, though, it couldn't happen."

Going to Canton

Unitas' football glory remained untarnished. There was never any doubt that he would enter the Pro Football Hall of Fame. The question was when. NFL rules mandate that a retired player must wait five years before he can be voted upon to join the hallowed hall.

Another big mystery regarding his induction was who Unitas' presenter would be. He certainly had an impressive number of candidates from whom to choose: Weeb Ewbank, Don Shula, Don McCafferty. When the time drew near, a poll ran throughout Baltimore, and there was even a pool in a local bar to try to guess who would have that honor bestowed upon him. When the incomparable quarterback announced his choice of Frank Gitschier, all the pool money had to be returned. Gitschier's name wasn't even on the board. In picking the unknown Gitschier, Unitas went back to his roots. Gitschier, Unitas' quarterback coach at Louisville, and the school's first quarterback in 1946, was "spellbound" when Unitas called.

"Coach, I guess you know I'm going into the Hall of Fame," said Unitas.

"I heard about it," said Gitschier.

"I'd like for you to be my presenter," said Unitas.

"Heck yeah, I'll do it," replied the excited Gitschier.

"Thanks."

"But one thing. If it's alright with you, I'd like to run it by coach Camp."

"Sure, go ahead."

Frank Camp, the former Louisville head coach who gave Unitas his shot at college ball when no one else would, approved of Gitschier's role. "I was totally surprised and so pleased by John's call that I felt like crying," said Gitschier. "Everybody in Baltimore was asking, 'Who the hell is this guy?' They had to give all the money back."

Unitas' selection of Gitschier was vintage Unitas. He had done the unexpected on the field on so many Sundays, and he pulled another surprise five years after he retired. Gitschier said, "When you think of all the wonderful coaches and players and other people he has known—and he picks me. John doesn't say why, he just says, 'Will you?' He's that kind of a person, a strong personality, and I think he is selective in friends and associates."

Unitas was inducted into Canton, Ohio's cherished hall the very moment he was eligible to join other Colts like Ewbank, Art Donovan, Gino Marchetti, Jim Parker, Lenny Moore, and Raymond Berry. He belonged there with his teammates. Nobody ever did more to popularize the game than Unitas did. There were others who contributed, but it was Unitas who led them, and his induction was universally hailed. He was the consummate pro, a superstar. But humility was his defining characteristic. It was never about him. "He never put himself first and I never met anyone else like him," said Gitschier.

His Induction

Unitas appeared mellow in Canton days before the official ceremonies. He wasn't much on celebrations and all the hoopla that went with it. If he had his way, Unitas would have flown into Canton on Saturday morning, participated in the induction formalities, and flown back to Baltimore the same night. His wife, Sandy, admitted as much. "He wanted to wait until Saturday to fly out here," she said. "But I told him he was coming out for the first-day events, and for all the events, and he was going to smile and do everything they told him to do." He told her that she was right.

Unitas would have preferred to have been on a golf course. But, although the induction was something special, he wasn't overwhelmed by it all. "It was nice to hear I was going into the Hall," said Unitas. "All people who get into pro sports look forward to something like that. I feel it's a great honor. But it wouldn't have bothered me not to have gone in. I'm happy to go in, but it's not the ultimate thing for me. Just being able to play the game when I did for as long as I did was the ultimate. The Hall of Fame is something extra."

Unitas' twice-widowed mother couldn't have been prouder. She realized how significant the recognition was. "I remember John had such determination to make good," she said. "There just wasn't anything that was going to defeat him in his ambition to be a quarterback and make the team. I would get upset when he took those beatings and sometimes even injured his shoulder or his lungs or his legs. But he always told me that as long as he could walk away from the stadium when the game was over, there was no reason to be upset."

Unitas had informed his mother of the induction over the phone. "I think it's real nice," he told his mother. "You know me, I don't place too much importance on things like this."

As low-key as Unitas was about his Hall of Fame enshrinement, his ex-teammate Dick Szymanski was ebullient in praising him. He was more outspoken than any of the other Colts who attended. In talking with John Steadman, a Baltimore sportswriter, Szymanski, who blocked for Unitas for eight years at center, couldn't say enough about the quarterback. In his opinion, Szymanski felt that Unitas was the finest all-around quarterback who ever played in the NFL. He said, "He never expected anything from you he wouldn't do himself. I believe he had the kind of toughness you find in an interior lineman, not a man playing a skilled position like a quarterback. When you have a quarterback who is [as] rugged physically as a tackle or a guard, you really have something. I have never seen another like him."

Two former greats, Sammy Baugh and Sid Luckman, agreed. "Sammy and I used to kid each other," said Luckman. "I'd say I was the best quarterback of all time. Then Sam would say that he was. But, in time, we gave up our little game. We both realized John Unitas was the greatest."

The night before the induction, at one of those Hall of Fame functions that Sandy had instructed her husband that he had to attend, she asked Mary Gitschier what Frank's introductory speech was about. "What's Frank going to say?" asked Sandy. "I don't know," replied Mary. Gitschier and Unitas had never discussed it. That's how much trust Unitas had in him. Unitas would hear it for the first time along with a huge crowd of approximately ten thousand people.

Much of the audience was from Baltimore; 15 buses had delivered a Unitas crowd. Significantly, Robert Irsay was in the audience, although he was not seated with the Colts fans. "The guy paid $19 million for the Colts because you were his idol," Unitas was told later. Unitas grinned without saying a word.

At the moment that Gitschier reached for the microphone, a halo-like rainbow appeared in the sky. It was as if the gods of football were pleased. His introduction was brief, the way Unitas would want it:

> This is a very great moment in my life, the life of my family, and we are most grateful and appreciative of being here and being part of these induction ceremonies. Now I want to talk about Johnny Unitas, my man. No one here is more totally aware of the talents given to him by God than Johnny Unitas. And when you use those talents to the utmost, the bottom line is dedication, desire, discipline, sacrifice, and when you put all that together, it spells John Unitas, extraordinary in the field of leadership, and it spells John Unitas, a man respected by all who have known him.
>
> But let's talk about some of the talents that [are] more apparent to most of us because John has entertained us over the years. The thing that amazes me more than anything else is the man's ability to stand in that pocket with all that violence and mayhem going on about him—some of which was to be inflicted upon him—and he stood back there and ate his lunch before he threw that ball. His courage is unquestionable. Now let's digress a moment back to what is now called the greatest football game in the history of professional football. The game between the Baltimore Colts and the New York Giants. To say the least, those calls were not only unpredictable [but] totally unbelievable when you assess the downs and the yardage situations at that time. The man has always done his homework, and he knew the strengths and weakness that a defensive person should know. He had no peer as a reader of defense. It is impossible for me to go any further in these ceremonies and not make the flat-out statement

that if John Unitas is not the greatest quarterback that
played professional football, there can't be anybody
greater.

Now I must say, most importantly, the man has
always had his priorities in the right order. Let me say
this to you: can you imagine how many famous people,
great people, this man has met in his lifetime? And he
selected an average college football player, an average
college football coach, an average recruiter—as a matter
of fact, a nobody—to be his presenter. That tells you
something about Johnny Unitas. From all his coaches in
high school, in college, with the Bloomfield Rams, and
all of professional football, and I want to include John's
high school coach, Max Carey, who is deceased, and
Mr. Carroll Rosenbloom. This is the greatest moment
of my life and I want to thank you, John Constantine
Unitas.

As Unitas approached the podium to a ringing, standing ovation, he
held up his hand to quiet the crowd. No one expected him to talk long.
His oratory was expected to be brief and to the point. That had always
been Unitas' nature:

They must be drinking over there. Thank you very, very
much Frank. It's a real privilege for me to be here. And
I want to thank you especially, Frank, for taking the
time out, along with your wife, Mary, and your boys, to
come here to Canton to enshrine me. I appreciate it. It
was a difficult decision to make, but when I boiled it
down, it was the only decision to make. I thought that
the time and effort you put forth with me in college—
to come back to Tennessee when you were earning your
masters degree [to] work with me on weekends to try
to push some sense in this stubborn Ukrainian head of
mine—that I appreciate it and I hope, and I know, you
appreciate coming here and I thank you for that. . . .

You know a man never gets to this station of life
without being helped, aided, shoved, pushed into doing

something the proper way, as the other enshrinees mentioned, and thanks to the families, so also I have to do this. My mother, who was always behind me pushing, shoving, moving, getting me to do things. Trying to make me speak. Really, she always used to say getting a word out of me was like pulling teeth. It probably was because I don't very often say a whole lot. My family, of course, my wife and kids. I thank all of them for being here, for being behind me, and I know my wife is the most critical of whatever you do, but she always does it in love, so she says. I appreciate that. Of course, my brother, Leonard, who is here from Orlando, and his wife; my sister, Millie, and her husband; and my sister, Shirley, and her husband and boys, who have come down from Pittsburgh. I appreciate that, and I appreciate them being here. Also, all the blue-and-white outfits out there from the Colts. These are Baltimore fans. There are a lot of players who played in Baltimore during the time I played who know what I am talking about. Coming into Baltimore stadium was coming into an outside insane asylum. These fans were always 100 percent behind us and I hope they get 100 percent behind the new regime to try and help aid them in getting them to the Super Bowl so we can put more Baltimore Colts in this Hall of Fame.

I won't take up a whole lot of your time. There is going to be a fine football game this afternoon and it is getting a little warm, but there are two other people that I wished could have been here. . . . [James] Max Carey was a great influence on me when I was in high school as a football player. He worked with me, talked with me, treated me like a son. I can always remember Max saying, "When the going gets tough, the tough get going, and that is what I expect out of you 110 percent at all times." I always tried to remember that and give 110 percent, whenever I was on the field or off, regardless what it was I felt, that I was consistent, and he always got 110 percent out of me.

Then there was a newspaper man [at] my first football game in Baltimore, a little, funny fat guy with a
beard, sitting down here, by the name of Cameron
Snyder, who came over to me and knew I was nervous
and said, "John, I just want you to remember this, that
the game you are playing today is a kid's game played
by men. Go out and do a job," and I thank you for that
Cameron.

It is hard to remember everyone, very difficult
because, as I said, a lot of people touch your life as you
are growing up, in small ways possibly, some are larger
than others. You know just by a word, a congratulatory
word, or say, "Gee, thanks for the entertainment you
have given us over the years." All these are great things
to remember, and I will remember them. I will remember this day, and I honestly want to be honest with you
that the players I played with over the years, the coaches
that I had—the Sanduskys, the players, the Nutters, the
Berrys, Marchettis, and Pellingtons, Ewbanks, Shulas,
all my coaches, McCaffertys—they are directly responsible for my being here, and I want you all to know that
because I have never forgotten that. I want to thank you
very, very much for your attention and the kind words
and may God bless all of you.

Unitas delivered his speech with directness and simplicity, and with that
same intense look he displayed during games. He was almost grim. He
played that way, with a simplicity that made the game look easy. He was
the only quarterback who could ever do that.

18

Adjustment

U NITAS' INDUCTION INTO THE HALL OF FAME WAS THE FINAL
highlight of his life, even though he never made a big deal of it.
He should have accumulated millions with his high-profile celebrity per-
sona, much like Joe DiMaggio did, but it never happened. Like DiMaggio,
Unitas was easily recognizable and revered. He was even more approachable than the moody, intensely private baseball icon, but dame fortune
never smiled on him the way she did on the Yankee immortal. Ernie
Accorsi, who worked for the Colts for five years beginning in 1970 and
admired everything Unitas stood for, succinctly described the quarterback's
quandary: "He didn't get a lot of breaks."

Unitas made his way from a hardscrabble hill in Pennsylvania to become
the greatest quarterback the NFL had ever known. He outlasted all the
other quarterbacks and won defiantly in the most brutal of sports. His
life after retirement should have been sweet, but it wasn't. His Midas touch
on the football field didn't work in the business world.

The multifaceted enterprise with his longtime friend, Dario Icardi, which
looked like a Fortune 500 corporation on paper, imploded. The Florida
real estate venture turned out to include a swampland, which was worth-
less. The other businesses with which Unitas was involved resulted in hard-
ship for him as well. They included a chain of bowling alleys, an air

freight company, and a prime rib restaurant. However, Unitas managed to endure. He never complained about the setbacks, and optimism kept him going. "He had faith in his fellow man and a tendency to trust people until he found out he shouldn't," explained longtime friend Lee Stotsky.

The Greatest Loss

Unitas lived in a changing world. That was never more evident than in 1984, when the Colts deserted Baltimore and relocated to Indianapolis. All the memorabilia of the old Colts were gone, taken out of the building in the dead of the night. Everything was dumped in vans and transplanted to another city. Unitas' jersey—and all the other things that meant so much to Baltimore—were gone.

The loss cut through the hearts of Baltimore fans, who lost their beloved Colts. No one felt the loss more keenly than Unitas did, however. Part of him froze on that cold, snowy night at midnight when 12 vans left like looters while the city slept. In the early morning hours, cries of anguish reverberated throughout the Maryland countryside. But Unitas never took a harder hit on a football field. It was reported that he wept in solitude.

Unitas felt betrayed. It had been his team, his town—then there was nothing. Unitas never forgave the Colts. He wanted no part of them; he didn't want his name associated with them anymore. Of the devastating effect of the loss of the Baltimore team, Unitas said, "Every given Sunday, those people looked forward to the Colts' games. The only thing they hated on Sunday [was] that they had to wait until next Sunday to go back to the stadium again and root. It was a tremendous love affair. As far as I'm concerned, they just raped the town, taking everything from the city and not giving anything back."

The Colts' franchise's move was devious. Unitas had been uneasy with Bob Irsay ever since Irsay bought the team in 1972. Unitas, who had been the soul of the team, had been banished to San Diego. Unitas never trusted the Colts' new owner.

When he purchased the Colts on July 13, 1972, Irsay had claimed, and then repeated over the years, that he would never move the team from Baltimore. In his very first press conference, he said: "I have bought the Colts to play in Baltimore. I have no thought of taking them elsewhere. We have a great team in a great sports town where they have sellouts. Why move?" A year later, he was quoted in a magazine article as saying, "One thing I want to emphasize is that I own 100 percent of the Colts and I'm not selling them and I'm not moving them." It was a recurring theme for Irsay throughout his 12 years in Baltimore.

Five years later, at Super Bowl XI in Pasadena, the first mention of Indianapolis was heard in a conversation with a reporter: "I like Baltimore and I want to stay there, but when are we going to find out something about our stadium? I'm getting offers from towns like Indianapolis to build me a new stadium and give me other inducements to move there. I don't want to, but I'd like to see some action in Baltimore." Two years later, he cancelled a meeting with the Los Angeles Coliseum officials about moving there.

Two other cities, Jacksonville and Memphis, courted Irsay. In 1979 he issued a statement that read: "We want to stay here and bring Baltimore and Maryland a championship like we have in the past. That's all we are committed to." A year later, he remarked, "I have visited no cities. I have talked to no people about moving the team." In 1981, he put his commitment in writing. In a letter to season-ticket holders, he said in part, "We are the Baltimore Colts. We want to play here and we want to give you the kind of team you can be proud of again. This is our commitment." He emphasized it by signing a new two-year lease for venerable Memorial Stadium.

But the moving vans were moving closer despite Irsay's denials. In 1983, at the team's practice facilities, he said, "We are not moving. I wouldn't be here if I was going to move, would I? I'll tell you what I could do—and don't think it hasn't crossed my mind—but I'm not going to do it. I could . . . be out of here Sunday, and you'd never know who was here, but I haven't done it." At a preseason conference at the airport on January 20, 1984, following reports that negotiations were occurring with officials in Phoenix, Irsay was irate in denying them: "I have no intention to move the goddamn team," he fumed. Two months later, the Colts were in Indianapolis.

Irsay's mendacity riled Unitas. Unitas had always been a man of his word, and he looked at the move as a heinous crime. He made his feelings known quite unmistakably that May at a public relations function in Phoenix. "Believe me, you're better off without him," said Unitas. "Irsay only used Phoenix like a prostitute. What he did to your governor and your mayor was an insult. Indianapolis comes along and they prostitute themselves to give Irsay everything he wants the same way Phoenix did. Baltimore did the same thing. They came back with a better offer than Indianapolis, but Irsay had already burned too many bridges.

"Joe Thomas did not want me in Baltimore. No way, he said, was I ever going to play another game with the Colts. My contract with Carroll Rosenbloom called for me to go to the front office for 10 years after I retired. [The new owners] said if I was going to do that, I had to work seven days a week, eight hours a day, which was not my agreement with Carroll. Well, within two weeks I had a newspaperman call me at 7:00 in the morning and ask me why I was going to San Diego. I didn't know a thing about it. These kind of people, why do you want to deal with them?"

Retiring His Jersey

Unitas then had to deal with a town without football. It left him with an empty feeling. There was no more sideline for him to stand on. The last time he ever did so with any distinction was on October 9, 1977, when the Colts retired his jersey before the scheduled game against Miami. Despite the acrimony he still harbored for the new management, Unitas agreed to participate in the pregame ceremony in Memorial Stadium. He felt he owed it to the fans who worshiped him for all the years he wore the No. 19 Colt's jersey. He said, "Thank you for letting me share part of your life every Sunday afternoon and thank you for sharing an important part of my life."

Unitas truly loved Baltimore and its residents. There was something about the gritty neighborhoods with its rows of gray houses that appealed to Unitas. It reminded him of the neighborhood in Pittsburgh where he grew up. More important, the people were real and that's what Unitas liked the most. The blue-collar feel was genuinely welcoming to him. It made him comfortable. "This is a good place with good people," he said. "Baltimore is home to me."

Shula was warm in his remarks during the pregame ceremonies honoring Unitas. And he didn't forget the fans that had cheered him when he coached the Colts for seven years. "I am proud to be back in Baltimore to take part in honoring John Unitas," said Shula before the sold-out crowd. "I have been fortunate to coach some great quarterbacks during my career, John, Earl Morrall, and now Bob Griese. But John was the greatest under pressure, the best at executing the two-minute drill before the end of the half or the end of the game. I really cherish my memories of seven years with the Baltimore Colts and John Unitas and offer my congratulations to John on his day."

Life After Football

Unitas missed the competition on the field after he retired. He would have played longer if the injuries he sustained had not stopped him. The fields on which Unitas competed became the plush lawns of golf courses. Golf became a love of his although it could never replace football. It was far removed from the killing fields, but it offered him competition.

Unitas had survived 18 years in the pro-football wars, despite the beatings he had taken on Sunday afternoons, which could have left others using a cane. He was reminded of football's lasting effects every morning when he awoke and left his bed. Yet he never complained. He just shrugged off the physical ailments. "Oh, I have a bad knee and a bad back," he said. "My knee has arthritis in it. My fingers are all bad. But outside of that, nothing. But it doesn't stop me from doing anything. I play golf, racquetball. I do whatever I want. If you know you have a headache and you get involved in something, your headache goes away, doesn't it? Pain is only in your mind. At least, that's how it is to me. Other people may not have my pain threshold. A lot of times my pain threshold could get me in [more] trouble than if it were slightly less."

Unitas, with his hunched shoulders, remained an icon around town long after the Colts had left. He never stopped going to Club 4100, a restaurant owned by Dino and Manny Spanomanolis. It was a neighborhood haven that occupied the first floor of a house. That, too, was like home to Unitas. He could relax and be treated like family at an establishment located in a working-class neighborhood in the Brooklyn Park section of town, away from the crowds and bright lights. He just wanted to be one of the guys, and he got to be one of the crowd at Club 4100. Unitas had been a regular since 1959 when the place opened.

After home games, many of the Colts players would head for 4100 and a steak dinner. Unitas was often with them. The restaurant was near the airport, which made it convenient for the players when they returned from a road game. It took a single phone call from one of the air traffic controllers to inform the Spanomanolis brothers that the Colts' charter had arrived, which was the signal to start filling the grill with steaks. Unitas was so comfortable at the Club 4100 that one time he lumbered in on crutches after being discharged from the hospital.

Setting the Record Straight

Although he was far removed from the playing field, Unitas often had to correct misconceptions of his role in two of the most important games in NFL history. Being a perfectionist, he never tired of correcting the stories. The errors involving the Super Bowl III contest against the Jets particularly riled him. It was misleadingly billed by the media as a duel between "Mr. Quarterback" and "Broadway" Joe Namath. In actuality, Unitas had watched from the sidelines with a tender throwing arm for most of the game. He only took the field after the Colts were shockingly behind, 16–0.

"I didn't even play until the end of the third quarter," said Unitas. "Any time they bring out these little excerpts and they bring that '69 game on, they all talk about Joe Namath being against Johnny Unitas.

"I say, 'Uh-uh.' They're blaming me for all that stuff. I didn't have anything to do with it until I took the team down and scored a touchdown in the fourth quarter. We were going for another touchdown when the game ended. I always tell people to blame Shula for that because if he had started me in the second half, I'd have got it."

The other moment he wanted clarified was the 1958 NFL championship overtime thriller against the Giants. Unitas acknowledged that the story wasn't wrong, but simply incomplete. In particular, during the third quarter, the Colts were leading 14–10, and had a chance to put the game away with another touchdown.

"We were down on the closed end of Yankee Stadium, on the 1-yard line," said Unitas. "We had four downs to get it in, but never did. We were on frozen turf and we couldn't get our footing very well." After two runs by Ameche and a quarterback sneak were futile, Unitas called a "423" in the huddle. It was a play in which Ameche was to line up as a halfback, take a pitch out to his right, stop, and throw a pass into the end zone.

"Well, Ameche never heard '400,'" said Unitas. "All he heard was '23.' So, he elects to run, and Jim Mutscheller, the tight end and the initial receiver, was standing all alone in the end zone by himself waiting for the ball.

"The commissioner at the time was Bert Bell, and he decreed that never should a championship game end in a tie. Nobody knew what was going to happen. The officials didn't know what to do and both teams were standing on the sidelines wondering, 'What do we do now?' The biggest thing I remembered was that some drunk suddenly appeared on the field and the New York cops [were] chasing him all over Yankee Stadium. They finally collared the guy, but when they were taking him away, he yelled, 'Damn, don't bother with me. Grab that guy wearing No. 19. He's the guy killing us.'"

Unitas' mind was set that he would always rather go for a touchdown than a field goal. It was a quality that only a champion could have. He never considered playing for the field goal in the overtime period, even after he maneuvered the Colts to the Giants' 8-yard line for a seemingly easy chip shot. Instead, he wanted a touchdown. He shrugged off Ewbank's instruction to keep the ball on the ground to avoid an interception. When Ameche was stuffed, Unitas took matters into his own hands. He brought the sold-out, frenzied stadium to its feet with a seven-yard pass to Mutscheller that would have been a touchdown if the tight end had fallen to his left instead of his right and landed out of bounds. Unitas scoffed at those who considered the play a gamble.

"Gamble? Some gamble," he said. "It wasn't a gamble. They didn't see what I saw. Nine times out of ten, Emlen Tunnell, the strong safety, would be on Mutscheller. This time it was Cliff Livingston, the linebacker, trying to take away the inside. So I checked off to a diagonal outside. Who's there to cover him? Linden Crow, the cornerback, and he's got to worry about Lenny Moore. Not a gamble. An educated move."

The Real Johnny Unitas

Unitas would talk about football, but he remained a private person. The Baltimore sports editor, John Steadman, enjoyed an amity with Unitas that enabled him to witness the quarterback in moments that no one else did. He respected and revered Unitas, and Unitas trusted him. And, if it was all right with Unitas, he chronicled such experiences in his widely read column. There was one that contained a letter that touched everyone, including NFL Commissioner Pete Rozelle, who called it "one of the most heartwarming and tenderly written letters I have ever seen." The column and letter described Unitas' biggest fan, an 11-year-old girl named Teresa Ariosa.

Teresa was deaf and had mild cerebral palsy with aphasia. Unitas and Teresa met at a fundraising carnival hosted by the Parents' League for Aphasia Youngsters. Unitas spent an hour selling tickets for the event with Teresa on his lap. Although she knew nothing about football, Teresa loved Unitas. He loved her as well. He made it a point to sit near her at church or to ask her parents about her.

Unitas always had a soft spot for kids. He demonstrated it another time at a photo shoot for an Easter Seals promotion. Unitas agreed to be photographed with a crippled youngster after practice. The Baltimore star waited patiently for an hour, and when the boy and his mother didn't show up, he took off his uniform, showered, and got dressed. He left the stadium with the photographer, and when they reached the parking lot, a cab pulled up beside them. The mother got out and humbly apologized for their tardiness. The photographer decided to take the photograph on the spot.

"Wouldn't it be better if I had my uniform on?" asked Unitas. The lensman agreed, but he told Unitas that he didn't want to inconvenience him any more than he already had. Unitas just shook his head, went back to the locker room, and returned fully dressed in his uniform. He knelt down beside the smiling youngster in braces and the Easter Seals photo was made.

That was the Unitas few people knew about. The solitary superstar wanted it that way. He cared about people, but shunned the publicity as he turned up any number of times in poor neighborhoods to visit sick children.

"If you're poor, you don't know it because you've never been rich," said Unitas. "You don't know the difference. I think it's a great help for most children if they have to make sacrifices, to do without. Because then, when they have an opportunity to have it, they certainly appreciate it. I wasn't going to throw anything away because I knew how I had to work to get it. I get more emotional for kids and animals than I do for football."

Unitas, on occasion, would do the unexpected. There was a bar in York, Pennsylvania, that the players frequented whenever they were in the area. The saloonkeeper, a passionate Colts fan, died unexpectedly. When Unitas found out, he surprised the bereaved family by attending the funeral in the half-empty church.

The unexpected was special and could only come from someone who cared. That was the unknown Unitas.

19

A New Era

U NITAS' ACCOMPLISHMENTS ON THE FOOTBALL FIELD CANNOT be calibrated in yards or touchdowns. He carried professional football on his sloping shoulders to the pinnacle of sports in America almost overnight during his first five years with the Baltimore Colts. There wasn't another quarterback like him. Others, like Bart Starr and Roman Gabriel, studied him. In the 1958 overtime NFL championship game, Unitas changed the art of quarterbacking. It took skill and courage, and Unitas used both to become the greatest quarterback who ever played the game.

After he retired, Unitas disliked the changes he saw in the game. He frowned at the use of headsets in players' helmets so that coaches could provide players with instructions on plays to call. He didn't like what was happening to the quarterback position he had mastered: "I think it's sad the way they've taken the game out of the hands of the quarterback. That's the big change now. They've taken the quarterback's personality out of the game. All the plays are called for him. Everything's sent in. He has his own immediate information on the field, but it doesn't come into play. He can't really work a game. Radios in helmets. I'd get very deaf all of a sudden. The five-yard bump rule, hell, you and I could get open. Liberalized pass-blocking rules, a bunch of big, fat guys just grabbing on.

But the big thing that's really gone is the way a quarterback used to be able to run the game."

Vilification

Unitas missed his role as quarterback, but he embarked diligently on his new role as wage earner for his family. However, his consulting job with the Baltimore Colts ended abruptly five years after it began. NFL Commissioner Pete Rozelle, whom Unitas once called "a pawn for the owners," ordered the Colts to release Unitas from any affiliation with the organization.

Unitas had allowed his name to be associated with a betting service, which was an abominable transgression for the image-conscious Rozelle. Unitas, however, balked at the suggestion of wrongdoing. "I never made a football bet in my life, but the implication now is that I am involved in something that's wrong. The Colts listed my name in their press guide as a 'consultant' to help their public image. It didn't make any difference at the time, but since I don't have a contract with them [and I'm not] on their payroll, how can Rozelle take this kind of stand? I'm not into gambling. I don't feel I'm doing anything wrong. We gather information and sell it to the people."

It didn't matter that Jim Brown was doing the same thing for a rival publication. The difference was that Brown didn't have an official identity with the Cleveland Browns.

Unitas was outspoken at some of the policies instituted by the league. He was particularly incensed that former players don't receive any monies from licensed products, like football trading cards or souvenir items sold at the Hall of Fame. "They don't pay anything to the players of old for the use of our names or pictures on cards," he said. "NFL Enterprises seems to think they have the rights to our names from the time we started playing until we're dead. The players don't think that's the way it ought to be. You don't see any football cards with the owners' pictures. We feel we've been kind of had and we have a right to protect our names."

Unfortunately, Unitas experienced severe financial problems with his business ventures and was forced to file for bankruptcy. He was millions of dollars in debt, and on February 22, 1991, he filed for protection under Chapter 11. The 57-year-old football legend was deeply troubled by the beatings he took in the business world, beginning with a land-deal fiasco in Orlando and an air-freight company that was grounded. It became a twisted world for Unitas. Once sought by fans for autographs and hand-shakes, he became sought after by process servers at the door of his Baldwin, Maryland, home. His bank accounts were being frozen by creditors, and a lien was placed on his $500,000 estate. Spared was Unitas' pension fund, valued at more than $600,000, which was exempt from being liquidated by creditors. It was the low point of Unitas' majestic life. The fortune he acquired as a player was gone. "This hurts," said Charles Tatelbaum, Unitas' attorney. "It pains him. Not just the embarrassment. It's not that he didn't succeed. He feels he let some people down."

An Honor

Still, Unitas remained beloved by sports fans and was offered a chance to throw a ceremonial ball before a baseball game. Instead of a baseball, he clutched a football in 1992 at Oriole Park. One more time he slipped on his famous No. 19 jersey, this time with Tom Matte by his side. He joked that he "was not going to have any grass stains" on the jersey when he took it off. When he left the tunnel behind home plate and appeared before the crowd, he did so to a standing ovation—even at a baseball game.

Hindered by a sore shoulder that needed surgery and a hand that was recently operated on, Unitas couldn't throw his signature pass. Instead, he took the snap on a cue from the cartoon character Orioles mascot and lateraled the ball to Matte, who completed the ceremonial toss. The crowd roared its approval.

Keeping His Hand In

Unitas needed that contact with football as much as when he played. It was so much a part of him. He wanted to be a part of a team always, and he almost achieved that goal in the fall of 1992 when best-selling author Tom Clancy hired Unitas to assist him in acquiring an expansion team for Baltimore. "He's one of the team," Clancy proudly announced, who as a youngster had watched Unitas play in Memorial Stadium. "If the group is awarded a franchise, he has a job on the team for as long as he wants." Baltimore, however, was not a lock to get a franchise despite Unitas' presence. There were four other cities, Memphis, St. Louis, Jacksonville, and Charlotte, vying for the two teams the league wanted to add. Eventually, when the league expanded to 30 teams, Baltimore was left empty by the addition of Charlotte and Jacksonville.

Unitas was in New York in 1993 to commemorate the 35th anniversary of the Colts' 23-17 overtime win over the Giants in the 1958 championship game. He sat in the press box at Giants Stadium and noticed that Giants quarterback Phil Simms had completed only nine passes for just 85 yards, something Unitas didn't expect from one of the league's premier quarterbacks.

"Eighty-five yards? Is that all?" muttered Unitas to writer Bob Glauber, who was sitting nearby. "The biggest problem in the whole NFL is that there aren't enough good quarterbacks. It's a problem because the colleges aren't playing the passing game and the guys coming out don't throw the ball all that much. You can't expect them to be good at the NFL level if they're not coming into the league with much experience at throwing.

"I don't think zone defenses are an excuse. I don't buy it. We played against all kinds of zones. There are things you can do as a quarterback to throw against a zone. The problem now is that you have coaches calling the games in high school, college, and in the pros so that the quarterback doesn't have the experience at calling his own plays. I asked Washington's Mark Rypien once if he wanted to call his own plays. He looked at me and said, 'Heck, no, that would be too hard.'"

Yet, Unitas studied quarterbacks and liked what he saw in some of them. He had a high regard for Dan Marino, a long-distance passer like himself. In 1983, Unitas suggested to Ernie Accorsi, the general manager of the Colts, that he draft the Pittsburgh product. He also had admiration for Troy Aikman, Joe Montana, John Elway, and Steve Young. All had multimillion dollar contracts during their careers, which Unitas easily would have had if he played with them. Outside of the final $250,000 contract Unitas got when he was sold to San Diego at the end of his career, the most he ever got playing for the Colts for 17 years was $125,000.

Gravely Ill

At the age of 53, Unitas was encumbered by physical discomfort. He had a painful rotator cuff in his right shoulder that could only be relieved by surgery. He also needed two knee replacements as a result of the 18 years of punishment he received on the playing field. However, he kept delaying the surgeries because of the cost. None of the needed shoulder and knee operations were covered by the medical benefits available to the players of Unitas' era. There were hundreds of other players like Unitas hobbling around in pain; that was another reason Unitas was so outspoken in his criticism of the NFL. He challenged the league to correct what he felt to be grave injustices.

Unitas finally did get his knee surgery in the spring of 1993, but it almost cost him his life. He momentarily died on the operating table when his heart stopped, but he was quickly resuscitated. A day later, Unitas underwent coronary bypass surgery and was in serious condition for days. He wasn't released from the hospital until almost two weeks later. It was quite an ordeal for the 60-year-old legend who had a tear in his eye when he related what he went through.

"I never had a chance to pray, but I'm thanking the Lord for being so good to me," he said. "For five days after the bypass, it was the weirdest feeling. I was out of it. I was flying missions to Mars, kind of like *Star Wars*. It was the result of all the medication. The operation at Kernan went fine. I had a wonderful roommate, a great kid, a 14-year-old MS patient. I was feeling good. It was the day after Friday evening, and I had dinner. Sandra went out of the room to get a soft drink. My daughter Janice was there with her husband. Then I had this shortness of breath. All hell broke loose. From that point, I was mostly out of town."

The outpouring of love for Unitas touched him. In addition to the hundreds of phone calls, Sandra was already holding two shopping bags of mail "from all over the world," she said. Unitas was thankful. "It's just a tremendous world when sports allows a person like me to play a game and, by so doing, is able to create an image for himself that's revered," said Unitas. "People don't have to be so kind, but they are. The obligation is immense and I tried to be a role model without ever being a big-timer. I've been out of the game for 20 years. For people to remember me in such a way shows how much good there is being able to play football. People don't have to be so kind, but they are."

It was a visibly tired Unitas who was released from the hospital. "It feels good to be able to walk out of here rather than be carried out," he joked. The doctor had told him that his heart attack could have been fatal if it had not occurred in a hospital. He also told him that he should be able to resume his normal routine in approximately two months, which seemed long to Unitas. But the heart surgery had taken a toll: "He can walk, although he still gets tired because he did have a heart attack and he did have emergency triple bypass," explained his doctor. "I would anticipate that he'll go into a full recovery, but he's still awfully weak from this."

A healthy Unitas was in New York a year later when he was named among a dozen or so other legends to the NFL's 75th Anniversary Team. It was an Oscar-like night at Radio City Music Hall, but Unitas was conspicuously missing. He had not heard about the evening and never got an invitation to attend the festivities. He had learned about the honor from John Steadman, the Baltimore sports editor who befriended him over the years.

"What are you talking about?" Unitas asked him.

"You've just been named to the 75th Anniversary Team," Steadman said.

"What's that?"

"They picked the best quarterbacks over 75 years, and you made it."

But Unitas never made the invitation list, and neither did any of his Colts teammates: Gino Marchetti, Raymond Berry, or Jim Parker. Strange indeed, and insulting. Unitas was acknowledged as the greatest quarterback in NFL history, and yet he was shunned. The NFL's attempt at an explanation was that it invited one player from each position. It tried to mollify the slight by announcing that it hoped to get Unitas on a conference call.

"It would have been nice to go over and see some of the guys," said Unitas about the slight. "But the NFL has not done one thing for the players." He then discussed the impact on Baltimore of losing its football team. "[Commissioner Paul] Tagliabue hasn't done anything for the city. He doesn't care about Baltimore. The only way they could bring back NFL football is to steal a team from Los Angeles or Tampa."

A New Baltimore Team

In 1996 Art Modell, the owner of the Cleveland Browns, was allowed to take his NFL franchise to Baltimore and rename it. Baltimore had a team again after 12 years. According to an agreement with the city of Cleveland, that city retained the Browns' heritage and records, including the name, logo, colors, history, playing records, trophies, and memorabilia. Modell tried to get the Colts name returned to Baltimore, and Unitas couldn't have been happier. His beloved Colts, in a new incarnation, could reappear 13 years after leaving Baltimore.

At the NFL owners meeting, Modell made a preliminary inquiry to Jim Irsay, who was running the Colts because of his father's illness, about purchasing the Colts' name. Tagliabue supported the change. The scenario that the commissioner envisioned was that Indianapolis could establish a new identity, and Baltimore could reclaim an old one from the past. Tagliabue deduced that there would be two positive results. However, Irsay stubbornly refused despite hints of a princely sum of money for the name.

"My gut feeling says it's something that's not going to happen," said Irsay when asked about the subject. "I would really emphasize that because I don't see myself parting with it, and it's my decision and my decision

only, but you always listen. I really do not have a strong desire to do anything. I think you can see in this day and age that $25 million, or some-
thing along that line, that's gone in a couple of signing bonuses for players.
That Colts' lineage, that symbol goes on for decades and decades. It's really
difficult to give up something like that for a dollar sign because it has
such a large meaning to your identification.

"You want to respect the fact that this team started in Dallas and went
to Baltimore, then Indianapolis. The Quentin Coryatts and Jim Harbaughs
were teammates of guys that were teammates of Bert Jones and Johnny
Unitas. It's like a lineage. I do feel the horseshoes are a very unique symbol and there's a lot of sentiment attached to that. I emphasize that when
you change the name, it's forever. It's something that goes on for decades.
That's the reason I don't know how to put a price tag on that sort of thing."

Despite the team's having no name, pro football was back in Baltimore.
Then a fan contest produced the brand-new name: Ravens. Modell clev-
erly revived the city's loyal fan base by declaring that his newly created
Ravens would train that summer at the Colts' old stomping grounds in
Westminster, Maryland. The announcement conjured up visions of the
old Colts, and the former players embraced the move, which brought
back warm memories for them. Some even visited Westminster when the
Ravens opened camp at Western Maryland College.

Unitas was one of the first to reach out to Modell and offer him support, and he was there for the Ravens' inaugural game against the Oakland
Raiders. It was like old times when the city's most popular athlete trotted onto the field for the pregame ceremonies at Memorial Stadium.
Approximately 40 former Colts had arrived in Ravens jackets, but when
Unitas slowly trotted on his bad knees to midfield and took off his jacket,
he displayed his No. 19 Colts jersey. The crowd, 62,124 strong, erupted
as if he were going to play once more. Unitas held the football high in his
aching right hand, but instead of throwing the ball, he handed it to the
referee. It was poignant because Unitas had filled the air with passes as
the greatest Colt of all, and had given the fans the most thrills they ever
had. "When Johnny U came out with the ball, it was all over for me," David

Modell, the owner's son, rhapsodized. "It was just one of the most special experiences I'll ever have. I'll remember that forever."

It was also an immensely nostalgic moment for the Ravens coach, Ted Marchibroda. Marchibroda had coached the Colts for the last five years in the 1970s after Unitas had left. He was flushed with emotion as a former Colt himself.

Unitas started the celebration when he reached out and hugged Marchibroda. Then, spontaneously, other Colts did the same with hugs and handshakes. Marchibroda was happy to see Unitas, once again a leader, showing the others the way.

"I told him that it was good to see him," said Marchibroda, "and that I sure wish he could suit up and play. That was a wonderful moment. To have those names from the past on the field just brought home everything that happened here."

Then the Ravens went out and did the unthinkable: they defeated the vaunted Raiders 19–14, much to the chagrin of the Raiders owner, Al Davis, who glared down from his box in dismay. The joy belonged to Marchibroda. "The link from the past to the present made this a special day," exclaimed a happy Marchibroda. "And then winning the game made the day, period."

Unitas had a football team again and so did a deserving city.

20

The Unexpected

S UNDAYS WERE SPECIAL AGAIN. UNITAS HAD A PLAYING FIELD
on which to walk. He went to all the Ravens home games and
stood to the left of the team's bench, where he watched the action with
the eyes of an eagle. At every game, the big TeleTron captured him on
the screen and the crowd would instantly respond with a roar. Unitas
would hold up his arm as high as he could, wave, and smile that crooked
smile that everyone got to know. He got to hear the cheers again and
he felt good.

The arm with which Unitas waved and greeted people was getting
progressively weaker. He practically had no strength in his once-invincible
right arm that had thrown passes from sunrise to sunset. It had deterio-
rated drastically in the 30 years since he had incurred the freakish injury.
In the final 1968 preseason game against Dallas, he had succeeded in escap-
ing from the pressure of several Cowboys only to throw a sidearm pass
awkwardly. Pain shot through his arm when he got smacked on his elbow.
On the plane back to Baltimore, Unitas winced saying, "It's really sore,
puffed up, black and blue." Lenny Moore remarked, "I've known my man
John since 1956, and that was the first time I've ever heard him admit he
had pain."

More Medical Problems

Unitas was dealing with tremendous pain. He had two artificial knees, a plastic replacement for the middle finger of his right hand, and the bypass heart surgery that had turned into a life-or-death situation. With his right arm totally useless, he couldn't put off the additional surgery any longer. In 1997 he went into an operating room once again for complex surgery. At the University of Maryland Hospital Medical Systems, Dr. Andrew Eglseder worked for five hours to repair the damaged arm. After the surgery, Unitas said, "Dr. Eglseder mentioned after what he found that he didn't know how I was able to play the last four or five seasons. The ligaments just reattached themselves where they weren't supposed to be and I guess I made the best of the situation." Unitas then began three months of rehabilitation with his old friend and therapist, Bill Neill, who had tended to him so many times in the past at Kernan Hospital. The therapy lasted four months, and when it was over, there was no improvement in Unitas' arm. At age 66, he faced the rest of his life with a useless right arm that continued to worsen. He developed atrophy in his index finger and thumb. He couldn't lift half of a pound with his right hand. He couldn't button his shirt or tie his shoes, and he could hardly write his name. Painfully, he held a pen between his thumb and pinky. But his adoring fans waited patiently in line for long periods of time at card shows as he slowly wrote his name because he was still Johnny Unitas— the greatest quarterback of them all.

Frustratingly, he couldn't extract a dollar from the NFL despite his disabilities. When he requested compensation, he was turned down. They positioned their rejection behind a legality that declared that for him to be eligible for any compensation, he had to apply by the age of 55. They added that "he was not totally and permanently disabled." The league also contended that it paid him a pension of $4,000 a month. Unitas never went to court with his grievance. He was not one to beg. If he pursued the legal channels, it would not have been difficult to find a jury to be sympathetic to his infirmity, which was so visible and humbling.

Unitas maintained that his arm didn't become impaired until he was 60 years old. He heard that he waited too long to initiate any legal action, but he was too honest to claim that the disability had surfaced earlier. "There was no way to do that before I turned 55 because the residual part of the injury hadn't become apparent," he said. "Any such legal redress would have been fraudulent, not legitimate, and I don't think anyone wants to listen to claims that are invented from fiction. [Now] I have no strength in the fingers. I can't use a hammer or saw around the house. I can't button buttons. I can't use zippers. Very difficult to tie shoes. I can't brush my teeth because I can't hold a brush. I can't hold a fork with the right hand. You give me a cup of coffee and I can't hold it. I can't comb my hair."

Among other things, Unitas undauntedly managed to continue his golf game, but it took some doing. Just to grip a club, he had to use his left hand to close the fingers of his disabled right one. Then he had to strap the hand securely to the shaft of his club with a Velcro strip. He had to follow that procedure with every shot he took. With time and patience he got to a 19 handicap. "I do it putting, too," said Unitas.

Still a Part of Baltimore

In 1997 Unitas appeared at a ceremony for the official closing of Memorial Stadium, which had served as the Ravens' home for two years. It was Unitas' home, too, and had been for a lot longer than that. It was the site of most of his memorable games, and if Unitas felt somewhat melancholy, it was understandable. The old stadium was the last tangible symbol that associated him and the city with the Colts. It was closed until its demolition in 2001. In a final symbolic moment, Unitas was supposed to throw a football, passing it downfield. He couldn't. He had to hand it off instead, something he hated doing when he played.

The Ravens' new stadium opened in 1998. It was a magnificent edifice with a capacity of 69,084 and cost $200 million to construct. Unitas was there for the opening, and he claimed his little patch of soil to the left of the Ravens' bench just like he had at Memorial Stadium. Only this time, the fans got to see more of the legendary quarterback. The new playground had not only one giant screen, but two. They were located in the end zones and measured 100 feet by 24 feet. They are the largest permanent display screens of any sports venue in the world. There was more of Unitas and more of his emblematic wave and smile.

It didn't take long for the expansion Ravens to reach the Super Bowl. They did so in 2000, their fifth year in Baltimore, and Unitas couldn't have been more pleased. Baltimore had a championship football team again. Unitas had been the last quarterback to bring it one, back in 1970. There was somewhat of a parallel between Unitas and the 2000 Ravens quarterback, Trent Dilfer.

Like Unitas, Dilfer wasn't wanted. He was let go by Tampa Bay after the 1999 season and signed with the Ravens as a free agent. He then led the Ravens into the playoffs and on to a convincing 34–7 victory in Super Bowl XXXV over the Giants, much like Unitas did in 1958 and 1959. He got the Ravens their first touchdown with a 38-yard pass to Brandon Stokely. The Ravens defense took over at that point and held the Giants to a paltry 152 yards to achieve an overwhelming victory.

Dilfer was gone after that season, but Unitas befriended the Ravens' rookie quarterback, Chris Redman, during the 2000 campaign. Redman had played at Louisville and was the recipient of the John Unitas Golden Arm Award as a senior. Unitas looked after the youngster when he arrived in Baltimore that spring. Redman didn't know anybody, didn't have a car or a place to live. Unitas took care of everything. His son, John Jr., a real estate broker, secured a house for the rookie. Then Unitas turned to a longtime friend and got Redman a car from his dealership. He worked with Redman and was his personal mentor, which excited Redman. How many young quarterbacks could ever get hands-on attention from the great Unitas?

The old artist was doing what he always did, grabbing a football and teaching the young rookie the nuances of the game. They talked often, and Redman had an open line to his teacher whenever he wanted to call. Being the perfectionist that he was, Unitas wasn't easy on Redman. The first touchdown pass he threw in a preseason game didn't get Unitas' full

John and Dorothy Unitas and their children at home in Baltimore a few days before Christmas in 1959. PHOTO COURTESY OF BETTMAN/CORBIS.

John, second wife Sandy, and son at John Unitas Day in Baltimore in 1977.
PHOTO COURTESY OF THE INDIANAPOLIS COLTS.

Unitas led Ewbank's Colts back to the NFL title game in 1959, beating the Giants again by the more comfortable margin of 31–16.

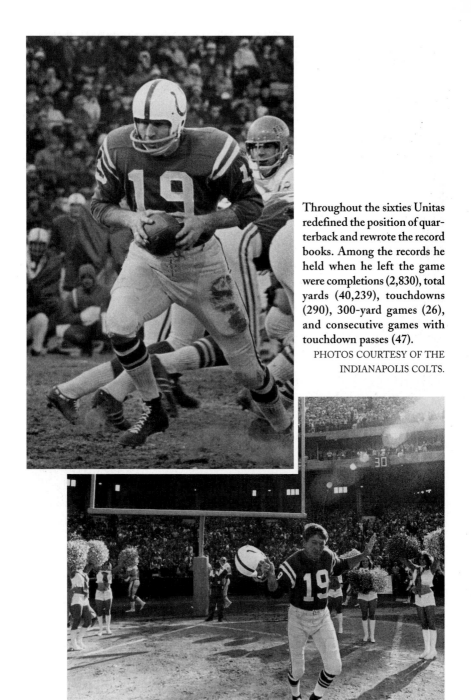

Throughout the sixties Unitas redefined the position of quarterback and rewrote the record books. Among the records he held when he left the game were completions (2,830), total yards (40,239), touchdowns (290), 300-yard games (26), and consecutive games with touchdown passes (47).

PHOTOS COURTESY OF THE INDIANAPOLIS COLTS.

Unitas brought the Colts to their fourth championship game under his reign in Super Bowl V against the Dallas Cowboys in 1971. Though he was knocked out of the game on this play, his team prevailed, 16–13.   PHOTO COURTESY OF AP/WIDE WORLD PHOTOS.

Visiting with President Richard Nixon at the White House during the 1971 championship season.   PHOTO COURTESY OF BETTMAN/CORBIS.

The 1972 season was a bitter disappointment for an aging Unitas, who was benched by a team that struggled to win five games. PHOTO COURTESY OF THE INDIANAPOLIS COLTS.

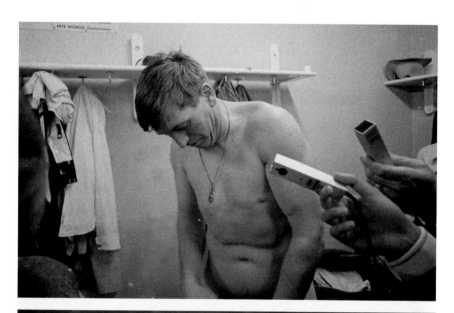

Unitas answers reporters' questions after playing in his final game as a Baltimore Colt (top). He would soon be traded to San Diego, where he finished out his Hall-of-Fame playing career.
TOP PHOTO COURTESY OF BETTMAN/CORBIS;
BOTTOM PHOTO COURTESY OF FOCUS ON SPORTS.

To Lou
Only The Best To
a Guy Who Knows
The Game!
Tony Veteri
H.L 36

Unitas with former NFL referee Tony Veteri. "Unitas was as accurate a passer as anyone, and one of the greatest competitors I ever saw," remarked Veteri

PHOTO COURTESY OF TONY VETERI.

The ever-popular Unitas acknowledges his fans.

approval. "You can't float that ball up there, Redman," he scolded. Perhaps Unitas saw himself in Redman. At 6'3" he was a good prospect with a lively arm. He had a future as tomorrow's quarterback.

His Passing

Unitas never got to help Redman realize that future. On September 11, 2002, Unitas was in his office with longtime friend Richard Sammis, on what seemed an ordinary day. Sammis, who shared his office space with Unitas, was with him for most of the day. "We were laughing and joking, and he did some business and made some calls," said Sammis. "I was with him from about 9:30 until 2:30, when he left and said he was going to work out like he does almost every day. When he was leaving, he said, 'I'll be back tomorrow.'" A half-hour later, Unitas collapsed and died while exercising at the Kernan Physical Therapy Center. The frantic attempt to resuscitate him failed. He died instantly from a massive heart attack.

Only a week before, Unitas had been at the Camden Club with his wife, Sandra, having lunch with Julia Ruth Stevens, Babe Ruth's daughter. The 85-year-old dowager made annual visits to Baltimore to visit the Babe Ruth Birthplace and Museum. The meeting was special because Unitas had recently donated his memorabilia to the same museum.

"He had debated the perfect place for his collection," said Mike Gibbons, the museum's director. "The possibilities were the Pro Football Hall of Fame, the University of Louisville, and here. This is where he achieved all his football glory. His family wanted to keep the collection together and display it for the fans, and we agreed that, come hell or high water, in this museum we would create a permanent facility for John's collection."

Stevens and Unitas chatted for about an hour and a half, and it was a conversation only the two of them could have had. They understood celebrity. Stevens started talking about her father and his death, how he was laid out in Yankee Stadium and eulogized. Unitas said, "There ain't going to be no eulogy for me." His wife interrupted, "Oh yes there will, and you won't be able to stop it because you won't be able to do anything about it."

Unitas' death was untimely. It came just before a 13-foot bronze statue of Unitas, with his trademark high-top shoes, was to be unveiled to a cheering crowd during the halftime of a Ravens contest against Jacksonville. Two days after the unveiling, the museum had scheduled a fundraiser featuring the largest assemblage of Colts players ever. Instead, without Unitas, the events turned into tributes for the stilled idol.

The Ravens owner, Art Modell, was shaken by Unitas' death. "This is stunning, sad, sad news," he said. "He was a good friend, my contemporary. He helped make me love this game more. It meant so much to me, my family, and our team when he embraced us when we first arrived. He is on the short list of players that you can count on one hand of the greatest to ever play. His impact was enormous."

Tom Matte was in Ocean City, Maryland, preparing for a radio show when the report of Unitas' passing reached him. "My producer told me that he just got word, although it wasn't positive, that John had a heart attack at the Kernan Center and passed away," the former running back recalled. "I told him to call me back when it was definite. I couldn't believe it. He looked so great. We did so many things together and he loved playing golf. I was with him only the weekend before at Towson State, where he signed on as spokesman. He was excited about it, too."

The disturbing news of Unitas' death reverberated throughout the country, first on the East Coast, when commuters were on their way home from work. It was a top story on the early television news shows the next day, but it reached the old Colts players sooner.

Gino Marchetti got the word as soon as he walked into his house in West Chester, Pennsylvania. Because it was the first anniversary of the September 11 terrorist attacks, Marchetti, like most Americans, said that he "was praying all day that he wouldn't hear any bad news." Once inside the house, he heard his wife on the phone saying, "Oh, no." "I thought those bastards had blown up another building," he said. "She told me John had died. I saw John three or four weeks ago, kidded him that he looked younger than ever."

Art Donovan was shaken. "I was so shocked," said Donovan, whose ready humor was somber now. "It's just a tragedy. A damn shame. Him dying like that. I think he was the greatest football player to ever play the game. There was nobody like Unitas. He was a breed apart. I've told people that I thought John and Joe DiMaggio were the two greatest living athletes and now they're both gone."

Bill Curry, who centered the ball to Unitas for three years, had a special memory of Unitas, which showed his greatness. Curry said, "Nothing in sports matches football training camp two-a-days for discomfort and disgust, and the guy was happy. I said, 'How can you be whistling, old man? It's hot out here!' He grinned, 'You better enjoy today, Billy. You're a long time dead.' 'What did you say?' I couldn't believe my ears. 'You're a long time dead, so why not enjoy every day, every practice? I love football practice.'"

Curry went on to describe Unitas' impact on professional football: "The thing that makes him so hard to describe, even for those of us who spent years with him in the trenches, is that despite his natural humility, his stoic mien, he really was larger than life. He really did personally transform the National Football League from the sandlot to the Great American Obsession."

Don Shula had coached Unitas for seven years. Although they didn't always agree with each other, Shula had the highest praise for Unitas and attributed much of his coaching success to the taciturn quarterback. "He was one of the toughest competitors I ever saw and overcame tremendous odds to become one of the greatest quarterbacks in NFL history," said Shula. "He was the first of the great modern quarterbacks, and his performances set the standard for everyone else who followed him at that position."

Buzz Nutter couldn't believe Unitas had died when he received the phone call at his office in La Plata, Maryland. He had handed the ball to Unitas for five straight years from his center position and sat heartbroken with the other Colts at the funeral. "Without being partial, John was the greatest quarterback who ever played," said Nutter. "He was in total control in the huddle at all times. If Weeb Ewbank sent in a play and John didn't like it, he'd change it. He just loved to play. In the 1958 championship game, the referee was explaining to him about overtime and all that, and John finally stopped him by saying, 'Let's get on with it and play the game.' He was respected by every player in the league and the officials, too. Everybody knew who he was. The league should recognize him with some kind of award, like the Lombardi Trophy."

The admirable union that Unitas had with Raymond Berry was perhaps the most celebrated in any sport. They spent more time on the field honing their skills than any two athletes. And Berry, who wasn't regarded too highly as a prospect when he came into the NFL, worked hour after hour with Unitas to become a Hall-of-Fame receiver. He was as much of an underdog as Unitas was when they met for the first time in 1956 at training camp. He had a deep love for Unitas.

"It gets clearer every year that to be able to be in Baltimore as a receiver and get to play 12 years with him, I have to classify as the best break I ever got in my career," said Berry. "The type of quarterback he was, the leader he was, he was totally focused on moving the football, scoring points, and winning. He never thought about records and individual things; he was all business. He was the toughest competitor you could hope for. He simply refused to lose. You pretty much had to drive a stake through his heart if you were going to beat him."

Two years before Unitas' death, he visited Berry. It was the first time they had gotten together in a number of years, and Berry cherished the visit. "I'm so glad I had that time with him," said Berry. "I had a chance to ask him about things I've always wondered about. I drilled him on his thinking, his calls, his strategy. It had been 30 years since we played together, and in the time we spent apart, I had the chance to reflect on the things that made him such a great quarterback. It was his uncanny instinct for calling the right play at the right time, his icy composure under fire, his fierce competitiveness, and his utter disregard for his own safety."

Ernie Accorsi, too, had a special bond with Unitas, which began the first day he walked into the Colts' office in 1971 as the team's new public relations director. However, his earliest memory of Unitas was as a youngster in 1956 when the Colts played a preseason game in Hershey, Pennsylvania, Accorsi's hometown. "I saw him throw his first NFL pass . . . saw the first preseason game he ever played," he said.

But Accorsi did not meet Unitas until 15 years later, and he never dreamed that his first look at Unitas that summer of 1956 would develop into a long and warm friendship. He recalled, "His last game for the Colts was in 1972, the final game of the season. We lost 16–0 in Miami, and the Dolphins went undefeated. The Hall of Fame had called me a couple of days before the game and told me to collect everything John had on. After the game, I walked over to John's locker with a plastic bag and started filling it with everything I could get, socks, shirts, tape, when he asked me what I was doing. I told him that the Hall of Fame wanted it all. 'They can't have my shoes,' barked Unitas. 'Are they that sentimental?' [I asked.] 'Hell no, it's great to cut the grass with them.'"

Accorsi also recalled his thoughts at Unitas' funeral as he sat there as a pallbearer: "I always think how tough he was. I try to take from him. If I was in a jam or needed some mental strength, I would think about him and I would get through it. If he was alive today and I called him, he'd be there for me. If he was your friend, it was for life. Not only was he the greatest quarterback who ever lived, he was one of the best friends I ever had."

Tex Schramm, who had been around pro football for more than 50 years and was instrumental in building the Dallas Cowboy dynasties of Tom Landry, was a great admirer of Unitas. "There were guys like Otto Graham and Sammy Baugh who were great passers, but Unitas was really the first great, unbelievable passing quarterback," said Schramm. "We never had anything like that before in the league. He could hit anything. And he did it late in close games. He was a player the people loved to watch. Unitas had something that you can't exactly put into words, a form of quiet leadership you don't see much of anymore, and it was more than that day in 1958. As the audience for pro football grew with that game and others that followed, Unitas represented something to the public."

Commissioner Paul Tagliabue recognized that, too. "Johnny Unitas will always be a legendary name in NFL history," he predicted. "One of the greatest quarterbacks to ever play the game, he epitomized the position with his leadership skills and his ability to perform under pressure. At a time when national television was beginning to focus on the NFL, Johnny U captured the public's imagination and helped drive the popularity of professional football."

Jim Irsay was 13 years old when his father bought the Colts. He grew up a Unitas fan. "He was a hero to so many people, including me," said Irsay. "Without question, Johnny was the reason football catapulted to the top of the professional sports world. He was a leader in so many ways, a man of indescribable talent and extraordinary character. Johnny leaves us with many great memories, and we are all grateful for what he gave us in his lifetime."

Unitas was a different kind of superstar. His humility toward his celebrity status allowed him to reach everyone. He became the people's quarterback. And he seemed at ease, pleased to be around everyday people. That was how he grew up and he never wanted to change.

Joe Montana, who, like Unitas, was proficient in the two-minute offense, had deep affection for Unitas. The only jersey he ever bought was Unitas' No. 19. "I wear it like a sweatshirt," said Montana. "[It's] the only jersey I do that with." Some have argued that Montana, having won four Super Bowls, was better than Unitas. Montana disagrees: "My hat's off to him all the way. He played in a lot tougher era. You could hold, could kick, and could bite each other back then."

The Giants' Dick Modzelewski played during that time. "The big thing between he and I was in the 1958 game," he said. "I sacked him three times. They had a third-and-19 to go, and I go to get him for the fourth time, and they ran a trap and got 20 yards. He always kidded me about that. I said it was the dumbest play you could ever call, and he would ask, 'Did it work?'" Twenty years after that unforgettable game, the players got together for a nationally televised six-man touch football game in New York's Central Park. "They told me that he and Raymond Berry got together and practiced for two days for a touch football game," said Modzelewski. "Then, they beat us again. I loved John to death. He was a super guy. I don't know anybody who disliked John."

It was Unitas' unyielding refusal to accept failure, even in a harmless touch football game, that made him such a revered figure for the millions of pro football followers. When he retired, one writer eloquently described Unitas' departure: "Superstars are constantly making the scene, but Johnny Unitas was maybe the last of the real sports heroes. He was the kind of athlete little kids could admire and copy, and whose stories were the kind you could read with your breakfast cereal. We won't see anyone quite like him again."

The funeral mass was held at the Cathedral of Mary Our Queen and was presided over by William Cardinal Keeler, the Archbishop of Baltimore. The services that September 17 morning were a testament to Unitas' influence. Two thousand mourners silently sat and stood outside on the sidewalk on Charles Street. His funeral was the largest ever to take place in Baltimore. Frank Gitschier, the head of Johnny Unitas Golden Arm Educational Foundation in Louisville, and Raymond Berry, eulogized Unitas. Gitschier called Unitas "the most approachable legend that I have ever seen or heard about." A teary Berry said, "You elevated all of us. . . . You made the impossible possible." Five of Unitas' eight children, Joseph, Janice Ann, Kenneth, John Jr., and Paige, spoke proudly of their father. Cardinal Keeler said that Unitas "was the kind of man who would shake the hand of a homeless person and say to that person it was a honor to shake his hand. He humbly and generously dealt with everyone."

The service was dignified and poignant. An old friend, John Ziemann, was touched by what he saw at the service. "I was standing there and watching my heroes with the Baltimore Colts come up with tears in their eyes," said Ziemann. "I thought I would never see that. It's the first time I ever saw tears in the eyes of the Baltimore Colts." Fittingly, as Unitas' casket emerged from the church, a plane flew overhead towing a banner that read, "Unitas We Stand."

Posthumous Honors

On the Sunday after the funeral, the Ravens hosted Tampa Bay. Unitas' protégé, Redman, made his first home start. Redman wanted to extend a special honor to Unitas by wearing black high-top shoes, a pair of which was unveiled on the patch of ground where Unitas used to stand by the Ravens' bench. Also a replica of Unitas' famous No. 19 jersey was emblazoned on the grass behind the shoes. Redman was fined $5,000 by the league afterward for wearing a pair, a first-time offense of the uniform dress code. The league allowed the players to add a small No. 19 to the backs of their helmets, however. But Redman didn't care about the fine. He was wearing the shoes.

Some six hundred miles away in Indianapolis, the Colts were playing the Miami Dolphins that same Sunday. Peyton Manning, too, wanted to wear black high-top shoes to honor Unitas, but he was told by a team official that he would face a $25,000 fine, maybe more. Manning was willing to pay the fine, but he later changed his mind because he determined that by wearing the shoes in defiance of the NFL, it would create a public controversy, which would be a dishonor to Unitas. Manning met Unitas when he was named the 1998 winner of the Johnny Unitas Golden Arm Award. At the presentation, Manning surprised Unitas by presenting him with a pair of his University of Tennessee high-tops. One of Manning's cherished photos is of him and Unitas standing together side by side holding the high-tops.

"He told me he liked the way I played the game," said Manning. "That was real neat. I can't tell you what a great compliment that was to have Johnny U say that. It would have been such an honor wearing the black high-tops again."

Unitas' signature black high-top shoes will always be venerated in NFL lore. "If you had a drawing of a pair of high-tops and a crew cut, it would only be one person, Johnny Unitas," said Joe Horrigan, vice president of communications and exhibits at the Pro Football Hall of Fame. "He was a caricature of football in the fifties."

A month after Unitas' death, Art Modell renamed the area in front of Gate A at the Ravens' stadium: Unitas Plaza. Modell was in Yankee Stadium in 1958, and that one dramatic game stimulated Modell to buy the Cleveland Browns. "That reconfirmed my love for football in spades," he said. "[We were] a new team seeking to establish our credentials, and I think there was some resentment on the part of the old Baltimore Colts. But not Johnny. He reached out for our family and our franchise."

One year after his death, Unitas received another honor. Towson University named its new stadium for him. Unitas Stadium became the only college stadium to be named after a professional athlete. Unitas' second wife, Sandra, said, "The stadium, which now stands in his memory, will for ages reverberate with the sights and sounds of athletic events and the young athletes he so loved."

At the halftime dedication, many former Colts paid their respects by unveiling the field sign. "It's nice to see something with Johnny's name on it," said Rich Volk, a former teammate. "It's important for the whole community to remember him. He really was Baltimore." Governor Robert Ehrlich Jr. also appeared at the dedication. The governor recalled that one of his favorite memories of Unitas was at a fundraiser in Washington. "During a question-and-answer session, someone asked him what he would be making today with the zillions of dollars players make today. He told them $3 million. The room was silent, stunned. Then he said, 'Of course, I am 66 years old.'"

Unitas alone ushered the league into the television era during the fifties and sixties. That one game in 1958 was so memorable that Lamar Hunt created the American Football League two years later. There is no minimizing the profound impact Johnny Unitas had on the game of professional football at a period in time when baseball was America's favorite sport.

Hall-of-Fame quarterback Len Dawson powerfully described Unitas' style on the field and off: "Unitas wasn't just a passer, he was a football player. He would do anything to win. He was the best of his time, a gunslinger when they didn't throw the ball as much as they do today.

He was a person who spoke his mind and fought for benefits for the old timers."

Johnny Unitas ushered in a new era of professional football by adhering to tried-and-true basics. He played with this heart, his mind, his faith, and his courage. He was a hero to his fans, and is a legend in the game.

Afterword

Johnny's Time

THERE IS A TIME IN EVERYONE'S LIFE—JUST ONE TIME—WHEN the sun seems brighter, the sky bluer, the music prettier. For some, it might be their high school or college years, the best job they ever had, or the best boyfriend or girlfriend of their lives. Try to make that unique time happen again, or attempt to relive a similar experience, and your heart will be broken. Wrap it up in a ribbon and put it in your heart: God only gives it to us once. There are no second acts in life.

For me and for you—for Baltimore and for much of Maryland, no matter if you are from Dundalk or Towson, from Patterson Park or West Baltimore, from Westminster or Druid Hill Park—it was Johnny Unitas' time. It was a time when the National Bohemian beer tasted the best it ever has and the crabs were never better. It was a time when we truly lived in "the land of pleasant living," when those wonderful television ads created by Doner Advertising really were true.

To understand how much it meant to all of us, you first had to understand the town in 1956 as only we understood it. There had never been anything of national athletic significance in Baltimore, at least not since the Orioles of the 1890s. Maryland had some great college football teams in the early and mid-fifties. But they were never embraced by fans in Baltimore and were generally greeted by a collective yawn. It was the

243

Baltimore Colts that became the city's college, the Colts' fight song its alma mater.

I didn't grow up in Baltimore. I was born and raised 80 miles to the north in Hershey, Pennsylvania. Traveling to Baltimore for sports events was never considered by my family. There wasn't anything there. Baltimore had no teams. It was largely ignored for just about every other reason, too. It was the best-kept secret in America. After all, my dad wasn't going to take me to the Block. You went to Philadelphia.

Then, during the summer of 1956, everything changed. It began happening on a summer night in Memorial Stadium when more than forty thousand people came to see a Colts' intra-squad scrimmage, pitting the "blue" against the "white." It was that night when a spindlylegged unknown, who had been cut by the Pittsburgh Steelers, with rubber bands holding up his rolled-up sleeves, played for both teams. He electrified the fans by throwing touchdown passes for the "white." They had come to salute the National Football League's 1955 rookie of the year, George Shaw; they left talking about a quarterback named Unitas, whose name many of them couldn't even pronounce. They hardly could have imagined that Johnny Unitas was going to change a city.

The Colts came to my hometown the following Saturday night to play their first exhibition game against the Philadelphia Eagles, a team that trained in our town and a team I detested from birth. In fact, I had started to root for the Colts in 1954, when they first came to Hershey and beat Philadelphia to begin their annual summer exhibition ritual. If you could beat the Eagles, you were OK with me. But that night in 1956, at age 14, I was getting that tingling feeling about this team that every kid gets for one team in his life that signals a lifelong love affair.

The first quarter ends. Out comes Shaw and in comes Unitas. I had never heard of him, and I wasn't very happy because I paid the entire $2.50 I had earned that day caddying double at the Hershey Country Club for a ticket to see Shaw play. Before very long, though, even the untrained eye of a young boy could see the magic lasers being fired all over the field

244

by this unknown backup. The team in blue and white moved relentlessly up and down the field through the air for a decisive victory. It may have been only an exhibition game—we didn't call them preseason games back then—but I had just watched Johnny Unitas play the first NFL game of his life.

The lasers never stopped whistling their way across the green fields on which the Colts played until they were silenced by a 1973 trade to the San Diego Chargers that seems senseless even to this day. The passes might have gotten a little softer as the years went on, but they nevertheless took Baltimore to one last championship in 1970.

The games and the numbers have now been chronicled by many. They have been rediscovered and written about and broadcast across the land—all of them finally representing an acknowledgment of what those of us who loved him all these years always knew: John Unitas was the greatest quarterback to ever play the game.

Every city and every team that has won a championship thinks their accomplishments and their heritage are unique. But there really has never been anything like Baltimore and the Colts. There will never be anything like them again.

If you don't believe me, go to 33rd Street. Walk around that vacant lot. Maybe on a Sunday afternoon in autumn. Maybe with your children or grandchildren. Listen hard and you can hear the voice of Roger Griswall or Harry Shriver echoing through the air: "Unitas complete to Berry. First down, Colts." Listen hard and you will hear the sounds one more time: "C-O-L-T-S . . . COLTS."

What lingers in our memory and what will live in our hearts are the men who made that time for us: Marchetti, Moore, Parker, Ameche, Berry, Pellington, Lipscomb, Donovan, Mutscheller, Dupre, Sandusky, Tasseff.

But however many names you properly want to put in the pantheon of the Baltimore Colts—however big a role you rightly want to ascribe to the coaches of that time, to the organization's staff, to the fans—there was one man who made it happen for all of them and for all of us. His name was John Constantine Unitas, and for Baltimore the time was Camelot.

> The rain may never fall till after sundown.
>
> By eight, the morning fog must disappear.
>
> In short, there's simply not a more congenial spot,
>
> For happily-ever-aftering than here in Camelot.

—Ernie Accorsi

An Interview
with Johnny Unitas

Baltimore, Maryland
October 3, 1989

I N AN EXCLUSIVE INTERVIEW, THE AUTHOR SPOKE WITH Johnny Unitas about his career with the Baltimore Colts. This never-before-published material reveals Unitas' own opinions, personal recollections, and unique personality.

Lou Sahadi: What was training camp like in 1958?

Johnny Unitas: In 1958, going into training camp in July, we came into camp with great expectations because of the type of season we had in 1957. I'm sure the coaches felt that with a little luck in 1957 we could have won the title. In 1958 coming into training camp, everybody was healthy, we had great expectations of being able to win the title in the NFL.

Sahadi: How did you feel going to camp, physically?

Unitas: Physically I was fine. Didn't have any particular type injuries at all from 1957. I guess the biggest thing we had [done was] to win one game out of three in 1957. We had to win one ball game to win it all, and then we lost our two ball games back to back: one to L.A. and one to San Francisco. And in the San Francisco ball game, the way they beat us was that [Dicky Moegle] actually came out of the back field—and Y. A. Tittle was quarterback at that time—and he went down and just pushed our defensive back, Milt Davis, to the ground and then caught the ball, which was thrown by Tittle, for the touchdown just to win the ball game. Of course, had we had instant replay, we would have been able to argue and scream about that.

So coming into the 1958 season, I think everyone came in with a tremendous outlook and great expectations because of the way we ended up, played the year previously. And the football team was just starting to gel, with the veterans like [Gino] Marchetti, and [Art] Donovan, and [Eugene] "Big Daddy" [Lipscomb] and all these people who were there. And with a crop of good rookies coming in, we felt we had a good opportunity.

Sahadi: How were the players with Weeb [Ewbank]?

Unitas: I always enjoyed Weeb as a coach. He sometimes would overlook things that the veterans did, but if the rookies would do the same thing, he'd jump on [them] with all four feet!

Sahadi: Like what?

Unitas: Well, you might be late for a meeting or something like that. If [Alan] Ameche walked in a little bit late, or Marchetti walked in a little late, somebody didn't say anything. But as soon as a rookie walked in late, it was a $100 fine. I think it made it a little difficult on him as a coach to do things like that. He'd overlook some things that the veterans would do, where when a rookie did it, he would jump on him. But the players liked Weeb.

His coaching ability was second to none as far as I was concerned, and I guess his greatest asset was his way of organization. Organizing practices, organizing the game plan, and then giving it to his assistant coaches and making sure that it got to the players. And the organization and the situations that he put you into . . . when you went into a ball game with Weeb, you almost knew pretty much what the other team was going to do in a given situation. And their defensive [plays] wouldn't change—that you learn through study of plays and those type things. But he was a great organizer. And practices ran like clockwork. We worked about an hour and a half, and that was it. And I don't think he could have wanted for anything better than that.

Sahadi: How was training camp?

Unitas: Training camp was hard. We worked twice a day, and then we had meetings all the time. I guess our meetings were a little bit different than [those] most people [had]. Weeb had a playbook, and in the book was his organizational ability. And he used to stand up at the head of the class and recite, or read everything to the players, and we had to sit down there with a pencil and paper, and we had to write out the proper fundamental for a "crackback block," the proper fundamental for a "shoulder block," the proper fundamental for a "downfield block." All those things. We wrote it out just like [we] were in school. 'Cause [Weeb] felt that you learned from reading and writing and studying, and actually playing on the field, and so on. And I think that's probably the old Paul Brown [influence], 'cause he was involved with Paul Brown for a number of years.

So we did a lot of schoolwork-type stuff in training camp. And everyone was expected offensively to know everyone's position on the ball club. In other words, I had to know what the tackles did, the guards did, the center did: I had to know what everybody did on every given play. And your offensive tackles had to know the same thing. That way you knew the continuity of the play—where it was going, what your responsibility was, but also what the guy next to you, his responsibility was. And we had tests, examinations. We'd come in one evening, and, "OK, you've had your plays, 4, 5, 6 plays. I want your offensive tackles. Give me your position, plus the rest in line. Quarterbacks, give me everybody's. Offensive back, give me your position," and so on. And you were graded on it. That was my third year, 1958. I was there 1956, 1957, 1958.

Sahadi: So going back to your start in professional football, Weeb gave you the shot. He was the one that made that important phone call, right?

Unitas: No, Don Kellett was the general manager. Don Kellett gave me the shot in 1956. He called me, asked me if I was still interested in playing in February 1956. I said, "Yes." He said, "I'm looking for a backup quarterback for [George] Shaw." [Gary] Kerkorian was the backup quarterback, and he had decided to retire. He was going back to law school. "So we're looking for a backup quarterback, and you got a good recommendation from coach Herman Ball"—who was with Pittsburgh in 1955—"and we'd like to give you a workout, a tryout. I'll send you a contract there." I think it was $7,000. So I said, "Fine." I felt that I would have a [good] opportunity in Baltimore because [they only had] one other quarterback there—another rookie and myself.

Sahadi: Was Ewbank the coach when you tried out?

Unitas: Yeah, Weeb was the coach in 1956. In fact, he was the coach in 1953.

Sahadi: That was his first head-coaching job, wasn't it?

Unitas: Yeah, 1953.

Sahadi: How did Weeb prepare you for the first game of the 1958 season? Did he say, "John, it's up to you"?

Unitas: In 1958, of course, I was the number one quarterback at the time. [Shaw] took over in 1956. So I was number one, George was number two. And we went into camp with that knowledge.

And we practiced. You'd put your whole offense in, and it'd come up to game time, and you'd have a game plan.

And it's the opening of the season, and you played your preseason ball games, and then you'd have films of, like, maybe Detroit. Detroit was our first ball game in 1958. So we had films on Detroit for at least two or three [games] and possibly what we had from last year. So [they'd] look at the films and they'd make their game plan up accordingly: [these are] our running plays, these are our pass offense, and so forth.

Usually what happened with Weeb [was] he always like to call the first three plays. So we always went on the field with three plays already called. Already knew what he wanted the first three plays. So we'd run that first play, unless the defense was stacked against it, come back with the second play, run that one, and come back with a third play.

Sahadi: Did he have a pattern for those plays?

Unitas: No, just maybe three things he decided he wanted to start with. And he might make a first down on the first one. You might get lucky and make a touchdown. A lot of times we opened up the ball game with a long pass just to let them know we're gonna go deep on 'em, just to test the water. But that's the way he was. He wanted to call those first three plays. And after that, that was it.

Sahadi: What was it like going into the Detroit game? Were any of the Colts injured?

Unitas: We went in the ball game 100 percent. We won the ball game 28 to something. Our concern with Detroit was with Bobby Layne and their defense; they'd always possessed a very, very difficult defense. Joe Schmidt called signals from the middle linebacker position, and Alex Karras and other folks on the football team had always been outstanding people. Defensively, we knew they were very difficult.

Sahadi: What did you have to do to beat them?

Unitas: [We] had to control the game . . . to score. [We] tried to keep the ball away. Another one of Weeb's idiosyncrasies: he wouldn't allow you to throw the football into [Dick] "Night Train" Lane's area. He respected Night Train a tremendous amount.

Sahadi: How did you feel about that?

Unitas: I said, "I can't do that, I can't let a guy have an open, free day on me. We gotta do something. We gotta throw at him, and just be careful with it." What happened, I went one time too many into his area and got it picked off [and run] back for a touchdown on me.

Sahadi: What did Weeb say?

Unitas: Oh, he was hollering and screaming. He was up in arms: "I told you! I told you! I told you!" We got back [and] we ended up winning the football game. But to play against Detroit, you had to be fairly methodical and ready to change the plays at the line of scrimmage because Joe Schmidt was so good at diagnosing, maybe studying, you to know what you might want to do. He would change those defenses on you, and you had to be ready to change that play.

Sahadi: So how did you figure to beat him, on short passes or deep?

Unitas: Well we'd very seldom get anything deep on him. And so you went for the medium-range passes, 15 to 18 yards.

Sahadi: To whom?

Unitas: To Raymond [Berry]. Lenny Moore, Jim Mutscheller in the tight-end position. And you ran the ball with Ameche and L. G. Dupre.

Then, if you threw the ball 30 times a game, it was an awful lot. Most of the time you threw the ball maybe somewhere like 20, 22, 23 times. Now they throw it 62, 70 times a ball game and come up with these 400-yard games. That's the way. You ought to be able to do that every week, if that's the case!

Sahadi: What was it like to play the Chicago Bears?

Unitas: We were always leery about going into Chicago and playing the Bears on their own home field, Wrigley Field. [We were] always fearful of [not] getting out of there alive because the Bears were always the most physical football team in the National Football League to us. We played them a number of years [and] always ended up hurt one way or another by some key personnel, or what have you.

They had excellent personnel. Bill George [was] middle linebacker, and Doug Atkins [was] defensive end. Richie Pettibone [was] safety. [J. C.] Caroline [was] the defensive back. Great material. All good players, and all hard-nosed players. And they played hard.

So we knew we were always in for a back-alley fight with these guys when we were playing the Bears. And we were fortunate. I think we had a pretty high score in that ball game, if I'm not mistaken. It's one of the higher scoring games of that year, 51–38. So that's very unusual. We outlasted them, is basically what we did, and we came out of the game in pretty good shape. No one was really banged up. Our defense played as well as they could, and our offense moved the ball extremely well. We threw the ball well, and we ran extremely well, and we had, I believe, a couple kickoff returns in that ball game, which helped.

Sahadi: What was the game plan going into that one, to throw on the Bears?

Unitas: Yeah, you've gotta throw against the Bears, but you gotta get time. They had such a good pass rush that you tried to keep the ball short. Quick slants, quick pops, and after they get them guys coming up on that short stuff, then you can go deep: 18 to 20 yards. I don't recall what the key play in that ball game [was], I really don't.

It was a wide-open football [game]. And we scored 51 points, they scored 38. That was the second-highest scoring game of that year. But we were always concerned about the Bears 'cause they were always a mean, tough group.

Sahadi: So beating the Bears by that much, did that give you confidence to say, hey, we can win the whole championship?

Unitas: Well, the biggest thing we did was stay healthy. We came out of the [Chicago] ball game without any injuries whatsoever. Little scratches, bruises, those things, which all heal—that's no big deal.

Things were starting to pick up. We just took off after the 1957 season, and we just kind of put things together. You could see everybody coming together. Where there was hesitation at one time, now you knew—bang—it was right there. You never hesitated on a call, guys never hesitated on making a cut one way or the other. They were able to read the defenses and know where the open areas were. So the football team was gelling, and gelling very quickly.

Sahadi: What was it like to play the Green Bay Packers?

Unitas: We had to take on the likes of Bart Starr and his group of people up there. Green Bay at that time—was the coach Blackman? I'm forgetting. Anyway, it was a good ball game for us up there. I remember our first kickoff. They had kicked off to us, and we had fumbled the ball. And the ball just lay there in the end zone and no one wanted to fall on it. And, I believe, they fell on it and got a touchdown, by the way. So we put ourselves in a bad position right away. And the big play of that ball game, if I recall right, was Andy Nelson intercepted a ball, which was thrown by Starr, I believe, and came right off to someone's shoe tops. The ball hit his shoe, and [Nelson] picked it up right in the air. So it wasn't a dead ball: it hadn't hit the ground, it hit the person's shoe. He picked it up, and I think he ran it back. That seemed to be the turning point in that ball game for us. We were able to outlast the Packers 24–17 in Milwaukee, which had always been a very tough place for us to win.

Sahadi: Now what is Weeb saying after all these games so far, anything unusual?

Unitas: Nothing unusual. He's just trying to see that everybody's in good shape, keeping them mentally alert. No mistakes, no mental errors. He was very particular about that. Physical mistakes he could excuse.

But there's no reason to have a mental error when you have time to study and work at it.

Next came a game with Detroit. Those years we used to play Detroit and [the] Bears and everybody in our division twice a season. Generally it made it very difficult after playing one time [to] come back and beat them again.

Sahadi: How did you prepare for the next game against Detroit, John?

Unitas: [Laughter.] This would be the fourth week now. We've had the Lions and Bears, Milwaukee, we came back from Green Bay, then we came back at Detroit again.

Sahadi: How do you prepare that quickly?

Unitas: Well, you really just almost duplicate your game plan from the first week. You look at films of Detroit, what they have done over the past three weeks, to see [if there are] any changes in their defense, what their thinking is, because a lot of defenses type themselves into playing the down, the yardage, and the position on the field as to how they want to rotate their defense. And with Detroit, of course, you're facing the Joe Schmidts and [Alex] Karrases and those types of guys again.

We came back and we were a fairly high-scoring team that year. We threw the ball, we ran the ball, our defense played superb, [and] we scored 40 points against a defense that we were only able to score 28 at home on. So it was a good, rock 'em sock 'em football game. Detroit really wasn't as tough as they at one time were. Bobby Layne was doing his thing. And we were able to come out and beat Detroit.

So everyone's kinda happy, and we're looking at these things, and we got a lot of incentive. We've got four or five wins in a row. I guess some people started talking about going undefeated, which [is] a bugaboo—you don't do those kind of things!

Sahadi: How was your season going at this point?

Unitas: My season was going well. I can't tell you statistic-wise or touch-downs or anything like that, but I was making the right calls, getting the ball to the right receivers, [and] reading the defenses properly. Up to that time, as I mentioned earlier, sometimes there's a hesitation in what you're doing, and when you hesitate, you just don't complete the ball. You're unsure of what you're doing. But in 1958, after being there for two years, I knew the offense extremely well. I guess that [all] I could do, [all] that any quarterback can do, is to study the defenses and learn the weaknesses and strengths of defenses and the recognition of them. Because that, after all, is going to be your bread and butter. You don't want to throw the football into areas that are over-crowded, and you want to keep it to the single coverage as [much as] you can, and get it to the right individual, and make the right calls. So we were doing that.

One of my concerns has always been that I check myself as to my play calling, as to what I did on first-and-10, what I would do on second-and-3, what I did on third down, and make sure I'm hitting each one of these different holes and not giving the defense any type of edge on my play callings. I wanted to be fairly even up and down that line so they couldn't dictate to me what I was going to do. So that's always been important to me. So I studied that quite a bit. And if one game I got into sort of a habit—I'd always come up with second-and-6 running up tackle—the next week I'd do just the opposite of that. So they may key on that for this coming week. All of a sudden I say, look I'm falling into this habit, unbeknownst to myself. I gotta change that up. So the next week would come up, I'd do just exactly opposite of what I did maybe the preceding week.

Then we come up with Washington. And Washington wasn't too good a football team. They hadn't been good for a good while.

Sahadi: Did the team feel complacent before that game?

Unitas: No, we were kinda feeling pretty good with a breather.

I think we always played Washington in the preseason ball game—
I think that was a contractual thing. We always faired very well against
Washington, and we ended up beating Washington this ball game
35–10. I think Eddie LeBaron was probably playing quarterback at
that time for them. And Sonny Jurgensen wasn't there at that point.
They had some good people, but not as many good people as we had,
and that was the big difference. Those years, you were only allowed to
carry 33 people, you know. It's not like having 48. So some guys had
the ability to play both offense and defense, and had to play that way.

Sahadi: Did they play much zone back in those days?

Unitas: Yeah, we played zone. Of course Baltimore was primarily a zone
football team on defense. And we played against a lot of teams who
played zones: man-to-man, combination, or weakside zones. And if
there's anything a young quarterback can do [it's] to learn defenses
and to be able to distinguish between zone, man-to-man, combination, and what they're trying to do to you, and where the weakness is
in defense, so that you understand what you're doing.

Sahadi: Is that something that can be taught to quarterbacks?

Unitas: [It's] very teachable, sure. That's something you learn by sitting
down and watching films, getting keys on people. [There are] certain
things that happen that tell you automatically once the ball's [in play]
what's going to happen.

So Washington went down fairly easily. So we're now 6–0. So now
we come back with the Green Bay Packers back here in Baltimore,
and we win that ball game 56–0. That was a game that took me out. I
ran with the football, and [got] tackled by the defensive back by the
name of John Symank. I was knocked down and Symank came into
me with his knees and broke three ribs and, unbeknownst to me, also
punctured my lung. That was in the third period.

Sahadi: You ran by design?

257

Unitas: No, just to get out of somebody's way. And it was rainy. And at the time I was taken off the field, I think we were ahead something like 28–0.

Then they took me to the hospital and x-rayed me, and they said, "You have some broken ribs." But that was it.

So I came back to the playing field. I didn't play the rest of the game, but by the time I got back, we were . . .

Sahadi: Did they tape you up?

Unitas: No. Not at that point. By the time I got back, we were ahead something like 49–0, and Bert Rechichar was playing tight end, and they had all the substitutes in there.

Sahadi: Which hospital had they taken you to?

Unitas: Union Memorial Hospital, 'cause it was right down from the stadium.

[I had] played with broken ribs before, so I felt that's all I had, but I wasn't going to get back in the ball game anyway at that late time.

So we went home that evening, and they [had given] me some codeine pills and everything because of pain. Steve Allen and Don Knotts and those other crazy guys [were] on TV, and my brother happened to be there with me at home. And I'm sitting down watching this television show, and those guys got up some kind of skit about wine-tasting. And they had me cracking up. I mean, I couldn't . . . my sides were . . . I was laughing so hard I'd just start hurting. I had to get out of the room it was so funny.

By 11:00 I excused myself. I was going to bed. I was just tired. At that time I had a split-level home, and I walked up four stairs. By the time I got to the fourth stair on the landing, I was holding onto the railing with both hands and trying to get my breath, and I could hardly breathe. And then I made it up another four stairs and I went on to bed.

The next morning I got up [and] I felt fine. [I] got a phone call from [the team doctor] that morning. And he said, "How are you?" I said, "I'm fine." He said, "I want you to bring your pajamas and get your butt to the hospital right now." I said, "Why?" He said, "Just come on down, we gotta do some tests."

Sahadi: You're still not taped up?

Unitas: No, I wasn't taped up. So I went on down, and they had to take more X-rays. He listened to my chest, and [said], "Put your pajamas on, you're going to bed." I said, "What for?" He says, "You're only operating on one lung, your other lung is collapsed." So I said, "Really?" He said, "Yeah."

So he put me in that bed, and they gave me two of these bottles. One bottle had water in [it], the other one had nothing in [it]. And these tubes [were] running into both bottles. He said, "I want you to blow on the one that has the water, and force that water out into the other bottle. So what they were trying to do is to put some force into the lungs so that the lung that was collapsed would pop up because a lung heals itself fairly readily. And I did that all afternoon, and finally, there was nothing.

So they brought in a doctor by the name of Jake Classen and he had me upstairs in bed. He says, "John, we're going to operate, and what we're going to do is, we're going to put an incision in your chest, and I'm going to insert this tube." The tube was about maybe a foot long.

Sahadi: This is that same day?

Unitas: It was in the evening. Monday. And so I said, "OK." And he says, "The whole object is to get the blood out from around your lung that's holding it collapsed."

So he cut me on the chest here and took that tube and popped it down in between the ribs so it gets down next to the lung, and they started up this little pump, looked like an oil derrick, and you could see the blood coming out. When they got to that point I just went on to sleep. And

I was in intensive care for about three days. So they had me pretty well sedated and everything. And by Thursday I was fine. I was up and walking around. I stayed in the hospital the rest of that week.

Sahadi: Was your injury known around the league?

Unitas: Oh sure it was known. And I came out of that the week we played the New York Giants. George Shaw took over as quarterback for that week, and I watched the game on TV. George played well. I was still in [the] hospital. The Giants beat us 24–21 on a field goal. And that was our first loss for the year.

Sahadi: What were your thoughts as you watched the game from your hospital bed?

Unitas: Well, I thought we played well, I really did. New York played a little bit better than we did, and they kicked a field goal to beat us. 'Cause Charlie Conerly, of course, the quarterback, and [Kyle] Rote and [Alex] Webster and those guys were all playing—[Andy] Robustelli. Those years you had great material, great personnel. I mean they're all household names. You take Robustelli and [Jim] Katcavage—you can probably name [them] yourself: Webster, [Frank] Gifford, [Kyle] Rote, Conerly, those type of people. You don't see those people too often anymore. So they played extremely well, and they won it in the last minute or so I guess it was.

Sahadi: Were you antsy?

Unitas: Oh, sure. You'd like to get in there, but you know you can't at that particular point. There's not much you can do about it. You're under doctor's care.

Sahadi: Did you see anything you would have done differently?

Unitas: No, it's hard to see anything from TV. So we came back the following week. I got out of the hospital that Monday, I guess it was, and went back to the stadium.

Sahadi: What did the doctor say?

Unitas: What they did, they had to get some padding. They built a piece of molded aluminum that went from my sternum all the way back to the backbone on my left-hand side. And then they covered it with about a half-inch, quarter-inch of sponge rubber on both sides. That attached to the shoulder pads and attached to my hip pads. I went down to an orthopedic brace maker to do this, and he made a plaster-of-paris cast of my left side. He built this thing up, and I attached it up and went out on the field.

Maybe Thursday, I guess, [I] tested it. I fell down, I rolled, I jumped, I got hit, and rolled, everything else. And I said, feels fine. So that week we were going back to see the big bad Bears. That was the tough part! [Shaw] is a tremendous quarterback, and we had great personnel defensively, offensively. We had a guy by the name of Alan "the Horse" Ameche, a fullback, and L. G. Dupre, a halfback, and Lenny Moore, a halfback and outside receiver as well. And [Shaw] did a tremendous [job] as well as Ameche and our offensive line. We beat the Bears 17–0 that afternoon.

I was ready to play. Matter of fact, in our pregame practice, Weeb said, "I want you to go out there and throw nothing but long ones. Just psych the Bears out, see that if you're gonna play, you're gonna play." So I said, "OK." Threw it out, just threw the ball long, no problem. No, I didn't need a practice. No problem throwing the ball. I'd throw the ball deep, and he said, "You had 'em all lookin'." Didn't know what was going to happen. And so then, of course, the game started and [Shaw] played the whole game. And they thought everything's going fine, there's no sense to put you in the ball game. He had a great ball game and everything went good.

Sahadi: In those days, you didn't have to announce whether the injured guys were questionable, probable, doubtful to play.

Unitas: I don't know if you did or not. There was always some kind of injury report, but coaches lie anyway.

So we came back and we won that ball game 17–0. And now we're coming back against the Rams, came back in Baltimore against the Rams. [Norm] Van Brocklin, [Tom] Fears, and those guys.

I started the game, and the very first play of the game, I threw a 70-yard touchdown pass to Lenny Moore. We opened up a ball game.

Sahadi: How did Shaw feel about you coming back? He had won what, two games?

Unitas: He won one, lost one. He lost [to the] Giants and won [against] Chicago. Well, [Shaw] was just a super-nice guy. We got along extremely well. There was never any animosity there. I've never had any animosity between myself and another quarterback as long as I played. I guess the personalities were just fairly even.

And we came back and I threw that long touchdown. One of the funniest things was that Dr. Classen, the guy who had operated on me, was sitting in the stands. He was upstairs; he was a specialist. And he told me after the ball game, he said, "John, I was sitting up there in the stands, and when you started the ball game and everybody was just on pins and needles, the guy two seats down from me—I heard him exclaim, 'What son of a bitch ever let him play?'" I said, "What'd you say, Doc?" He said, "I didn't have the nerve to say anything."

So we came out and we won the ball game. Was it 31–14? [It was] 34–7.

Sahadi: You played the whole game?

Unitas: Yeah, I played the majority of the ball game. I think [Shaw] came in the latter part.

Sahadi: Did you say, all right, Weeb, I'm coming out?

Unitas: No, I had nothing to do with that. Weeb was the boss, he ran the team. He ran it from the sidelines. I did all the play calling and all that stuff. He ran the field goals and the personnel changes and those kinds of things.

[The] following week we came up with the 49ers. That's always a tough game. That was at home; 35–27 we beat the San Francisco 49ers. We went into the halftime behind in the game, 27–7.

Sahadi: Weeb's gotta come over saying, John, what the hell's going on?

Unitas: Naw. They had us 20–0 right about a minute or so before the game at halftime, and I threw an interception to Matt Hazeltine. They went in and scored another time, and it put us behind 27–7 at halftime.

The thing about that was that the Steelers were playing the Bears the same day. The Bears were getting beat. So it meant if we win this ball game [and] the Bears get beat, we win the Western Division title.

So Weeb went in that halftime and announced that, but he just said that what we had to do this halftime—and this was his whole halftime speech—was that our defense had to keep San Francisco from scoring any more points and our offense had to score 28 points to win the ball game. And he says, "That's all I'm going to say."

We went out and we scored 28 points, and our defense held Tittle, [Hugh] McElhenny, Joe Perry, Billy Wilson, all those guys, [to] zero points in the second half.

I guess one of the highlights of that ballgame was a great run by Lenny Moore. I don't know the total amount of yards he ran, but the last 15 yards, he ran backward into the end zone. He got turned around, he got hit, spun around, and he kept his feet moving. He broke the tackle and just went the last 15 yards into the end zone. That was on a run. And then we scored a touchdown.

But the last series, going downfield to score the winning touchdown, is [how] we came up with a fourth-and-1 situation. And I called time-out. So I walked off the field to go to Weeb to ask him for some help. I said, "What do you want in this kind of situation?" Well, Weeb during the ball game was very nervous. If you know Weeb at all, he's a very nervous guy during [a] ball game, and it was really sometimes difficult for Weeb to make a decision during the heat of the battle. So he used to send stuff into the huddle like, "Make the first down, score the touchdown," things like that. So I came over [to] the sidelines [and] asked him, "What do you want?" He walked away from me. He walked right down the sidelines, and I was following him. I said, "Weeb, what do you want me to do here?" And he kept hawing around, da-da-da-da. And he was just running away from me, and I was following him up and down the sideline. Finally the official blew the whistle, and I said, "Oh, forget it, I'll do it myself."

[I] walked out on the field and I called a power off-tackle play with a short yardage down with Ameche carrying. It was fourth-and-1. The situation was we had to make the first down to continue the drive to score the touchdown. So we get to the line of scrimmage and these guys are all bunched up in the one hole, and I notice the defensive back playing off [Moore] about 10 yards—Lenny Moore, the outside receiver.

Sahadi: What yard line?

Unitas: Probably about the 20. Theirs. So I checked off at the line of scrimmage to [a] hitch pattern. [Moore] took one quick move then stopped, then raised up. I popped the ball to him, picked up about five yards for a first down, then we went on in for the score and ended up winning the football game 35–28. Chicago lost, Pittsburgh beat Chicago, [and] we won the Western Division title, so we're home free.

Sahadi: What did you do after you won the Western Division title?

Unitas: We came down for the last two weeks, which was usually what we did in the last two weeks of the year. [Then] we'd always go to the West Coast, for fear of weather conditions, and we always played L.A. and San Francisco back-to-back. So we went out there, and everyone was looking forward to it because we had our Western Division title won. We could go out there and have some fun. We knew we weren't going to have much curfew for the first three to four days of practice. You go out there and raise hell and have a little fun. We stayed out there for 10 days.

Sahadi: What did Weeb say when you got out there?

Unitas: He says, "Well, we're here to play football, we're here to win football games."

We knew we won our Western Division title, we're going to have some fun for the first couple days. We'll get things to do, take a tour, maybe the movies, go fishing, do some things like that. 'Cause Carroll Rosenbloom was the owner, and he always wanted his players to enjoy what they were doing. So we did for the first couple of days, and then we got down to business. Then we ended up losing both ball games out there. Really didn't matter: we ended up losing 28–30 to the Rams.

Sahadi: Did you start that game?

Unitas: Yeah, I started it, and we started some new kids in the backfields and just kind of worked those kids out. And then we lost that ball game 30–28. And then we went to San Francisco and lost [that] one badly 21–12. I don't recall too much about either one of those ball games.

Sahadi: What kind of guy was Carroll Rosenbloom?

Unitas: [Rosenbloom] was a man who was concerned about the people that worked for him, his players, his coaches. And he would go to [great lengths] to see that they had whatever comforts were needed, as far as doctors and those type of things, medical help. We always had [a] first-class organization, from the top to the bottom.

[Rosenbloom] just didn't feel like there was any reason for anybody in the sport of football, on his football team, to play with pain. Unfortunately that's never been the way it is in football. It's a physical game and you never play 100 percent, except the first day of spring practice. But [Rosenbloom] would see that you always had the best facilities and the best medical help that he could supply.

He was a gracious man, generous man, to the point he was a businessman. And he always knew that if he took care of his players and saw to their needs and the coaches' needs, then he was going to get

100 percent [in] return. So in one way he was generous, but he was generous to a point that, hey, it was going to be good for him, too.

You could go to him and talk to him at any time, and if you had some type of a business thing you wanted to get into or needed some help somewhere, he had the connections around the country in various businesses. And he was always open to that.

Sahadi: What did Rosenbloom say to you after the division-clinching game against San Francisco, anything?

Unitas: Not really, he was just proud of the guys, the way we came back in the second half. He'd go around to talk to everybody in the dressing room.

I'll say one thing for Carroll, what he did was, before the season started, once we were cut down to our final 33 players, he always made his beginning-of-the-year speech. And what it amounted to was the fact that he considered this team as a family group, and what was said in these meetings was to be left in here.

During that period of time, for every win that we had, he and his fellow guys that he hung around with would donate $10,000 in a fund for every ball game we won, for the players. And for every game we won, it was $10,000. And whether we won six games or five games or four games or ten games, you had that money sitting there for you at the end of the season. Once the season was over, it would be split up for the players as a bonus. And that was prior to the fact that they weren't allowed to have any incentives. So that was one thing that Baltimore had going with it. And also he was very big with a fellow by the name of Lou Chesler, who was in the development business down in Florida. He just mentioned to the guys at one time that there were some good stocks available, and he would guarantee the stocks against any particular losses.

Sahadi: Speaking of Florida, what's your opinion of the fact that [Rosenbloom], an accomplished swimmer, drowned in Golden Beach and was never found?

Unitas: Well, I don't think that's in everyone's mind that [Rosenbloom] would go out there by himself. He wasn't a stupid man. And to go out in the ocean when there are gale warnings up, as I understood it, seemed to be a stupid thing to do. But I'm sure there are people around who don't feel that he went out there by himself.

Sahadi: Do you feel there could have been foul play?

Unitas: Who knows? I don't know that there was ever an investigation.

Sahadi: He was an accomplished swimmer.

Unitas: Yes, he was. But I don't care how accomplished you are, you don't go out in the ocean when the weather's that bad.

Sahadi: Isn't there a story about Weeb sending spies to watch your opponents' practices in hopes of learning their patterns?

Unitas: Well, they used to do that all the time. They used to send people, at least [when Weeb was] with Cleveland. I think he was telling us a story [about how] he sent someone to spy on someone's practices, and the guy would climb up the trees on the outside of the stadium and sit in a tree with binoculars and look at people. Even he had some idiosyncrasies. When we were getting ready to play Chicago, he always accused George Halas of doing the same thing. Weeb would have guys go up and go through the stadium to see if there was anybody up there. That's what they used to do when he was [a] Cleveland Brown.

Sahadi: So he got that from Paul Brown also?

Unitas: Sure, and Weeb [was] always concerned when we were playing other teams and we were on the road. He knew that we were going to see other players who were in the same towns, like for preseason ball games and everything. And he would always caution us to talk to the guys, be nice to them, and he [said], "Find out all you can, but don't tell them nothing."

Sahadi: I heard that in his pregame talk before that famous 1958 Colts-Giants game, Weeb went around to every player and singled them out for things, saying, "We're a team of castoffs and rejects." Is that true?

Unitas: Yes, he actually did that. [He] talked about Donovan, talked about Marchetti: "Nobody wanted you, Cleveland didn't want you."

In fact, he [had] made a big trade; a lot of guys came from Cleveland to Baltimore. And then the other guys were from the Dallas Texans, who never had a home spot to play in, just went from one stadium to the other stadium. I don't think they ever played a home game. I'm not positive of that, but that's what I heard.

And he went down the whole list: "Unitas, Pittsburgh didn't want you. Donovan . . . Marchetti . . . But I wanted you, I took you."

Sahadi: Did you feel any different after that?

Unitas: Oh no, that's just his typical thing to try and get the people aroused and to try and get a team where they're hungry to go outside and play. A lot of coaches look at that and that's what they're supposed to do, but I never felt that you need those kind of things. Why do I need someone to tell me to try to do my job? To me, that's foolish.

And another thing, one of the questions always bothered me by reporters was, "Are you up for the game?" Now what a stupid-ass question that is. What do you mean? Did someone have to get *you* up to go to work in the morning to make a living to feed your family? But some people are that way, and they just felt they had to make speeches.

Sahadi: Did Weeb do speeches before every game?

Unitas: Oh yeah, every game. He always had something he was going to say.

Sahadi: I read that after that game, Weeb said, "George Shaw was the hero of the day." Is that possible? He didn't even play.

Unitas: Against New York?

Sahadi: Yeah.

Unitas: [Shaw] held the ball for the kicker. And the holder is just as important as the kicker. Without a good hold, the kicker can't make a good kick.

Sahadi: So [Weeb] felt [that Shaw was] under pressure to perform?

Unitas: Yes.

Sahadi: Rosenbloom supposedly was a bettor. The Colts didn't go for the field goal and needed to cover the spread with a touchdown. I know that you have been asked the question, but was there any connection between Rosenbloom's gambling and your actions on the field?

Unitas: No.

Sahadi: Let's dispel it once and for all.

Unitas: No, there's nothing to that. I don't think anybody on our ball club knew that Rosenbloom bet until probably after his death, whenever they had this film that they did, sort of an exposé of his death. [There were] a lot of questions and implications in the TV thing that they did, and they said, of course, that Rosenbloom was a large bettor. He had a bag man who would bet for him as much as $1 million a game. I never knew anything like that. Hell, I never knew that people bet on football games until about three-quarters of the way through my career. I never knew anything like that.

So I came off the field after that game was over and, of course, one of the questions that reporters asked me [was], "Why did you go for the six points instead of the field goal?" And just being funny, I said, "Well I gave six points." And boy, I got my ass handed to me by the commissioner and everybody else. I said, "I was just kidding."

But I got that question an awful lot of times, that Rosenbloom said to play and we should go for the touchdown and not the field goal. I said, "No, I don't control whether we go for the touchdown or the field goal." Weeb would control the field goal because he would be the guy to send the field goal team. If [he doesn't] send [them] in, then

I'm going for six. And there was no reason to kick the field goal from that close position anyway. They weren't going to stop us at that close range. They did that earlier in the game at the other end of the field, and the reason they stopped us was because the ground, the turf, was completely frozen. We could get no footing up there, one way or another. And what happened on the last play is that I had called a play called 428. With us, a 28 is a pitchout, going to the right side. The four designates a pass off of the pitchout.

Sahadi: Describe it: 4–28 was a pitch to Lenny Moore?

Unitas: No, I split [Moore] out, and I had Ameche split out in a halfback position. So I called the pass, the pitchout to Ameche, who was supposed to just take about a step and raise up and hit Mutscheller, throw it to Mutscheller, the tight end.

Well what happened in the huddle, with all the noise, [was that] Ameche only heard 28. And if you're able to see the film and catch the end zone shot of the film, [Moore] came down to the inside and took Lindon Crow with him, and Mutscheller hit the linebacker and then released to the outside and was standing there all by himself. So had Ameche seen him and thrown it to him, we would have blown, probably, New York right off the field after that.

Sahadi: So Ameche just went in straight ahead.

Unitas: And got caught. I mean, tried to run a pitchout and couldn't get outside. So that led up to the next series of plays . . . because I just felt [Ameche] got caught, [that] he was getting ready to throw the ball but he got caught. So the series of plays after that was when Conerly hit Kyle Rote coming across the middle on a quick look-in pass, and then Kyle Rote was hit [and] fumbled the ball. Alex Webster had been trailing the play, the ball bounced up into Alex's arms, and Alex took the ball way down to about the 3-yard line. And that's when they went ahead.

Sam [Huff] was too busy trying to decide what I was trying to do. He got into position in the last drive, where I was hitting [Berry] in front of [Harland] Svare and then behind Svare. And the defense was playing a little bit loose on us. [Huff], usually his position on the field was that he's up in tight between those two tackles. Their defense was such that they would keep [our] offensive linemen off [Huff] so that he could go up and down a line to make a tackle.

What happened, [Huff] became frustrated because we were just eating Svare up with a short, quick slant inside, quick slant behind him, in front of him. [Huff] just got a little antsy to try to get back, got out of his position, to get back to try to help. So what happened, on a series of downs prior to that, I got caught by [Dick] Modzelewski, and I got sacked. I noticed [Huff] was moving back out at that point. So I know that Modzelewski's coming like a big train; we can trap him. My own main difficulty was being able to get the tackle through to not get [Huff] out of the way. But since he's moved back out of that pocket, now he allowed himself vulnerability to that tackle coming across. So I changed a play at the line of scrimmage and ran a trap up the middle with Ameche. We trapped Modzelewski, [Jim] Parker trapped him. [Buzz] Nutter blocked back down on the left guard, Rosey Grier, or rather, [Art] Spinney. Spinney trapped Modzelewski, and Nutter blocked down on [Grier]. And then George Preas came across over here and picked up [Huff], and Ameche took off for about 35 yards up the middle.

Sahadi: Was that the same plan for the winning touchdown?

Unitas: No, the winning touchdown was what we call a 16 power play.

Sahadi: And there was no time-out, you just went right back out after you got the first down?

Unitas: Yeah, there was plenty [of] time, we didn't need a time-out at all.

Sahadi: I thought maybe you had a time-out to talk about a field goal. Did you look down the sidelines?

Unitas: No. I never worried about a field goal until they came in on the field. A lot of times I'd motion them the hell off!

Sahadi: What did you tell Ameche when you called that play?

Unitas: I just said, "This is the 16 power. This [is] the game right here. We can win the ball game with this play." And Lenny Moore made a hell of a block. Sixteen power play, which is really just a short running play for us, [is] just a scoring play. [It] was a weakside setup, where [Moore was] in the back and Ameche's in fullback position.

Sahadi: Did Lenny Moore split?

Unitas: No, [Moore's] in his halfback position, and [his] main block is the linebacker, at that time Cliff Livingston. And there wasn't any way that those guys were going to stop that particular play. I think they pretty much knew it too. And when I turned around and handed the ball to Ameche, there was a hole as big as this room here that he could have walked through.

Sahadi: Who blocked who on the line?

Unitas: Well, George Preas came down on the end, Alex Sandusky blocked on the tackle, [Nutter] came on [Huff], Spinney blocked on Grier, Lenny Moore came and hit Livingston, and Ameche just ran off of George Preas' block.

Sahadi: Did you speak with any of the Giants after the game?

Unitas: After I handed the ball off, I just headed to the dressing room. I was getting off the field 'cause the field became mayhem after, with all those people coming out of the stands. You get hurt out there.

Sahadi: Could you describe Bobby Layne?

Unitas: Oh, he was tough, absolutely crazy. Bobby's biggest wish in his life—biggest thing he wanted to do in life—was to [have] his last breath [when] he spent his last dollar. Always said he never watched a football game. Said, "The clock just ran out on me." Says, "Give me enough time, I'm going to beat you."

Sahadi: What about Raymond Berry? What made Berry great?

Unitas: Self-made guy. If you look at him—and you've seen him all the time on TV and seen him play—you'd never think that he was a football player. [Berry] ran the 40 in about 4.9, 4.8. And he had uncanny moves. And he worked on every one of these different moves. And everything was precise with [Berry].

He would come in on a Monday morning after a Sunday game. He would go look at films on Sunday night or Monday of the upcoming team. And he'd come in on Tuesday when we report back to practice. And he'd have a list. He'd have a yellow pad. He'd sit down and say, "These are the things I can do against this guy we're playing this week. I've got inside move, like an outside move." Maybe four or five different things he wanted to work on this particular week. He said, "It's all I want to do." It wasn't anything fancy: "These are the things that will work on him, and this is how we want to do it." He says, "I'll let you know just what I can do and when I can do it. You have to figure the rest of it out. I'll take care of that. I'll give the flare control. I'll isolate people, and I'll get you that single coverage list to work on." So that's all we'd do that week after practice, every night for a good 45 minutes, just running those particular patterns.

Sahadi: So you threw extra to him?

Unitas: Oh, constantly. A hard worker, diligent guy, and he had his ideas of what he could do, what he couldn't do. And he didn't change it. And he'd just come back and say, "I've got a five-step inside move, outside back at 18." OK, so then I'd set the offense accordingly so I could occupy different people to make sure he ended up on the single coverage. Then if they changed coverages on me, then I'd just have to go elsewhere with the ball.

Sahadi: Was there anybody in particular he used to beat on all the time?

Unitas: He used to beat everybody. He was so dependable. And Bobby Layne said one time about him, after we beat the hell out of them in Miami—we beat Pittsburgh in Miami in the preseason ball game. Then Saturday we were all at the airport together, Pittsburghs and Baltimores. I was talking to [Layne]. [Berry] came walking down through the concourse there, and [Layne] looked at him, said, "Goddamn, no wonder he can get open. He got moves when he walks."

Sahadi: Did Raymond Berry have any idiosyncrasies?

Unitas: Raymond was very religious. And Raymond always, when he would take a nap or go to sleep, always wore these black blinders on his eyes.

And we were all sitting in Detroit one time waiting to go [after] the ball game. And where we stayed in Detroit was down in slum haven, just down from the Tiger Stadium there. I forget the name of the hotel. We were all in the bus waiting, and last guy out of the hotel was [Berry]. And as he came walking up to the bus, this panhandler came over, grabbed hold of him, and wanted some money. So [Berry] reached in his pocket, took out three $1 bills, gave them to the guy, and the guy took them and looked at [Berry] like he was kind of goofy. And the guy turned around and started to walk away, and [Berry] grabbed hold of him, pulled him back, took out his Bible, and read a verse to him. And the guy stayed there and listened to him. And [Berry] shut the Bible, walked in on the bus, and nobody said one word.

Sahadi: What about Lenny Moore?

Unitas: [Moore] to my way of thinking, was probably the best running back that I'd ever been involved with . . . on the Baltimore Colts operation. And there weren't too many in the whole league really [who] could surpass [Moore] at what he did, and did well.

He was a natural runner, he was so difficult. He and I were rookies together in 1956, I believe. And I had trouble getting the ball to [Moore] an awful lot of times. At training camp, I hit him on the hip, and we would make a good connection. So I asked George Shaw one time, "Would you take this group this time, let me see what I'm doing wrong with Lenny?" And as [Moore] approached the line of scrimmage, he turned sideways. Instead of hitting the line of scrimmage head on, [Moore] would come up and then slide, turn sideways, and just kind of squeeze through those holes and just glide. I was hitting him on the outside for the inside hip all the time and not getting a good exchange. So I couldn't believe that. I said, "Now I know what in the world I was doing wrong here, so I can resolve that."

[Moore] was the first guy I had ever seen who taped his ankles, and then he wore high-tops—he didn't wear low cuts. He taped over [his shoes] so he looked like he had spats on all the time. So it gave him some added support to his ankles. I assume that's why he did it.

He didn't do it for show, 'cause that stuff never existed then. There wasn't any high-fives, or low-fives, or behind-the-back stuff in those days. It was pretty much, you get down, you play and have a good time, and you go out and win.

And that's where he got the name "Spats," because that's what they looked like. But he was a natural runner. He really didn't have to work an awful lot of pass patterns because everything came naturally to him.

Sahadi: What was Moore like off the field?

Unitas: He liked to make fun of [Eugene] "Big Daddy" [Lipscomb] and [Jim] Parker. He liked to poke fun at [Parker] all the time. He would imitate him, and he'd get Parker and make silly bets with Parker that he couldn't drink three bottles of pop at the same time, that kind of stuff. And Parker would fall for it. Jim Parker loved soda water, what they call pop. Pepsi-Cola, whatever it was. We always had it in the dressing room. So he'd go over and get three bottles and open them up and put all three bottles in his mouth at one time and drink that stuff and it was running down his face. [Moore] would just laugh, giggle, carry on. He thought that was the funniest thing in the world.

We had an instance in the intrasquad game, and the first offense was playing against the first defense. So that meant [Moore] and Ameche were the running backs, I was the quarterback, and [Marchetti], "Big Daddy" Lipscomb, and those guys were in the side. And we had been running an off-tackle play. And we ran that thing, I guarantee you, four or five times in a row, and kept picking up yardage. And Lipscomb got so frustrated, and he stood up and just hollered, "You can't run that son of a bitch here every time." And [Moore] busts out laughing. He says, "Run it again."

Sahadi: How did it end up?

Unitas: Oh, [we] picked up more yardage. So after that, we got away from him and just went somewhere else.

Sahadi: What made Alan Ameche a great player?

Unitas: He had one of the greatest attitudes in the world. He loved to run the football. And the harder it got, the harder he played, and the better he became. He was an outstanding runner. I think the first play he ever ran from the line of scrimmage, his rookie season, he went 70 yards against the Chicago Bears.

Ameche was constantly late for everything.

Sahadi: For team meetings?

Unitas: For everything. He was just on the borderline of being late. He always waited until the last minute. He loved to play cards, and they played a lot of cards at training camp: poker, gin, bridge—good bridge player. And he was always the last one to walk through the door for a meeting.

Weeb was on him constantly. He would just berate Ameche constantly. Weeb felt he had to do that, to get after Ameche to make him play. And you really didn't have to.

Weeb got so excited one time, he got after Ameche's butt during a ball game, something like that. [Ameche] ran, he was running so hard. He had the ball and he ran over the sidelines, and hit the table and broke the table. Weeb got all excited: "See, see, see what I made him do?" And you didn't have to do that to Ameche.

He was always right on the verge of getting fined constantly, getting fined for not taping his ankles, fined for lateness of the meeting. But he was there. He was a player.

Sahadi: He never taped his ankles?

Unitas: Oh yeah, but sometimes at practice he wouldn't or something like that. It was a fine. And everything was fined. If you were late for a meeting it was $50. If you missed a meeting it was $100. If you were late for practice it was $50. They were always taking your money away from you. And that's the way they felt they had to do it.

But we always ended up maybe with $500 to $600 [in] fines at the end of the year, [so] we either had a party or we turned around and gave it to the kids.

Sahadi: What made Ameche a great runner?

Unitas: He just loved it. He loved to play the game. He was very competitive in just about anything he did. He ran the ball maybe 35 or 36 times each game and he took a beating, but he gave out a lot of punishment, too.

Sahadi: Is there one particular run that stands out in your mind?

Unitas: Any time you called on him, he had the ability to go the distance for you. He had good speed. But he just loved to run a quick volley and he played extremely well. One thing he never did: he never made a mental error. Never missed an assignment, never made a mental error.

Sahadi: What was Ameche like off the field?

Unitas: He was a big opera buff. And [in] his latter part of years, once he became very successful businesswise, he gave an awful lot of his time and money to help the blacks and the poor people.

Sahadi: Did he ever play opera music . . .

Unitas: In his home.

Sahadi: Did he ever play opera music in the clubhouse?

Unitas: Oh no, we never played music in the clubhouse. Now they have carpets and music and hair dryers.

Sahadi: Why was Gino Marchetti probably one of the best defensive ends of the time?

Unitas: Well he had the ability. And again, he was a guy who [would] probably play for nothing. He just loved it. He loved the competition, and he loved the camaraderie of the people we played with. And he enjoyed it.

[Marchetti], I could tell you—when Jim Parker first came to Baltimore, I guess we were rookies in 1956, [Parker], of course, came from Ohio State—and it was never any problem with [Parker] on his run blocking because that's all they did. It was 1957 he came in?

Sahadi: Yes.

Unitas: OK, so 1957, and we never questioned his ability to block on runs 'cause that's all they did over at Ohio State. They never threw the ball. So the big question was, could [Parker] pass protect? So we were in training camp, and this is after about three weeks of training camp. So they decided to give [Parker] a test of pass protection to see whether he could pass protect or not. And so after practice we set up two dummies. We set up a dummy inside of [Parker] and a dummy outside of [Parker]. Then [Marchetti], who [Parker] would have to block, was playing his defensive end. And we limited the amount of space that [Marchetti] had to work in, which gave [Parker] a certain amount of space to work in.

So I took the snap. I went back to my allotted 7 yards [and] just stood there. Well [Parker] was supposed to block [Marchetti]. Well the first time [Parker] came up, [he] came up a little bit high and [Marchetti] went between his legs and came up and got the quarterback. Now remember, we've got everyone standing around watching. So [Parker] doesn't think anything of that. So the next time I took the ball, [Parker] crouched down and closed his legs, and [Marchetti] jumped completely over top of him. So now [Parker] doesn't know what to do, crouch down, stand up, or what.

So next time I took the ball, he tried to do both, crouched down, stood up, and [Marchetti] took him, just threw him out of the way. [Parker] was getting a little frustrated, and he started to stutter. [Art] Donovan was standing over with the other guys, and they were all kind of giggling, laughing. And [Parker] said to Donovan, "Wwwwwhat do I do now?" And Donovan said, "Well if I was you, Jim, I'd just applaud."

Sahadi: Did Gino Marchetti have any personality quirks you could share?

Unitas: One of [Marchetti's] idiosyncrasies, I guess, was the fact that any time he wore a white shirt, he stayed out. He said, "There's no sense of me going home and wasting a white shirt. We gotta go out and have some fun." If he wore one to practice, it meant he might not get home until like 10:30, 11:00 that night. Gino never knew anybody's name.

Sahadi: Teammates?

Unitas: Yeah. In training camp, you had 65 guys coming into camp. He never learned anybody's name. To this day, when he sees me, he calls me "kid." I said, "Gino, how come you don't call anybody by their name?" He says, "Too many people out there to remember and most of them are going to be gone anyway, so no sense of me learning everybody's name." But the players who [made the final cuts], he knew what their names were. But to this day he calls me kid. "Hey kid, how ya doing?"

Sahadi: He had great anticipation, quickness?

Unitas: Great quickness. He wasn't what you'd call extremely fast, but he had great quickness and strength. Yet he was not the type of guy that you have now. [Marchetti] probably couldn't bench press 150 pounds. Nobody ever did weights in those times. But he had the upper body strength where he could take a big tackle and get him off balance and just throw him aside.

Bob St. Clair was a guy who played with [Marchetti] at [the] University of San Francisco, and [St. Clair] used to hate to play on [Marchetti] because he just couldn't do anything with him.

In the championship game, the Giants had a guy who played at Vanderbilt, I believe, [who] was a fullback, Phil King, who's now passed away. And they were running the ball. And [King] was a rookie, I guess, that year. And his job was to block [Marchetti] from pass protection. Well, he held [Marchetti] a couple times, and [Marchetti] told him, "Don't hold me again, 'cause I'll kick your head off." Or something to that effect. And the story I got from Conerly was that [King] came back and he said, "Hey, Mr. Marchetti told me not to hold him. That's the only way I can block him," And [Conerly] says, "Well, then, don't hold him."

Sahadi: That's the respect he had.

Unitas: Yeah.

Sahadi: He broke his ankle that game, didn't he? How'd that happen?

Unitas: [Marchetti], yeah. [Eugene] "Big Daddy" [Lipscomb] did it. They were in on the tackle and the big pileup. [Lipscomb] came in and [Marchetti] just happened to be in that position, and [Lipscomb] fell on him. But yet he never went off the field. They put him on a stretcher, and he wouldn't let them take him into the dressing room. He wanted to see the remainder of the game on the sidelines.

Sahadi: What can you tell me about Eugene "Big Daddy" Lipscomb?

Unitas: He was the first big guy in professional football. Well, Doug Atkins was there—he was 6'8", 285. [Lipscomb] was 6'8". [He had] great lateral movement. Great coordination. Again was not a strong person. Could have . . . difficulty getting rid of the blocker in front of him to get to the passer. Very seldom did he get to the passer. . . . He put enough pressure to drop the guys back. . . . His greatest asset was his lateral movement. [He was] able to catch the runner before he turned up. Matter of fact, in 1958 I guess it was, he was credited with making about 80 to 85 percent, was in on about 85 percent of every tackle for that season because there was lateral movement making the tackle.

Sahadi: What was Lipscomb like in person?

Unitas: He was just a fun guy. Sometimes he was moody, but most of the time he was great. He was great with kids.

[Lipscomb] was scared to sleep by himself. When he would sleep by himself, he would put the dresser in front of the door because [he] had experienced a very traumatic thing in his lifetime when he saw his mother stabbed to death on a street corner in Detroit.

Sahadi: Was he a recreational drug user?

Unitas: No. That situation with [Lipscomb] was a one-time situation. Probably one of his biggest faults was that he would get in with the wrong people. He used to hang around, I guess, up on Pennsylvania Avenue in Baltimore and just get in with the wrong crowd.

The situation, from what I was able to learn, was that he got with this one guy, who apparently was a pusher, on this dope. The guy had taken some heroin and had taken [Lipscomb] down to his apartment, and they cooked it up. What the guy wasn't aware of [was] that the heroin, instead of being a 90–10 cut, was 100 percent pure. And the detectives that we talked to said that [Lipscomb] just lived 10 seconds. Once that stuff hit the veins, it went right to his heart, killed him instantly.

Sahadi: How well did you get along with Art Donovan? What was he like?

Unitas: Just naturally funny. Big Irish guy, the brunt of an awful lot of jokes. And tells stories. He's so sincere, when he tells everything he just brings the house down.

[Donovan] was a good football player. He was in the Battle of the Bulge, as was [Marchetti], and they came back. He was in the marine corps.

He played football with Baltimore. He didn't have great speed—it would take him a day and a half to run the 40, but he had great quickness on the line of scrimmage. And it was very difficult to move him. And he loved the game. He was just a funny guy.

You could go up to Donovan with your hand closed, and he would back away from you.

Sahadi: Why?

Unitas: He's scared of worms and things like that.

Sahadi: How well did Donovan get along with coach Ewbank?

Unitas: Donovan thinks very highly of Weeb, even though he calls him "a weasel bastard." In fact, he stayed with Weeb down in Miami, Ohio, this past year. And Donovan tells a story: he says before he left, Weeb handed him a bill for $35 for the use of the room. I don't know whether it's true or not, but Donovan tells the story.

Sahadi: Did you have a roommate on the road? Who was your roommate?

Unitas: I roomed with George Shaw . . . I roomed with Jerry Hill. I roomed with Andy Nelson for a while. In the latter part of [my] career, I roomed with Earl Morrall, who was the other quarterback. I guess that was probably most of my roommates there.

Sahadi: Did you like your roommates pretty well? Did they let you get your rest?

Unitas: [Morrall] loved to talk.

Sahadi: How did you stop him?

Unitas: Just fall asleep. Didn't answer him! (Laughs)

[Morrall's] big thing: Saturday nights we always stayed at the motel, and the girl at the front desk would always give [him] a little bag of these Hershey silver-bell kisses 'cause he loved chocolate. He's a chocoholic. And he'd eat that stuff constantly.

Author's note: Unitas was never comfortable doing long interviews. The three hours I spent with him were priceless. Looking back, I wish there could have been three hours more. I cherish that afternoon in a Baltimore hotel room to this day.

Appendix

Johnny Unitas' Statistics

When he retired in 1973,
Unitas held 22 NFL records
and had been league MVP three times
while also appearing in 10 Pro Bowls.

Consecutive Game Touchdown Passing Streak

GAME NO.	DATE	OPPONENT AND SCORE	ATTEMPTS	COMPLETIONS	YARDAGE	INTERCEPTIONS
1.	12/09/1956	**At Los Angeles, 7–31** TD Pass: 3, to Mutscheller	29	14	147	1
2.	12/16/1956	**At San Francisco, 17–30** TD Pass: 31, to Berry	16	11	124	1
3.	12/23/1956	**Washington, 19–17** TD Pass: 53, to Mutscheller	18	10	161	1
4.	9/27/1957	**Detroit, 34–14** TD Pass: 44, to Mutscheller 35, to Dupre 35, to Berry 3, to Dupre	23	14	241	3
5.	10/05/1957	**Chicago, 21–10** TD Pass: 8, to Mutscheller 9, to Ameche	26	17	184	1
6.	10/13/1957	**At Green Bay (Mil.), 45–17** TD Pass: 12, to Mutscheller 29, to Mutscheller	17	7	130	2
7.	10/20/1957	**At Detroit, 27–31** TD Pass: 15, to Mutscheller 72, to Moore 52, to Mutscheller 4, to Moore	21	16	239	1
8.	10/27/1957	**Green Bay, 21–24** TD Pass: 52, to Berry 6, to Moore	31	16	188	2
9.	11/03/1957	**Pittsburgh, 13–19** TD Pass: 5, to Berry	9	2	56	3

GAME NO. DATE	OPPONENT AND SCORE	ATTEMPTS	COMPLETIONS	YARDAGE	INTERCEPTIONS
10. **11/10/1957**	**At Washington, 21–17** TD Pass: 67, to Berry 11, to Berry	30	17	247	0
11. **11/17/1957**	**At Chicago, 29–14** TD Pass: 66, to Mutscheller	23	11	245	0
12. **11/24/1957**	**San Francisco, 27–21** TD Pass: 8, to Ameche	25	16	230	0
13. **12/01/1957**	**Los Angeles, 31–14** TD Pass: 3, to Moore 10, to Berry 50, to Moore	30	18	271	1
14. **12/08/1957**	**At San Francisco, 13–17** TD Pass: 82, to Moore	37	23	296	2
15. **12/15/1957**	**At Los Angeles, 21–37** TD Pass: 2, to Moore	29	14	223	2
16. **9/28/1958**	**Detroit, 28–15** TD Pass: 26, to Berry 14, to Berry	43	23	250	1
17. **10/04/1958**	**Chicago, 51–38** TD Pass: 12, to Berry 77, to Moore 2, to Mutscheller 33, to Moore	23	10	198	1
18. **10/12/1958**	**At Green Bay (Mil.), 24–17** TD Pass: 54, to Mutscheller	35	16	238	1
19. **10/19/1958**	**At Detroit, 40–14** TD Pass: 37, to Mutscheller	17	11	221	0

GAME NO.	DATE	OPPONENT AND SCORE	ATTEMPTS	COMPLETIONS	YARDAGE	INTERCEPTIONS
20.	10/26/1958	**Washington, 35–10** TD Pass: 17, to Berry 48, to Berry	15	8	183	0
21.	11/02/1958	**Green Bay, 56–0** TD Pass: 2, to Moore 5, to Ameche	16	5	99	0
—.	11/09/1958	**At New York, 21–24**	INJURED, DID NOT PLAY			
—.	11/16/1958	**At Chicago, 17–0**	INJURED, DID NOT PLAY			
22.	11/23/1958	**Los Angeles, 34–7** TD Pass: 58, to Moore 12, to Mutscheller	18	12	218	0
23.	11/30/1958	**San Francisco, 35–27** TD Pass: 7, to Berry	33	17	229	1
24.	12/06/1958	**At Los Angeles, 28–30** TD Pass: 3, to Berry 5, to Moore 22, to Mutscheller	38	23	214	3
25.	12/14/1958	**At San Francisco, 12–21** TD Pass: 38, to Mutscheller	25	11	157	0
26.	9/27/1959	**Detroit, 21–9** TD Pass: 18, to Berry 40, to Mutscheller	30	13	230	0
27.	10/03/1959	**Chicago, 21–26** TD Pass: 7, to Berry 4, to Mutscheller 13, to Mutscheller	38	17	221	3

GAME NO.	DATE	OPPONENT AND SCORE	ATTEMPTS	COMPLETIONS	YARDAGE	INTERCEPTIONS
28.	**10/11/1959**	**At Detroit, 31–24** TD Pass: 68, to Moore 39, to Mutscheller 53, to Berry	25	13	257	2
29.	**10/18/1959**	**At Chicago, 21–7** TD Pass: 25, to Moore 1, to Dupre	30	16	233	2
30.	**10/25/1959**	**Green Bay, 38–21** TD Pass: 8, to Berry 3, to Ameche 2, to Berry	29	19	206	0
31.	**11/01/1959**	**Cleveland, 31–38** TD Pass: 3, to Moore 8, to Richardson 10, to Berry 5, to Mutscheller	41	23	397	3
32.	**11/08/1959**	**At Washington, 24–27** TD Pass: 19, to Mutscheller 4, to Mutscheller	35	15	265	2
33.	**11/15/1959**	**At Green Bay (Mil.), 28–24** TD Pass: 7, to Berry 13, to Berry 24, to Mutscheller	33	19	324	0
34.	**11/22/1959**	**San Francisco, 45–14** TD Pass: 21, to Berry 3, to Moore	19	10	141	1
35.	**11/29/1959**	**Los Angeles, 35–21** TD Pass: 55, to Berry 17, to Moore	24	14	242	1

GAME NO. DATE	OPPONENT AND SCORE	ATTEMPTS	COMPLETIONS	YARDAGE	INTERCEPTIONS
36. **12/05/1959**	**At San Francisco, 34–14** TD Pass: 7, to Berry 13, to Berry 64, to Moore	36	21	273	0
37. **12/12/1959**	**At Los Angeles, 45–26** TD Pass: 7, to Berry 11, to Berry 9, to Richardson	27	13	110	0
38. **9/25/1960**	**Washington, 20–0** TD Pass: 12, to Berry	35	17	232	1
39. **10/02/1960**	**Chicago, 42–7** TD Pass: 66, to Moore 27, to Berry 18, to Moore 43, to Mutscheller	27	14	307	0
40. **10/09/1960**	**At Green Bay, 21–35** TD Pass: 1, to Hawkins	31	16	216	4
41. **10/16/1960**	**Los Angeles, 31–17** TD Pass: 22, to Moore	23	12	176	2
42. **10/23/1960**	**At Detroit, 17–30** TD Pass: 22, to Berry 3, to Mutscheller	40	20	253	2
43. **10/30/1960**	**At Dallas, 45–7** TD Pass: 68, to Berry 52, to Berry 70, to Berry 20, to Moore	16	8	270	0

GAME NO.	DATE	OPPONENT AND SCORE	ATTEMPTS	COMPLETIONS	YARDAGE	INTERCEPTIONS
44.	11/06/1960	**Green Bay, 38–24** TD Pass: 45, to Berry 1, to Hawkins 21, to Berry 16, to Berry	29	20	324	1
45.	11/13/1960	**At Chicago, 24–20** TD Pass: 36, to Moore 39, to Moore	33	16	266	2
46.	11/27/1960	**San Francisco, 22–30** TD Pass: 10, to Berry 6, to Hawkins 65, to Moore	30	16	356	5
47.	12/04/1960	**Detroit, 15–20** TD Pass: 80, to Moore 38, to Moore	40	22	357	3
	12/11/1960	**At Los Angeles, 3–10** STREAK BROKEN	38	17	182	1

Johnny Unitas Career Stats

YEAR	GAMES	COMP	ATT	YRDS	TDS	INTS
1956 Baltimore	12	110	198	1,498	9	10
1957 Baltimore	12	172	301	2,550	24	17
1958 Baltimore	10	136	263	2,007	19	7
1959 Baltimore	12	193	367	2,899	32	14
1960 Baltimore	12	190	378	3,099	25	24
1961 Baltimore	14	229	420	2,990	16	24
1962 Baltimore	14	222	389	2,967	23	23
1963 Baltimore	14	237	410	3,481	20	12
1964 Baltimore	14	158	305	2,824	19	6
1965 Baltimore	11	164	282	2,530	23	12
1966 Baltimore	14	195	348	2,748	22	24
1967 Baltimore	14	255	436	3,428	20	16
1968 Baltimore	5	11	32	139	2	4
1969 Baltimore	13	178	327	2,342	12	20
1970 Baltimore	14	166	321	2,213	14	18
1971 Baltimore	13	92	176	942	3	9
1972 Baltimore	8	88	157	1,111	4	6
1973 San Diego	5	34	76	471	3	7
Totals	211	2,830	5,186	40,239	290	253

Postseason

YEAR	COMP	ATT	YRDS	TDS	INTS
1958 vs. N.Y. Giants[x]	26	40	349	1	1
1959 vs. N.Y. Giants[x]	18	29	264	2	0
1964 vs. Cleveland[x]	12	20	95	0	2
1969 vs. N.Y. Jets[z]	11	24	110	0	1
1970 vs. Cincinnati[y]	6	17	145	2	0
1971 vs. Oakland[yy]	11	30	245	1	0
1971 vs. Dallas[z]	3	9	88	1	2
1971 vs. Cleveland[y]	13	21	143	0	1
1972 vs. Miami[yy]	20	36	224	0	3
Totals	**120**	**226**	**1,663**	**7**	**10**

[x] NFL Championship game

[y] AFC Divisional Playoff game

[yy] AFC Championship game

[z] Super Bowl

300-Yard Passing Games by Season

1956 (1) 314, Johnny Unitas at Detroit 11/18/56   17-30-314-0-1

1958 (1) 349, Johnny Unitas   26-40-349-1- 1
at New York Giants 12/28/58

1959 (2) 397, Johnny Unitas vs. Cleveland 11/01/59   23-41-397-4-3

324, Johnny Unitas vs. Green Bay 11/15/59   19-33-324-3-0
at Mil.

1960 (4) 307, Johnny Unitas vs. Chicago 10/02/60   14-27-307-4-0

324, Johnny Unitas vs. Green Bay 11/06/60   20-29-324-4-1

356, Johnny Unitas vs. San Francisco   16-30-356-3-5
11/27/60

357, Johnny Unitas vs. Detroit 12/04/60   22-40-357-2-3

1961 (2) 302, Johnny Unitas vs. Chicago 10/29/61   20-36-302-2-2

314, Johnny Unitas at San Francisco   19-34-314-3-0
12/16/61

1962 (2) 367, Johnny Unitas vs. Washington   25-36-367-4-1
12/08/62

385, Johnny Unitas vs. Minnesota 12/16/62   19-34-385-4-2

1963 (4) 376, Johnny Unitas vs. Detroit 11/10/63   17-24-376-2-1

355, Johnny Unitas at Washington 12/01/63   24-37-355-3-1

344, Johnny Unitas vs. Minnesota 12/08/63   17-22-344-3-0

323, Johnny Unitas vs. Los Angeles Rams   21-37-323-1-0
12/15/63

1965 (3) 319, Johnny Unitas vs. Detroit 10/10/65   18-24-319-3-1

324, Johnny Unitas at San Francisco   23-34-324-4-0
10/31/65

305, Johnny Unitas vs. Philadelphia   19-32-305-2-1
11/21/65

1966 (2) 342, Johnny Unitas vs. Washington   22-31-342-3-2
          11/06/66

339, Johnny Unitas at San Francisco   20-30-339-4-1
          12/18/66

1967 (3) 401, Johnny Unitas vs. Atlanta 09/17/67   23-32-401-2-1

353, Johnny Unitas vs. San Francisco   22-37-353-2-0
          10/01/67

370, Johnny Unitas at Atlanta 11/12/67   17-20-370-4-0

1969 (2) 319, Johnny Unitas at New Orleans   20-28-319-3-0
          10/19/69

300, Johnny Unitas vs. San Francisco   19-37-300-2-3
          10/26/69

1972 (1) 376, Johnny Unitas vs. New York Jets   26-45-376-2-0
          09/24/72

Unitas' Longest Touchdown Passes (50+ Yards)

89 John Unitas to John Mackey at Los Angeles Rams 10/30/66

88 John Unitas to Tom Matte vs. Atlanta 9/17/67

83 John Unitas to John Mackey at Minnesota 9/18/66

82 John Unitas to Lenny Moore at San Francisco 12/08/57

80 John Unitas to Lenny Moore vs. Detroit 12/04/60

80 John Unitas to Jimmy Orr at Chicago 10/21/62

80 John Unitas to Lenny Moore vs. Minnesota 12/16/62

79 John Unitas to John Mackey at Chicago 10/09/66

77 John Unitas to Lenny Moore vs. Chicago 10/04/58

75 John Unitas to John Mackey vs. Dallas 1/17/71 (playoffs)

74 John Unitas to Lenny Moore vs. Minnesota 11/15/64

72 John Unitas to Lenny Moore at Detroit 10/20/57

72 John Unitas to Lenny Moore vs. Minnesota 10/01/61

70 John Unitas to Raymond Berry at Dallas 10/30/60

70 John Unitas to Lenny Moore at Minnesota 9/13/64

68 John Unitas to Lenny Moore at Detroit 10/11/59

68 John Unitas to Raymond Berry at Dallas 10/30/60

68 John Unitas to Lenny Moore vs. Chicago 10/29/61

68 John Unitas to Ray Perkins vs. Oakland 1/03/71 (playoffs)

67 John Unitas to Raymond Berry at Washington 11/10/57

66 John Unitas to Jim Mutscheller at Chicago 11/17/57

66 John Unitas to Lenny Moore vs. Chicago 10/02/60

65 John Unitas to Lenny Moore vs. San Francisco 11/27/60

64 John Unitas to Lenny Moore at San Francisco 12/05/59

64 John Unitas to Raymond Berry vs. Detroit 11/10/63

64 John Unitas to Tom Matte at Atlanta 11/12/67

63   John Unitas to Eddie Hinton vs. Buffalo 12/03/72

61   John Unitas to John Mackey vs. Minnesota 12/08/63

61   John Unitas to Jimmy Orr at San Francisco 12/18/66

60   John Unitas to Jimmy Orr at Minnesota 11/17/63

59   John Unitas to Lenny Moore vs. New York Giants 12/27/59
      (playoffs)

59   John Unitas to Jimmy Orr vs. Washington 12/08/62

58   John Unitas to Lenny Moore vs. Los Angeles Rams 11/23/58

58   John Unitas to John Mackey vs. Green Bay 10/27/63

57   John Unitas to John Mackey vs. San Francisco 9/25/66

56   John Unitas to John Mackey at Minnesota 11/17/63

55   John Unitas to Raymond Berry vs. Los Angeles Rams 11/29/59

55   John Unitas to Jimmy Orr vs. Atlanta 9/17/67

55   John Unitas to Roy Jefferson at Boston 10/04/70

54   John Unitas to John Mackey vs. Chicago 11/29/70

53   John Unitas to Raymond Berry at Detroit 10/11/59

53   John Unitas to Eddie Hinton vs. Cincinnati 12/26/70 (playoffs)

52   John Unitas to Jim Mutscheller at Detroit 10/20/57

52   John Unitas to Raymond Berry vs. Green Bay 10/27/57

52   John Unitas to Raymond Berry at Dallas 10/30/60

52   John Unitas to Lenny Moore at Green Bay 9/20/64

52   John Unitas to Lenny Moore vs. Philadelphia 11/21/65

52   John Unitas to John Mackey at Detroit 11/25/65

52   John Unitas to John Mackey at Dallas 12/13/69

51   John Unitas to John Mackey vs. Detroit 10/16/66

51   John Unitas to Tom Mitchell vs. Green Bay 11/09/69

50   John Unitas to Lenny Moore vs. Los Angeles Rams 12/01/57

50   John Unitas to Jimmy Orr at Detroit 11/02/62

Seasonal Highlights

November 30, 1958
Unitas tossed a touchdown pass in a 23rd straight game, surpassing the prior NFL streak of 22 games by quarterback Cecil Isbell (Green Bay).

1959 Season
Unitas finished the season as the only NFL player ever to toss 30+ touchdown passes in a 12-game season.

December 11, 1960
Unitas' 47-game streak with a touchdown pass ends at Los Angeles.

1960 Season
Unitas ended season as the only NFL player ever to toss for 3,000+ yards in a 12-game season. Unitas finished as NFL leader in scoring passes for a league-record fourth straight time.

1961 Season
Unitas tied an NFL record with his fourth season of most pass attempts, besting quarterback Sammy Baugh's (Washington) mark. Unitas topped NFL in attempts from 1959–61 to set a league record.

1963 Season
Unitas concluded season with eight team records and an NFL-record 237 completions, besting 235 by quarterback Sonny Jurgensen (Philadelphia, 1961).

September 18, 1966
At Minnesota, Unitas tossed his 213th touchdown pass, besting the NFL record of 212 by quarterback Y. A. Tittle.

October 30, 1966
Unitas was 13-22-252 passing at Los Angeles to become the NFL's all-time leader in passing yards with 28,375, besting quarterback Y. A. Tittle's total of 28,339.

September 17, 1967
Unitas passed for 401 yards at Atlanta, the first 400+ game in Colts history.

December 3, 1967
Against Dallas, Unitas teamed with wide receiver Raymond Berry for a 63rd touchdown connection, an NFL record that stood until the eighties.

January 22, 1973
Unitas went to San Diego after concluding his Colts career as the NFL's all-time leader in passing yards.

Unitas Touchdowns

DATE	RESULT	OPPONENT	RECEIVER/YARDAGE
10/21/56	L, 27–58	@CHI	Mutscheller, 36
10/28/56	W, 28–21	GB	Mutscheller, 7; Berry, 43
11/25/56	W, 56–21	LA	Womble, 43; Mutscheller, 12; Mutscheller, 43
12/09/56	L, 7–31	@LA	Mutscheller, 3
12/16/56	L, 17–30	@SF	Berry, 31
12/23/56	W, 19–17	WASH	Mutscheller, 53
9/29/57	W, 34–14	DET	Mutscheller, 44; Dupre, 35; Berry, 35; Dupre, 3
10/05/57	W, 21–10	CHI	Mutscheller, 8; Ameche, 9
10/13/57	W, 45–17	GB@M	Mutscheller, 12; Mutscheller, 29
10/20/57	L, 27–31	@DET	Mutscheller, 15; Moore, 72; Mutscheller, 52; Moore, 4
10/27/57	L, 21–24	GB	Berry, 52; Moore, 6
11/03/57	L, 13–19	PIT	Berry, 5
11/10/57	W, 21–17	@WASH	Berry, 67; Berry, 11
11/17/57	W, 29–14	@CHI	Mutscheller, 66
11/24/57	W, 27–21	SF	Ameche, 8
12/01/57	W, 31–14	LA	Moore, 3; Berry, 10; Moore, 50
12/08/57	L, 13–17	@SF	Moore, 82
12/15/57	L, 21–37	@LA	Moore, 2
9/28/58	W, 28–15	DET	Berry, 26; Berry, 14
10/04/58	W, 51–38	CHI	Berry, 12; Moore, 77; Mutscheller, 2; Moore, 33
10/12/58	W, 24–17	GB@M	Mutscheller, 54
10/19/58	W, 40–14	@DET	Mutscheller, 37
10/26/58	W, 35–10	WASH	Berry, 17; Berry, 48

DATE	RESULT	OPPONENT	RECEIVER/YARDAGE
11/02/58	W, 56–0	GB	Moore, 2; Ameche, 5
11/23/58	W, 34–7	LA	Moore, 58; Mutscheller, 12
11/30/58	W, 35–27	SF	Berry, 7
12/06/58	L, 28–30	@LA	Berry, 3; Moore, 5; Mutscheller, 22
12/14/58	L, 12–21	@SF	Mutscheller, 38
12/28/58	W, 23–17	@NYG	Berry, 15
9/27/59	W, 21–9	DET	Berry, 18; Mutscheller, 40
10/03/59	L, 21–26	CHI	Berry, 7; Mutscheller, 4; Mutscheller, 13
10/11/59	W, 31–24	@DET	Moore, 68; Mutscheller, 39; Berry, 53
10/18/59	W, 21–7	@CHI	Moore, 25; Dupre, 1
10/25/59	W, 38–21	GB	Berry, 8; Ameche, 3; Berry, 2
11/01/59	L, 31–38	CLE	Moore, 3; Richardson, 8; Berry, 10; Mutscheller, 5
11/08/59	L, 24–27	@WASH	Mutscheller, 19; Mutscheller, 4
11/15/59	W, 28–24	GB@M	Berry, 7; Berry, 10; Mutscheller, 24
11/22/59	W, 45–14	SF	Berry, 12; Moore, 3
11/29/59	W, 35–21	LA	Berry, 55; Moore, 17
12/05/59	W, 34–14	@SF	Berry, 7; Berry, 13; Moore, 64
12/12/59	W, 45–26	@LA	Berry, 7; Berry, 11; Richardson, 9
12/27/59	W, 31–16	NYG	Moore, 59; Richardson, 12
9/25/60	W, 20–0	WASH	Berry, 12
10/02/60	W, 42–7	CHI	Moore, 66; Berry, 27; Moore, 18; Mutscheller, 43
10/09/60	L, 21–35	@GB	Hawkins, 1
10/16/60	W, 31–17	LA	Moore, 22
10/23/60	L, 17–30	@DET	Berry, 22; Mutscheller, 2

DATE	RESULT	OPPONENT	RECEIVER/YARDAGE
10/30/60	W, 45–7	@DAL	Berry, 68; Berry, 52; Berry, 70; Moore, 20
11/06/60	W, 38–24	GB	Berry, 45; Hawkins, 1; Berry, 21; Berry, 16
11/13/60	W, 24–20	@CHI	Moore, 36; Moore, 39
11/27/60	L, 22–30	SF	Berry, 10; Hawkins, 6; Moore, 65
12/04/60	L, 15–20	DET	Moore, 80; Moore, 39
12/18/60	L, 10–34	@SF	Pricer, 13
9/17/61	W, 27–24	LA	Moore, 3
9/24/61	L, 15–16	DET	Moore, 8
10/01/61	W, 34–33	MIN	Moore, 72; Moore, 23
10/29/61	L, 20–21	CHI	Perry, 21; Moore, 68
11/05/61	W, 45–21	GB	Hawkins, 4; Moore, 38; Orr, 19; Orr, 4
11/19/61	W, 16–0	STL	Moore, 17
11/26/61	W, 27–6	@WASH	Mutscheller, 10
12/03/61	W, 20–17	SF	Orr, 41
12/16/61	W, 27–24	@SF	Smolinski, 19; Mutscheller, 25; Orr, 20
9/16/62	W, 30–27	LA	Mackey, 2; Mackey, 38; Berry, 21; Orr, 14
9/23/62	W, 34–7	@MIN	Mackey, 11
9/30/62	L, 20–29	DET	Orr, 31
10/14/62	W, 36–14	@CLE	Owens, 24; Matte, 18; Owens, 9
10/21/62	L, 15–35	@CHI	Orr, 8; Orr, 80
11/04/62	W, 22–3	@SF	Moore, 6
11/18/62	L, 13–17	@GB	Orr, 34
12/02/62	L, 14–21	@DET	Berry, 5; Orr, 50

DATE	RESULT	OPPONENT	RECEIVER/YARDAGE
12/08/62	W, 34–21	WASH	Orr, 11; Orr, 59; Bielski, 11; Orr, 23
12/16/62	W, 42–17	MIN	Orr, 6; Berry, 10; Orr, 30; Moore, 80
9/15/63	L, 28–37	NYG	Orr, 34; Mackey, 32
9/22/63	W, 20–14	@SF	Orr, 7
10/13/63	W, 20–3	SF	Moore, 11
10/20/63	W, 25–21	@DET	Lockett, 11
10/27/63	L, 20–34	GB	Moore, 13; Mackey, 58
11/10/63	W, 24–21	DET	Berry, 64; Mackey, 42
11/17/63	W, 37–34	@MIN	Mackey, 56; Hill, 2; Orr, 60; Orr, 13
12/01/63	W, 36–20	@WASH	Mackey, 30; Berry, 2; Orr, 28
12/08/63	W, 41–10	MIN	Berry, 24; Mackey, 61; Mackey, 27
12/15/63	W, 19–16	LA	Matte, 14
9/13/64	L, 24–34	@MIN	Orr, 19; Moore, 70
9/20/64	W, 21–20	@GB	Moore, 52; Mackey, 40
9/27/64	W, 52–0	CHI	Berry, 36; Orr, 37; Hill, 27
10/04/64	W, 35–20	LA	Orr, 46; Orr, 43; Orr, 35
10/12/64	W, 47–27	STL	Berry, 6
10/25/64	W, 34–0	@DET	Berry, 9; Orr, 19
11/01/64	W, 37–7	SF	Berry, 20
11/15/64	W, 17–14	MIN	Moore, 74; Hawkins, 27
11/29/64	W, 14–3	@SF	Berry, 35
12/13/64	W, 45–17	WASH	Berry, 30; Mackey, 22
9/19/65	W, 35–16	MIN	Orr, 9; Mackey, 31
9/26/65	L, 17–20	GB@M	Berry, 5
10/03/65	W, 27–24	SF	Moore, 1

DATE	RESULT	OPPONENT	RECEIVER/YARDAGE
10/10/65	W, 31–7	DET	Orr, 17; Orr, 32; Mackey, 35
10/17/65	W, 38–7	@WASH	Mackey, 34; Berry, 3
10/24/65	W, 35–20	LA	Berry, 8; Orr, 15; Orr, 25
10/31/65	W, 34–28	@SF	Berry, 5; Lorick, 31; Orr, 12; Orr, 6
11/07/65	W, 26–21	@CHI	Mackey, 37; Lorick, 49
11/21/65	W, 34–24	PHIL	Moore, 52; Orr, 22
11/25/65	T, 24–24	@DET	Hawkins, 5; Mackey, 52; Mackey, 15
9/18/66	W, 38–23	@MIN	Mackey, 83; Berry, 40; Mackey, 26; Matte, 4
9/25/66	W, 36–14	SF	Mackey, 57; Wilson, 7
10/09/66	L, 17–27	@CHI	Mackey, 79
10/16/66	W, 45–14	DET	Matte, 28; Mackey, 51; Orr, 3; Berry, 17
10/23/66	W, 20–17	MIN	Berry, 13
10/30/66	W, 17–3	@LA	Mackey, 89; Mackey, 17
11/06/66	W, 37–10	WASH	Orr, 42; Berry, 8; Berry, 1
12/04/66	W, 21–16	CHI	Berry, 23
12/18/66	W, 30–14	@SF	Berry, 11; Mackey, 18; Orr, 61; Richardson, 31
1/08/67	W, 20–14	PHIL	Berry, 14
9/17/67	W, 38–31	ATL	Matte, 88; Orr, 55
9/24/67	W, 38–6	@PHIL	Richardson, 10; Richardson, 31
10/01/67	W, 41–7	SF	Matte, 19; Perkins, 33
10/08/67	W, 24–3	@CHI	Mackey, 34
10/15/67	T, 24–24	LA	Hawkins, 14; Richardson, 31
10/22/67	T, 20–20	@MIN	Mackey, 3

DATE	RESULT	OPPONENT	RECEIVER/YARDAGE
10/29/67	W, 17–13	@WASH	Hawkins, 22
11/05/67	W, 13–10	GB	Hawkins, 10; Richardson, 23
11/12/67	W, 49–7	@ATL	Richardson, 25; Mackey, 11; Matte, 64; Richardson, 5
11/19/67	W, 41–7	DET	Hawkins, 17
12/03/67	W, 23–17	DAL	Berry, 5
12/17/67	L, 10–34	@LA	Richardson, 12
10/13/68	W, 42–14	@SF	Mackey, 6
12/15/68	W, 28–24	@LA	Pearson, 9
9/21/69	L, 20–27	LA	Mitchell, 13; Orr, 41
10/05/69	W, 21–14	@ATL	Mackey, 6
10/19/69	W, 30–10	@NO	Richardson, 15; Mitchell, 5; Perkins, 47
10/26/69	L, 21–24	SF	Matte, 23; Orr, 6
11/09/69	W, 14–6	GB	Mitchell, 51; Perkins, 3
11/16/69	L, 17–20	@SF	Perkins, 11
12/13/69	L, 10–27	@DAL	Mackey, 52
10/04/70	W, 14–6	@BOS	Jefferson, 55
10/11/70	W, 24–20	@HOU	Jefferson, 17; Jefferson, 31
10/18/70	W, 29–22	@NYJ	Mitchell, 11
10/25/70	W, 27–3	BOS	Maitland, 8; Jefferson, 15; Orr, 26
11/01/70	W, 35–0	MIA	Hinton, 32
11/15/70	T, 17–17	BUF	Mackey, 25
11/22/70	L, 17–34	@MIA	Jefferson, 4; Mitchell, 2
11/29/70	W, 21–20	CHI	Jefferson, 7; Mackey, 54
12/06/70	W, 29–10	PHIL	Mackey, 13
12/26/70	W, 17–0	CIN	Jefferson, 45; Hinton, 53

DATE	RESULT	OPPONENT	RECEIVER/YARDAGE
1/03/71	W, 27–17	OAK	Perkins, 68
1/17/71	W, 16–13	DAL	Mackey, 75
12/05/71	W, 24–0	BUF	Perkins, 5
12/19/71	L, 17–21	NE	Hinton, 31; Hinton, 18
9/24/72	L, 34–44	NYJ	Havrilak, 40; Matte, 21
10/01/72	W, 17–0	@BUF	T. Mitchell, 27
12/03/72	W, 35–7	BUF	Hinton, 63

Information compiled by Craig Kelley (Indianapolis Colts) and Terry Musolf (of Madison, Wisconsin).

Johnny Unitas' Career Game-by-Game Passing (1956–1972)

1956	OPPONENT	COMP–ATT	YRDS	PCT	TD	INT	LG	RESULT
9/30/56	**Chicago**	—	0	0.0	0	0	0	W, 28–21
10/06/56	**Detroit**	0–2	0	0.0	0	1	0	L, 14–31
10/14/56	**at Green Bay (Mil.)**	—	0	0.0	0	0	0	L, 33–38
10/21/56	**at Chicago**	9–19	131	47.4	1	1	36	L, 27–58
10/28/56	**Green Bay**	8–16	128	50.0	2	1	43	W, 28–21
11/11/56	**at Cleveland**	5–14	21	35.7	0	0	6	W, 21–7
11/18/56	**at Detroit**	17–30	314	56.7	0	1	54	L, 3–27
11/25/56	**at L.A. Rams**	18–24	293	75.0	3	1	43	W, 56–21
12/02/56	**San Francisco**	18–30	179	60.0	0	2	23	L, 17–20
12/09/56	**at L.A. Rams**	14–29	147	48.3	1	1	30	L, 7–31
12/16/56	**at San Francisco**	11–16	124	68.8	1	1	31	L, 17–30
12/23/56	**Washington**	10–18	161	55.6	1	1	53	W, 19–17
1956 Total		**110–198**	**1,498**	**55.6**	**9**	**10**	**54**	

1957	OPPONENT	COMP-ATT	YRDS	PCT	TD	INT	LG	RESULT
9/29/57	**Detroit**	14–23	241	60.9	4	3	44	W, 34–14
10/05/57	**Chicago**	17–26	184	65.4	2	1	26	W, 21–10
10/13/57	**at Green Bay (Mil.)**	7–17	130	41.2	2	2	52	W, 45–17
10/20/57	**at Detroit**	16–21	239	76.2	4	1	72	L, 27–31
10/27/57	**Green Bay**	16–31	188	51.6	2	2	52	L, 21–24
11/03/57	**Pittsburgh**	3–9	56	33.3	1	3	29	L, 13–19
11/10/57	**at Washington**	17–30	247	56.7	2	0	67	W, 21–17
11/17/57	**at Chicago**	11–23	245	47.8	1	0	66	W, 29–14
11/24/57	**San Francisco**	16–25	230	64.0	1	0	43	W, 27–21
12/01/57	**L.A. Rams**	18–30	271	60.0	3	1	50	W, 31–14
12/08/57	**at San Francisco**	23–37	296	62.2	1	2	82	L, 13–17
12/15/57	**at L.A. Rams**	14–29	223	48.3	1	2	62	L, 21–37
1957 Total		**172–301**	**2,550**	**57.1**	**24**	**17**	**82**	

1958	OPPONENT	COMP–ATT	YRDS	PCT	TD	INT	LG	RESULT
9/28/58	**Detroit**	23–43	250	53.5	2	1	29	W, 28–15
10/04/58	**Chicago**	10–23	198	43.5	4	1	77	W, 51–38
10/12/58	**at Green Bay (Mil.)**	16–35	238	45.7	1	1	54	W, 24–17
10/19/58	**at Detroit**	11–17	221	64.7	1	0	54	W, 40–14
10/26/58	**Washington**	8–15	183	53.3	2	0	48	W, 35–10
11/02/58	**Green Bay**	5–16	99	31.3	2	0	63	W, 56–0
11/09/58	**at N.Y. Giants**	—	0	0.0	0	0	0	L, 21–24
11/16/58	**at Chicago**	—	0	0.0	0	0	0	W, 17–0
11/23/58	**L.A. Rams**	12–18	218	66.7	2	0	58	W, 34–7
11/30/58	**San Francisco**	17–33	229	51.5	1	1	50	W, 35–27
12/06/58	**at L.A. Rams**	23–38	214	60.5	3	3	22	L, 28–30
12/14/58	**at San Francisco**	11–25	157	44.0	1	0	38	L, 12–21
1958 Total		**136–263**	**2,007**	**51.7**	**19**	**7**	**77**	

WORLD CHAMPIONSHIP GAME

12/28/58	**at N.Y. Giants**	26–40	349	65.0	1	1	60	W, 23–17, OT

1959	OPPONENT	COMP-ATT	YRDS	PCT	TD	INT	LG	RESULT
9/27/59	**Detroit**							
		13–30	230	43.3	2	0	40	W, 21–9
10/03/59	**Chicago**							
		17–38	221	44.7	3	3	35	L, 21–26
10/11/59	**at Detroit**							
		13–25	257	52.0	3	2	68	W, 31–24
10/18/59	**at Chicago**							
		16–30	233	53.3	2	2	32	W, 21–7
10/25/59	**Green Bay**							
		19–29	206	65.5	3	0	23	W, 38–21
11/01/59	**Cleveland**							
		23–41	397	56.1	4	3	71	L, 31–38
11/08/59	**at Washington**							
		15–35	265	42.9	2	2	66	L, 24–27
11/15/59	**at Green Bay (Mil.)**							
		19–33	324	57.6	3	0	56	W, 28–24
11/22/59	**San Francisco**							
		10–19	141	52.6	2	1	25	W, 45–14
11/29/59	**L.A. Rams**							
		14–24	242	58.3	2	1	55	W, 35–21
12/05/59	**at San Francisco**							
		21–36	273	58.3	3	0	64	W, 34–14
12/12/59	**at L.A. Rams**							
		13–27	110	48.1	3	0	24	W, 45–26
1959 Total		**193–367**	**2,899**	**52.6**	**32**	**14**	**71**	

WORLD CHAMPIONSHIP GAME

12/27/59	**N.Y. Giants**							
		18–29	264	62.1	2	0	59	W, 31–16

1960	OPPONENT	COMP-ATT	YRDS	PCT	TD	INT	LG	RESULT
9/25/60	**Washington**	17–35	232	48.6	1	1	23	W, 20–0
10/02/60	**Chicago**	14–27	307	51.9	4	0	66	W, 42–7
10/09/60	**at Green Bay**	16–31	216	51.6	1	4	33	L, 21–35
10/16/60	**L.A. Rams**	12–23	176	52.2	1	2	29	W, 31–17
10/23/60	**at Detroit**	20–40	253	50.0	2	2	33	L, 17–30
10/30/60	**at Dallas**	8–16	270	50.0	4	0	70	W, 45–7
11/06/60	**Green Bay**	20–29	324	69.0	4	1	49	W, 38–24
11/13/60	**at Chicago**	16–33	266	48.5	2	2	39	W, 24–20
11/27/60	**San Francisco**	16–30	356	53.3	3	5	65	L, 22–30
12/04/60	**Detroit**	22–40	357	55.0	2	3	80	L, 15–20
12/11/60	**at L.A. Rams**	17–38	182	44.7	0	1	23	L, 3–10
12/18/60	**at San Francisco**	12–36	160	33.3	1	3	45	L, 10–34
1960 Total		**190–378**	**3,099**	**50.3**	**25**	**24**	**80**	

1961	OPPONENT	COMP–ATT	YRDS	PCT	TD	INT	LG	RESULT
9/17/61	L.A. Rams							
		10–22	132	45.5	3	0	64	W, 27–24
9/24/61	Detroit							
		10–16	105	62.5	0	1	36	L, 15–16
10/01/61	Minnesota							
		13–27	284	48.1	1	1	43	W, 34–33
10/08/61	at Green Bay							
		11–24	141	45.8	1	2	34	L, 7–45
10/15/61	at Chicago							
		19–36	278	52.8	1	0	27	L, 10–24
10/22/61	at Detroit							
		22–36	244	61.1	0	2	32	W, 17–14
10/29/61	Chicago							
		20–36	302	55.6	4	1	38	L, 20–21
11/05/61	Green Bay							
		22–35	218	62.9	2	2	68	W, 45–21
11/12/61	at Minnesota							
		14–31	138	45.2	0	4	25	L, 20–28
11/19/61	St. Louis							
		21–36	257	58.3	0	1	45	W, 16–0
11/26/61	at Washington							
		18–33	197	54.5	0	5	44	W, 27–6
12/03/61	San Francisco							
		15–27	216	55.6	2	1	72	W, 20–17
12/09/61	at L.A. Rams							
		15–27	164	55.6	1	2	45	L, 17–34
12/16/61	at San Francisco							
		19–34	314	55.9	1	2	24	W, 27–24
1961 Total		229–420	2,990	54.5	16	24	72	

1962	OPPONENT	COMP-ATT	YRDS	PCT	TD	INT	LG	RESULT
9/16/62	L.A. Rams							
		19–35	245	54.3	4	2	38	W, 30–27
9/23/62	at Minnesota							
		13–21	133	61.9	1	2	44	W, 34–7
9/30/62	Detroit							
		14–31	166	45.2	1	3	33	L, 20–29
10/07/62	San Francisco							
		8–15	82	53.3	0	0	16	L, 13–21
10/14/62	at Cleveland							
		18–31	225	58.1	3	1	24	W, 36–14
10/21/62	at Chicago							
		16–27	255	59.3	2	3	80	L, 15–35
10/28/62	Green Bay							
		18–30	161	60.0	0	1	17	L, 6–17
11/04/62	at San Francisco							
		9–17	156	52.9	1	0	40	W, 22–3
11/11/62	at L.A. Rams							
		16–27	232	59.3	0	2	32	W, 14–2
11/18/62	at Green Bay							
		17–28	237	60.7	1	1	34	L, 13–17
11/25/62	Chicago							
		11–24	91	45.8	0	1	28	L, 0–57
12/02/62	at Detroit							
		19–33	232	57.6	2	2	50	L, 14–21
12/08/62	Washington							
		25–36	367	69.4	4	1	59	W, 34–21
12/16/62	Minnesota							
		19–34	385	55.9	4	4	80	W, 42–17
1962 Total		**222–389**	**2,967**	**57.1**	**23**	**23**	**80**	

1963	OPPONENT	COMP-ATT	YRDS	PCT	TD	INT	LG	RESULT
9/15/63	**N.Y. Giants**							
		19–33	219	57.6	2	2	34	L, 28–37
9/22/63	**at San Francisco**							
		23–44	288	52.3	1	0	26	W, 20–14
9/29/63	**at Green Bay**							
		19–30	267	63.3	0	2	42	L, 20–31
10/06/63	**at Chicago**							
		21–36	182	58.3	0	1	18	L, 3–10
10/13/63	**San Francisco**							
		11–25	159	44.0	1	0	38	W, 20–3
10/20/63	**at Detroit**							
		9–24	123	37.5	1	1	29	W, 25–21
10/27/63	**Green Bay**							
		11–23	233	47.8	2	2	58	L, 20–34
11/03/63	**Chicago**							
		11–18	127	61.1	0	1	26	L, 7–17
11/10/63	**Detroit**							
		17–24	376	70.8	2	1	64	W, 24–21
11/17/63	**at Minnesota**							
		14–23	248	60.9	4	0	60	W, 37–34
11/24/63	**at L.A. Rams**							
		20–34	237	58.9	0	1	30	L, 16–17
12/01/63	**at Washington**							
		24–37	355	64.9	3	0	49	W, 36–20
12/08/63	**Minnesota**							
		17–22	344	77.3	3	0	61	W, 41–10
12/15/63	**L.A. Rams**							
		21–37	323	56.8	1	1	55	W, 19–16
1963 Total		**237–410**	**3,481**	**57.8**	**20**	**12**	**64**	

1964	OPPONENT	COMP-ATT	YRDS	PCT	TD	INT	LG	RESULT
9/13/64	at Minnesota 11–26		209	42.3	2	0	70	L, 24–34
9/20/64	at Green Bay 7–12		154	58.3	2	0	52	W, 21–20
9/27/64	Chicago 11–13		247	84.6	3	1	37	W, 52–0
10/04/64	L.A. Rams 10–18		232	55.6	3	0	46	W, 35–20
10/12/64	at St. Louis 8–20		117	40.0	1	0	31	W, 47–27
10/18/64	Green Bay 14–27		157	51.9	0	0	20	W, 24–21
10/25/64	at Detroit 12–24		210	50.0	2	2	59	W, 34–0
11/01/64	San Francisco 14–29		222	48.3	1	1	32	W, 37–7
11/08/64	at Chicago 16–32		241	50.0	0	0	30	W, 40–24
11/15/64	Minnesota 15–31		289	48.4	2	0	74	W, 17–14
11/22/64	at L.A. Rams 6–18		142	33.3	0	0	62	W, 24–7
11/29/64	at San Francisco 8–15		135	53.3	1	0	35	W, 14–3
12/06/64	Detroit 13–20		243	65.0	0	1	59	L, 14–31
12/13/64	Washington 13–20		226	65.0	2	1	30	W, 45–17
1964 Total		158–305	2,824	51.8	19	6	74	

NFL CHAMPIONSHIP GAME

| 12/27/64 | at Cleveland 12–20 | | 95 | 60.0 | 0 | 2 | 23 | L, 0–27 |

1965	OPPONENT	COMP-ATT	YRDS	PCT	TD	INT	LG	RESULT
9/19/65	**Minnesota**							
		14–22	224	63.6	2	2	52	W, 35–16
9/26/65	**at Green Bay (Mil.)**							
		14–32	210	43.8	1	2	57	L, 17–20
10/03/65	**San Francisco**							
		18–30	236	60.0	1	1	61	W, 27–24
10/10/65	**Detroit**							
		18–24	319	75.0	3	1	38	W, 31–7
10/17/65	**at Washington**							
		12–18	221	66.7	2	1	58	W, 38–7
10/24/65	**L.A. Rams**							
		18–27	251	66.7	3	0	28	W, 35–20
10/31/65	**at San Francisco**							
		23–34	324	67.6	4	0	31	W, 34–28
11/07/65	**at Chicago**							
		11–20	228	55.0	2	2	49	W, 26–21
11/14/65	**at Minnesota**							
		—	0	0.0	0	0	0	W, 41–21
11/21/65	**Philadelphia**							
		19–32	305	59.4	2	1	52	W, 34–24
11/25/65	**at Detroit**							
		14–34	188	41.2	3	2	52	T, 24–24
12/05/65	**Chicago**							
		3–9	24	33.3	0	0	23	L, 0–13
12/12/65	**Green Bay**							
		—	0	0.0	0	0	0	L, 27–42
12/18/65	**at L.A. Rams**							
		—	0	0.0	0	0	0	W, 20–17
1965 Total		**164–282**	**2,530**	**58.2**	**23**	**12**	**61**	

WESTERN CONFERENCE PLAYOFF

12/26/65	**at Green Bay**							
		—	0	0.0	0	0	0	L, 10–13, OT

PLAYOFF BOWL

1/09/66	**Dallas at Miami**							
		—	0	0.0	0	0	0	W, 35–3

1966	OPPONENT	COMP-ATT	YRDS	PCT	TD	INT	LG	RESULT
9/10/66	at Green Bay (Mil.)	14–20	106	70.0	0	3	18	L, 3–24
9/18/66	at Minnesota	14–22	241	63.6	4	2	83	W, 38–23
9/25/66	San Francisco	14–30	225	46.7	2	1	57	W, 36–14
10/09/66	at Chicago	18–38	274	47.4	1	2	79	L, 17–27
10/16/66	Detroit	18–27	218	66.7	4	0	51	W, 45–14
10/23/66	Minnesota	17–28	214	60.7	1	0	27	W, 20–17
10/30/66	at L.A. Rams	13–22	252	59.1	2	1	89	W, 17–3
11/06/66	Washington	22–31	342	71.0	3	2	42	W, 37–10
11/13/66	at Atlanta	10–25	121	40.0	0	2	19	W, 19–7
11/20/66	at Detroit	9–19	93	47.4	0	5	24	L, 14–20
11/27/66	L.A. Rams	2–11	35	18.2	0	1	24	L, 7–23
12/04/66	Chicago	13–21	148	61.9	1	1	26	W, 21–16
12/10/66	Green Bay	11–24	140	45.8	0	3	25	L, 10–14
12/18/66	at San Francisco	20–30	339	66.6	4	1	61	W, 30–14
1966 Total		**195–348**	**2,748**	**56.0**	**22**	**24**	**89**	

PLAYOFF BOWL

| 1/08/67 | Philadelphia at Miami | 19–33 | 193 | 57.6 | 1 | 1 | 19 | W, 20–14 |

1967	OPPONENT	COMP-ATT	YRDS	PCT	TD	INT	LG	RESULT
9/17/67	**Atlanta**							
		22–32	401	68.8	2	1	88	W, 38–31
9/24/67	**at Philadelphia**							
		21–34	267	61.8	2	0	31	W, 38–6
10/01/67	**San Francisco**							
		22–37	353	59.5	2	0	37	W, 41–7
10/08/67	**at Chicago**							
		19–37	149	51.4	1	3	34	W, 24–3
10/15/67	**L.A. Rams**							
		21–34	288	61.8	2	1	47	T, 24–24
10/22/67	**at Minnesota**							
		20–34	235	58.8	1	1	40	T, 20–20
10/29/67	**at Washington**							
		19–33	242	57.6	1	1	23	W, 17–13
11/05/67	**Green Bay**							
		15–32	126	46.9	2	1	23	W, 13–10
11/12/67	**at Atlanta**							
		17–20	370	85.0	4	0	64	W, 49–7
11/19/67	**Detroit**							
		12–22	157	54.5	1	1	31	W, 41–7
11/26/67	**at San Francisco**							
		16–27	211	59.3	0	1	31	W, 26–9
12/03/67	**Dallas**							
		22–39	275	56.4	1	3	33	W, 23–17
12/10/67	**New Orleans**							
		10–24	148	41.7	0	1	33	W, 30–10
12/17/67	**at L.A. Rams**							
		19–31	206	61.3	1	2	34	L, 10–34
1967 Total		**255–436**	**3,428**	**58.5**	**20**	**16**	**88**	

1968	OPPONENT	COMP–ATT	YRDS	PCT	TD	INT	LG	RESULT
9/15/68	San Francisco —		0	0.0	0	0	0	W, 27–10
9/23/68	at Atlanta —		0	0.0	0	0	0	W, 28–20
9/29/68	at Pittsburgh —		0	0.0	0	0	0	W, 41–7
10/06/68	Chicago —		0	0.0	0	0	0	W, 28–7
10/13/68	at San Francisco	1–2	6	50.0	1	0	6	W, 42–14
10/20/68	Cleveland	1–11	12	9.1	0	3	12	L, 20–30
10/27/68	L.A. Rams —		0	0.0	0	0	0	W, 27–10
11/02/68	at N.Y. Giants —		0	0.0	0	0	0	W, 26–0
11/10/68	at Detroit —		0	0.0	0	0	0	W, 27–10
11/17/68	St. Louis —		0	0.0	0	0	0	W, 27–0
11/24/68	Minnesota —		0	0.0	0	0	0	W, 21–9
12/01/68	Atlanta	5–10	54	50.0	0	0	22	W, 44–0
12/07/68	at Green Bay —		0	0.0	0	0	0	W, 16–3
12/15/68	at L.A. Rams	4–9	67	44.4	1	1	37	W, 28–24
1968 Total		11–32	139	34.4	2	4	37	

1968, cont. OPPONENT	COMP-ATT	YRDS	PCT	TD	INT	LG	RESULT
WESTERN CONFERENCE CHAMPIONSHIP GAME							
12/22/68 **Minnesota**							
	—	0	0.0	0	0	0	W, 24–14
NFL CHAMPIONSHIP GAME							
12/27/68 **at Cleveland**							
	—	0	0.0	0	0	0	W, 34–0
SUPER BOWL III							
1/12/69 **N.Y. Jets at Miami**							
	11–24	110	45.8	0	1	21	L, 7–16

1969	OPPONENT	COMP–ATT	YRDS	PCT	TD	INT	LG	RESULT
9/21/69	L.A. Rams	20–42	297	47.6	2	3	47	L, 20–27
9/28/69	at Minnesota	8–22	68	36.4	0	1	11	L, 14–52
10/05/69	at Atlanta	18–24	164	75.0	1	1	21	W, 21–14
10/13/69	Philadelphia	19–34	250	55.9	0	2	30	W, 24–20
10/19/69	at New Orleans	20–28	319	71.4	3	0	47	W, 30–10
10/26/69	San Francisco	19–37	300	51.4	2	3	42	L, 21–24
11/02/69	Washington	10–20	139	50.0	0	1	49	W, 41–17
11/09/69	Green Bay	15–25	145	60.0	2	3	51	W, 14–6
11/16/69	at San Francisco	2–8	14	25.0	1	1	1	L, 17–20
11/23/69	at Chicago	3–3	29	100.0	0	0	21	W, 24–21
11/30/69	Atlanta	13–23	164	56.5	0	0	24	W, 13–6
12/07/69	Detroit	—	0	0.0	0	0	0	T, 17–17
12/13/69	at Dallas	12–28	193	42.9	1	3	52	L, 10–27
12/21/69	at L.A. Rams	19–33	260	57.6	0	2	45	W, 13–7
1969 Total		178–327	2,342	54.4	12	20	52	

1970	OPPONENT	COMP-ATT	YRDS	PCT	TD	INT	LG	RESULT
9/20/70	**at San Diego**							
		15–31	202	48.4	0	1	25	W, 16–14
9/28/70	**Kansas City**							
		5–15	58	33.3	0	2	17	L, 24–44
10/04/70	**at Boston**							
		3–7	64	42.9	1	0	55	W, 14–6
10/11/70	**at Houston**							
		15–30	227	50.0	2	1	31	W, 24–20
10/18/70	**at N.Y. Jets**							
		12–24	206	50.0	1	3	48	W, 29–22
10/25/70	**Boston**							
		12–21	155	57.1	3	0	42	W, 27–3
11/01/70	**Miami**							
		11–19	142	57.9	1	1	32	W, 35–0
11/09/70	**at Green Bay (Mil.)**							
		9–17	125	52.9	0	1	33	W, 13–10
11/15/70	**Buffalo**							
		15–29	221	51.7	1	1	25	T, 17–17
11/22/70	**at Miami**							
		22–36	203	61.1	2	2	29	L, 17–34
11/29/70	**Chicago**							
		23–40	258	57.5	2	5	54	W, 21–20
12/06/70	**Philadelphia**							
		10–18	113	55.6	1	1	19	W, 29–10
12/13/70	**at Buffalo**							
		13–31	236	41.9	0	0	32	W, 20–14
12/19/70	**N.Y. Jets**							
		1–3	3	33.3	0	0	3	W, 35–20

1970, cont. OPPONENT	COMP-ATT	YRDS	PCT	TD	INT	LG	RESULT
1970 Total	**166–321**	**2,213**	**51.7**	**14**	**18**	**55**	
AFC DIVISIONAL PLAYOFF GAME							
12/26/70 **Cincinnati**	6–17	145	35.3	2	0	53	W, 17–0
AFC CHAMPIONSHIP GAME							
1/03/71 **Oakland**	11–30	245	36.7	1	0	68	W, 27–17
SUPER BOWL V							
1/17/71 **Dallas at Miami**	3–9	88	33.3	1	2	75	W, 16–13

1971	OPPONENT	COMP-ATT	YRDS	PCT	TD	INT	LG	RESULT
9/19/71	N.Y. Jets	1–3	(–9)	33.3	0	0	(–9)	W, 22–0
9/26/71	Cleveland	0–5	0	0.0	0	2	0	L, 13–14
10/03/71	at New England	6–7	73	85.7	0	0	20	W, 23–3
10/10/71	at Buffalo	3–9	60	33.3	0	1	35	W, 43–0
10/17/71	at N.Y. Giants	2–5	7	40.0	0	0	12	W, 31–7
10/25/71	at Minnesota	3–5	25	60.0	0	0	10	L, 3–10
10/31/71	Pittsburgh	7–15	32	46.7	0	1	13	W, 34–21
11/08/71	L.A. Rams	—	00	0.0	0	0	0	W, 24–17
11/14/71	at N.Y. Jets	8–22	116	36.4	0	0	N/A	W, 14–13
11/21/71	at Miami	9–17	78	52.9	0	2	20	L, 14–17
11/28/71	at Oakland	10–16	119	62.5	0	0	24	W, 37–14
12/05/71	Buffalo	11–21	134	52.4	1	1	28	W, 24–0
12/11/71	Miami	16–19	142	84.2	0	0	17	W, 14–3
12/19/71	New England	16–32	165	50.0	2	2	31	L, 17–21

1971, cont. OPPONENT	COMP-ATT	YRDS	PCT	TD	INT	LG	RESULT
1971 Total	**92–176**	**942**	**52.3**	**3**	**9**	**35**	

AFC DIVISIONAL PLAYOFF GAME

12/26/71 at Cleveland							
	13–21	143	61.9	0	1	26	W, 20–3

AFC CHAMPIONSHIP GAME

1/02/72 at Miami							
	20–36	224	55.6	0	3	27	L, 0–21

1972	OPPONENT	COMP-ATT	YRDS	PCT	TD	INT	LG	RESULT
9/17/72	**St. Louis**							
		22–36	257	61.1	0	2	43	L, 3–10
9/24/72	**N.Y. Jets**							
		26–45	376	57.8	2	0	40	L, 34–44
10/01/72	**at Buffalo**							
		13–29	197	44.8	1	2	N/A	W, 17–0
10/08/72	**San Diego**							
		13–21	117	61.9	0	0	17	L, 20–23
10/15/72	**Dallas**							
		11–22	97	50.0	0	1	19	L, 0–21
10/22/72	**at N.Y. Jets**							
		—	0	0.0	0	0	0	L, 20–24
10/29/72	**Miami**							
		—	0	0.0	0	0	0	L, 0–23
11/06/72	**at New England**							
		—	0	0.0	0	0	0	W, 24–17
11/12/72	**at San Francisco**							
		0–0	0	0.0	0	0	0	L, 21–24
11/19/72	**at Cincinnati**							
		—	0	0.0	0	0	0	W, 20–19
11/26/72	**New England**							
		—	0	0.0	0	0	0	W, 31–0
12/03/72	**Buffalo**							
		2–2	64	100.0	1	0	63	W, 35–7
12/10/72	**at Kansas City**							
		—	0	0.0	0	0	0	L, 10–24
12/16/72	**at Miami**							
		1–2	3	50.0	0	1	3	L, 0–16
1972 Total		**88–157**	**1,111**	**56.1**	**4**	**6**	**63**	

CAREER WITH COLTS

2,796–5,110 completed/attempted

39,768 yards

54.7 percent

287 touchdowns

246 interceptions

CAREER WITH SAN DIEGO

34–76 completed/attempted

471 yards

44.7 percent

3 touchdowns

7 interceptions

CAREER TOTAL

2,830–5,186 completed/attempted

40,239 yards

54.6 percent

290 touchdowns

253 interceptions

Information compiled by Craig Kelley (Indianapolis Colts) and Terry Musolf (of Madison, Wisconsin).

Bibliography

Accorsi, Ernie. "Johnny's Time." *Baltimore* magazine, January 2003.

Barnhardt, Laura. "A Golden Legacy Begins on a New Playing Field." *Baltimore Sun,* October 12, 2003.

Breslin, Jimmy. "The Passer Nobody Wanted." *Saturday Evening Post,* May 1, 1958.

Curry, Bill. "Unitas, the Teammate, Was Larger Than Life." ESPN.com. September 11, 2002. http://sports.espn.go.com/nfl/columns/curry_bill/1430697.html.

Donovan, Art. *Fatso.* New York: Avon Books, 1988.

Eisenberg, John. "John Unitas: 1933–2002: Youngster's Drive Couldn't Be Sacked." *Baltimore Sun.* October 20, 2002.

Eisenberg, John. "Special Talent, Special Guy." *Baltimore Sun,* September 15, 2002.

Forbes, Gordon. "Unitas Gets NFL Snub." *USA Today,* September 8, 1994.

Jaus, Bill. "Just Think, Unitas Is Still Around." *Chicago Today,* December 29, 1971.

Kiel, Stephen and Andew A. Green. "At Club 4100 Memories." *Baltimore Sun,* September 16, 2002.

Klein, Dave. *The Game of Their Lives.* New York: Random House, 1976.

McMullen, Paul. "Unitas, Ruth Linked Forever." *Baltimore Sun,* September 13, 2002.

Morgan, Jon. "Colts' Legend Johnny Unitas Dead at 69." *Baltimore Sun,* September 22, 2002.

Nack, William. "Post-NFL Pain." *Sports Illustrated.* May 7, 2001.

329

NFL Productions, *HBO Sports of the 20th Century,* 2000.

Schefter, Adam. "Legendary Unitas Dies at 69." *Denver Post,* September 12, 2002.

Steadman, John. "Letter Reveals Love Affair: Teresa, John." *Baltimore New-American,* January 6, 1966.

Steadman, John. "Szymanski Recalls the Unitas Years." *Baltimore American,* July 27, 1979.

Steadman, John. "Unitas Credits Family, Friends for Recovery from Heart Bypass." *Baltimore Sun,* March 17, 1993.

Steadman, John. "Unitas Played Babysitter." *Baltimore News-Post,* December 20, 1959.

Index